Light Troops in the Seven Years War

Irregular Warfare in Europe and North America 1755–1763

James R. McIntyre

Helion & Company

Helion & Company Limited
Unit 8 Amherst Business Centre
Budbrooke Road
Warwick
CV34 5WE
England
Tel. 01926 499619
Email: info@helion.co.uk
Website: www.helion.co.uk
Twitter: @helionbooks
Visit our blog at http://blog.helion.co.uk/

Published by Helion & Company 2023
Designed and typeset by Mach 3 Solutions (www.mach3solutions.co.uk)
Cover designed by Paul Hewitt, Battlefield Design (www.battlefield-design.co.uk)

Text © James R. McIntyre 2023
Cover: A jäger of Schaumburg-Lippe-Bückeburg Jäger Corps, 1760. Original artwork
by Alexandr Chernushkin © Helion & Company 2023. Cavalry attacking carts, during
the Seven Years War, by F. Oetinger. (Anne S.K. Brown Military Collection)
Illustrations © as individually credited
Maps by George Anderson © Helion & Company 2023

ISBN 978-1-804513-43-9

British Library Cataloguing-in-Publication Data.
A catalogue record for this book is available from the British Library.

For details of other military history titles published by Helion & Company Limited,
contact the above address, or visit our website: http://www.helion.co.uk

We always welcome receiving book proposals from prospective authors.

Contents

Preface

The Seven Years War is known for its great battles; Rossbach, Leuthen, and Minden stand at the head of the list for the European continent. In North American, smaller in numbers engaged, but no less intense in ways were Monongahela, Carillon and the Plains of Abraham. These clashes continued to dominate the literature of the conflict since the ink on the treaties of Paris and Hubertusburg was still damp. Often lost in this focus on great battles is the fact that between them, and sometimes during them, there occurred a continuous Small War of raids, skirmishes, and ambushes. These actions made up the war the French called petite guerre, and the Germans kleiner Krieg, in today's parlance, commentators refer to it as irregular warfare and it is to this aspect of the conflict the following pages are dedicated. This aspect of the Seven Years War has often been overlooked or dealt with only superficially. As *Colonel* Jean Colin of the French army observed at the beginning of the twentieth century, 'It is a general fact in the history of wars, for example, that skirmishers have played an often essential, always important role, and yet little is said about it.'[1] In part, this is due to its complexity. As Christopher Duffy noted, 'For the historian the efficacy of der Kleine Krieg can be as difficult to pin down as its practitioners, for it worked for most of the time on two quite separate planes—at the major operational level, by biting at enemy flanks and communications, and at a tactical level of a most basic kind'.[2] The irregular warfare aspect of the Seven Years War tends to languish in the background among the more climactic events. In the following pages, however, the dynamic is reversed. The Small War, or petite guerre, takes centre stage, while the major engagements will fall into the background. The Small War constituted a distinctly different type of fighting at the tactical level than the major engagements between the field armies. It consequently demanded a distinct type of soldier. Irregular warfare therefore constituted a form of warfare often conducted by specialist 'light troops.'

While light troops have likely been a part of warfare since the beginnings of human conflict, that the eighteenth century witnessed a re-emergence and

---

1   Jean Colin, *L'Infanterie au XVIIIe Siècle: La Tactique* (Paris: Bergerevrault, 1907), p.1.
2   Christopher Duffy, *Instrument of War: The Austrian Army in the Seven Years War* (Chicago: The Emperor's Press, 2000), p.395.

proliferation of irregular warfare is without question.[3] Beginning in the last war of Louis XIV, if not before, what the French referred to as petite guerre once more assumed an important role in the tactical repertoire of European commanders.[4] This fighting demanded a distinct type of soldier, one capable of greater individual initiative, stealth, marksmanship, physical endurance and resourcefulness.

On the European continent, these soldiers included Croats, Hussars and Pandours initially from the far eastern fringes of the Austrian Hapsburg empire, jäger from the central and western German states, Cossacks from the Russian empire and compagnes franches from France. At the same time, European involvement in North America, with the small numbers of European regular troops involved, the local terrain and its use of native auxiliaries, produced its own form of Small War. This was a hybrid of European and North American practices. As will be seen below, British officers brought with them their experiences fighting on the Continent against the light troops of eastern Europe and used these methods, where applicable, in the North American environment. In creating this hybrid of European and Native tactics, the British followed a path already blazed by their opponents in New France which the inhabitants referred to as the Petite Guerre, but which differed in several important ways from the warfare that characterised the tactics with the same term in Europe.[5] Both sides developed their own specialist light troops. On the French side, they were known as the Troupes de la Marine and the Canadian militia, while on the British side the colonists developed the rangers and the British regular army developed light companies.

As implied above, the following pages will demonstrate that in both theatres there were numerous similarities between the types of tactics employed and the attributes this type of fighting demanded of both soldiers and officers. These similarities appeared in contemporary writings on the Small War in both theatres as well.

At the same time, the following will show that what are usually considered minor operations could produce major effects. A well-conducted raid by one side, for instance, could force an enemy commander to re-evaluate or even completely alter his plan of campaign. This was especially the case if the raid interfered with enemy logistics, as will be seen in the two examples covered in depth in the following pages.

In order to accomplish the above goals, the following work adopts a thematic approach. Chapters that examine the development and conduct of Small War in specific theatres, as well as the recruiting and organization of

---

3   For a broad history of irregular warfare, the most useful one-volume text remains Robert Aspery, *War in the Shadows the Guerrilla in History: Two Thousand Years of the Guerrilla at War from Ancient Persia to the Present*. (New York: William Morrow and Company, 1994). A much shorter overview, which explores some important problems in terminology is available in Beatrice Heuser 'Introduction: Exploring the Jungle of Terminology', in *Small Wars and Insurgencies*, 25:4 (25 July 2014), pp.741–753.

4   For a very useful history of the wars of Louis XIV, see John A. Lynn, *The Wars of Louis XIV 1667-1714*. (London: Longman, 1999).

5   See the glossary for further elaboration.

various formations, first in Europe and then in North America specifically, are interspersed with chapters that closely analyse operations from those respective theatres.

The first chapter establishes the parameters of irregular warfare, or Small War (the terms will be used interchangeably, see the Note on Terminology) and presents an overview of the return of irregular warfare in Europe from the late seventeenth century through the end of the War of the Austrian Succession. It sketches in broad terms the re-emergence of what I refer to as Small War. Likewise, it describes some of the early formations raised specifically for Small War and their tactics.

The second chapter examines some of the early writings on Small War by various military professionals. These writings proliferated following the rapid expansion in the use of light troops in the War of the Austrian Succession and continued into the early stages of the Seven Years War. As will be seen, the writings on Small War tended to focus on two main themes: the types of officers and men best suited to serve as light troops and how to successfully apply the tactics these troops were raised to perform. The writings on Small War therefore form an appropriate bridge between the two conflicts. At the same time, they demonstrate a ready acceptance of the practice of Small War by military professionals, or at least a vocal minority of them.

The third chapter examines the role of light troops and Small War in the European theatre during the Seven Years War. Trends concerning the use of light troops established in the first chapter will be addressed further, with representative examples from the eastern and western theatres. The eastern theatre in Europe should be taken to include the region where Austria, Prussia and Russia along with Sweden constituted the primary belligerents. The western theatre is the area of operations of France and the Allies, Great Britain, Prussia, Hanover, and a number of the smaller German states. The means of raising light troops used by the various major powers are discussed. Some of the more notable formations raised during the war are highlighted as well.

The fourth chapter presents some examples of actions involving light troops during the Seven Years War. It highlights the actions of some of the formations described in the preceding chapter. Various tactics employed by light troops are examined through the lens of specific actions over the course of the Seven Years War. The western theatre of the conflict serves as the main focus for most of the analysis in this chapter, as the following section highlights an example from the eastern theatre.

The fifth chapter analyses the 1758 raid on Domstadtl in some depth as it gives an example of how the tactics of Small War could be applied on a large scale to achieve an operational or even strategic effect. The commanders, the development of the plan of the raid, and its execution are all examined in detail. Further, its effects on Frederick II's plans for the 1758 campaign are discussed.

The sixth chapter then, briefly traces the development of irregular warfare in North America, focusing on the various methods developed by the French colonists in what is now Canada, the British colonists along the eastern seaboard, and the Native Americans. As French and later British colonists developed settlements, they altered the tactics they brought with them from Europe to adapt to the realities of the terrain and conflict with the indigenous peoples of North America. In similar fashion, they adopted certain fighting practices of their native foes as these tactics demonstrated time and again their efficacy. The factors contributing to the development of certain formations, such as the colonial rangers will be discussed in detail. Likewise, the tactics utilized by the various groups will be discussed at length.

The seventh chapter focuses on an examination of the Fort Bull Raid in 1756, with special attention as to how the relations between the French forces and their Native Allies helped shape the expedition. The raid itself is discussed in some detail as are its effects on the intended British strategy for 1756. This chapter neatly bookends the one on the Domstadtl raid and provides an illustrative example of the operational, even strategic effects that could result from the actions of Small War in the North American context.

The eighth chapter provides an overview of the use of the tactics described above in the French and Indian War. The theme that emerges is interaction as the British and French fought one another, and Native Americans joined both sides as allies. The resultant clashes have long been seen by historians as the genesis for the light infantry companies in the British army. The chapter will examine this proposition in some depth, with special attention given to the influence colonial ranger practices exerted on the development of the British light infantry. What emerges from this examination is that this influence was often quite personal and individualistic, being transmitted through specific figures such as Robert Rogers, Thomas Gage and George Augustus Howe. Further, the chapter asserts that not only did ranger practices play into the development of the British light infantry, but the previous experiences of various officers, such as George Howe, fighting in Europe against irregular formations contributed to their development as well.

The conclusion pulls the various strands of Small War from Europe and America together. In doing so, it highlights the similarities as well as the differences that exemplified practices of Small War on both continents. Among the themes that emerge are the similarities in tactics, and even discipline, or perhaps more accurately the lack thereof among the practitioners of Small War on both continents. Another similarity that appears involved the importance of leadership for effective partisan units.

What emerges is that there seems to have been some communication of ideas among contemporaries of various fighting practices in both theatres and that this communication exerted an impact on how light troops were used. By the same token, there seem to have existed commonalities in the practices of Small War on both continents as well. Beyond the similarities and differences which characterised Small War between Europe and North America, the concluding section discusses the reasons underlying the diminution of Small War in Europe following the end of the Seven Years War as well as those for its persistence in North America. It will challenge the scope of the perceived decrease of Small War in Europe as well.

Acknowledgements

While it is usual to begin the Acknowledgements by thanking the publisher for their assistance in bringing the work to fruition, in this case, it seems most apropos to begin by thanking Alexander Burns. Alex posted a call for proposals from Andrew Bamford at Helion, which served as the impetus for this project.

From there, Andrew expressed an interest in the work from its inception and has guided it through the various stages of development to the final product here. He has been patient and supportive throughout and offered sage direction to the author at several crucial moments. The same can be said of Rob Griffith at Helion who oversaw the final stages of the production process. Both men were patient and supportive throughout.

The following pages have been a long time coming. My interest in light troops in the wars of the eighteenth century goes back some 20 years to research on the Continental riflemen in the American War of Independence. The early research into these soldiers led to an interest in light troops more generally. At the same time, I grew more interested in the conflict which set the stage for the American Revolution and subsequent War of Independence, the Seven Years War.

As the research progressed, numerous people made suggestions, and guided me towards sources which made this a better book. Ken Bunger has always been unstinting in offering his vast knowledge of the Seven Years War, and the various histories thereof. Likewise, George Satterfield, an expert on petite guerre in the Age of Louis XIV unreservedly shared some of the fruits of his research with me at a point in the research that helped to organize my thinking on the subject more broadly. George Nafziger deserves much recognition as well. George has acquired a profound knowledge of various archives as well as a trove of documents over the course of his career. Likewise, he has made a business of making these materials more accessible to the general public. Both of these he shared freely with me while I researched this work. The sections pertaining to light infantry in the Army of Louis XV would have been much shorter and superficial without George's unselfish sharing of a lifetime spent digging through various archives. Along those same lines, I must thank Dr Stephen Summerfield as well. He shared with me much of his vast research on the units and uniforms of the various fighting forces of the Seven Years War, especially the Prussian freikorps. The discussion of various units included in the following pages benefited significantly from the material he so graciously shared. Finally, I would be remiss if I did not acknowledge the excellent tutelage I received from the late Russell F. Weigley while an undergraduate at Temple University in Philadelphia, Pennsylvania. Professor Weigley demonstrated in his teaching, mentoring and research the true meaning of the phrase 'gentleman and a scholar'.

I would like to thank as well, the members of the Seven Years War Association and especially the subscribers and contributors to the *Journal of the Seven Years War Association*. Their passion supported my growing interest in eighteenth century warfare in general and the Seven Years War in particular. The membership of the organization themselves are a trove of knowledge on the conflict currently under investigation as well as numerous other wars of the eighteenth century and beyond. Likewise, the curators and contributors of the website Project Seven Years War at Kronoskaf (www.kronoskaf.com), which serves as an excellent resource for information on all aspects of the conflict.

All of this points to a network of passionate scholars who have all given freely to me of their time and expertise. Any shortcomings in factual accuracy or interpretation in the pages that follow are certainly mine and not theirs.

On a personal note, I would like to thank my wife Catherine whose excitement for my projects, and wise counsel when maybe I should 'take a break from the past', have always helped me to stay focused and sane. Likewise, our children: Jessica, Zayne and Nathanael have always helped me to stay rooted in the present and not get too lost in the past.

A Note on Terminology

As soon as one ventures into the thrilling world of irregular warfare one is confronted by a seemingly impenetrable mass of terminology, so much so that an entire historiographical article was dedicated to making some sense out of the various terms and how they are applied.[1] What the following note hopes to achieve is to clarify the meanings of the terms that will see the most use in the following pages with some justification as to why those terms are applied in the manner they are. It addresses the variation in terminology for the same concepts as well. To serve as a further aid to understanding, this work contains a glossary to which readers can refer for further explanation and clarification.

First, the terms irregular warfare, kleiner Krieg, petite guerre and Small War will be used synonymously throughout the text to specify the types of operations light troops generally specialized in, including raids, ambushes and generally disrupting their opponents' concentrations. In the case of kleiner Krieg and petite guerre, both of these terms were used by contemporaries to describe these actions. Likewise, both translate as Small War. As for irregular warfare, light troops often undertook missions for which regular line troops were not well suited. Finally, the use of varied terms prevents the text from becoming monotonous.

Determining a general term for the inhabitants of North America stood among the most challenging aspects of this project. It has been complicated by the changes in convention which have occurred over time, and the terminology in vogue from place to place. Terms noted in the research included: Amerindians, Indians, Native inhabitants, Native Americans, and First Peoples. Finally, a sort of compromise emerged from the research. Where a term is used in a direct quote, that term is used to maintain the integrity of the quote. Even if the term is no longer deemed generally acceptable, this seems the best way to preserve the accuracy of the speaker. In all other instances, the term Native American will be used as it is an accurate descriptor and generally recognizable.

As for the various formations discussed in the following pages, these will be identified as they occur in the text. They are contained in the glossary as well, which is meant to serve as a general reference.

---

1   Heuser, 'Introduction', pp.741–753.

Glossary

Amusette – (lit. plaything) This was a very long musket which fired a one-pound ball. It was therefore rated as an artillery piece. These were often issued to jäger, Frei battalions and Freikorps. They were referred to as wall-guns as well as they were often fired from walls when the unit was in garrison. Their main purpose seems to have been sniping, especially at enemy artillery crews.

Canadian Militia – A force raised from the male populace of New France. While militia were generally utilized for local defence, troops of the Canadian militia often took part in offensive operations as well.

Chasseur – (lit. hunter) These were light troops raised by the French and sometimes armed with rifles. Chasseurs à cheval referred to their mounted component, while chasseurs à pied refers to those who fought on foot.

Compagnie Franches – (lit., free companies) Units raised by the French, beginning during the reign of Louis XIV, to engage in irregular warfare.

Croat –Term applied to the troops raised on the south-eastern border of the Austrian Empire, who served as irregular troops in western and central Europe.

Freikorps – (lit. free corps) These were units usually containing a combination of mounted and foot-soldiers who served as irregulars and at times as line forces in the armies of Prussia and various other German states.

Jäger – (lit. hunter) The name was applied to troops armed with a short hunting rifle, and generally raised from the gamekeepers of the states that composed the German areas of the Holy Roman Empire. Jäger were of two types, jäger zu Fuss, or foot jäger, and jäger zu Pferd or mounted jäger.

Kleiner Krieg – (lit. Small War) The German term for the irregular war of ambushes, raids and skirmishes that occurred alongside the major battles.

Little War – The term applied to the tactics of ambushes, raids and skirmishes that occurred alongside the major battles.

Pandour – Term applied to various light troops, often but not always mounted, who were drawn from the Austrian borders with the Ottoman Empire beginning in the 1740s. They were considered by many contemporaries as experts at Small War. While tactically quite efficient, they earned a reputation for brutality as well, especially with their treatment of civilians.

Partisan – Someone who took part in the actions of Small War.

Petite Guerre – (lit. Small War) This term possesses two connotations. In Europe, it was simply the French term for the irregular war of ambushes, raids and skirmishes that occurred alongside the major battles. In North America, it referred to the hybrid style of warfare developed by the French colonists and employed by the Canadian militia and Troupes de la Marine which involved raids, ambushes and deliberate savagery as means to terrify their British and sometimes Native American antagonists. 'Petite Guerre is the designated term for the method of asymmetrical warfare inspired by the irregular warfare of North American Aboriginal peoples. The method has often been labelled as barbaric and as contrary to the ethics and morality of its time.'[2]

Raiding party – The basic tactical unit of Native American warriors in North America. It varied in size depending on the objective.

Rangers – New England troops trained to fight in ways similar to those of their Native American opponents. The term derived from the fact that they patrolled or 'ranged' between different forts hoping to interdict Native American raiding parties.

Troupes de la Marine – Regular soldiers who were assigned to garrison posts in New France. Their name derived from the fact that in France their administration fell under the auspices of the Bureau de la Marine.

Equivalent General Officer Ranks for the Major Belligerents

British	Austrian	Prussian	Russian
Major General	Generalfeldwachtmeister (GFWM)	General-Major (GM)	General Field Marshal (GFM)
Lieutenant General	Feldmarschalllieutenant (FML)	General-Lieutenant (GL)	General of Infantry (GdI) General der Cavallerie (GdC)
General (full)	Feldzeugmeister (FZM) (Infantry) General der Cavallerie (GdC)	General der Infanterie (GdI) General der Cavallerie (GdC)	Feldzeugmeister (FZM) (Infantry) Lieutenant General

---

2   Jérôme Lacroix-Leclair and Eric Ouellet, 'The *Petite Guerre* in New France, 1660-1759: An Institutional Analysis', *Canadian Military History*, 11:4 (Autumn 2011), p.49.

1

The Re-Emergence of Partisan Warfare in Europe, 1700–1748

Warfare between 1700 and 1799 is usually characterised as encompassing great battles between armies that grew progressively larger across the century.[1] Long lines of brightly uniformed figures blasting away at one another with flintlock muskets until one side finally drove the other from the battlefield with the cold steel of the bayonet. While the preceding imagery certainly portrays an aspect of the picture, it does not reveal the entire panorama. On the fringes of these epic clashes, at times in tandem with them, there throbbed a continuing smaller-scale war, what contemporaries referred to as petite guerre or kleiner Krieg; what is today referred to as irregular warfare.

Irregular warfare in the eighteenth century consisted of raids and counter-raids, ambushes and the gathering of contributions and forage. These minor actions often served to gain intelligence from opponents, disrupt their operations and generally to cause havoc and enhance the level of friction experienced by those on the receiving end. In order to maintain their rapid mobility, the irregulars took prisoners less often than their line units. As a result, if an irregular formation was unlucky enough to lose out to a line unit in combat, they could expect little mercy themselves.[2] Likewise, they developed a reputation for plunder. While at times the reputation was deserved, the troops in question were often merely taking supplies from their opponents. Consequently, the Small War often fed upon itself, at least in the realm of logistics. Much the same case could be made concerning prisoners.

When prisoners were taken, they were seen as sources of information on enemy strength and dispositions. The information thus gained was often put to use in developing raids to interdict supply columns, gain additional prisoners, especially officers, and to plan and execute ambushes to disrupt troop movements. Troop movements could be disrupted in several ways.

Ambushes of enemy scouting parties and patrols deprived them of tactical intelligence and made movements hazardous. By the same token,

---

1   John A. Lynn, 'The Evolution of Army Style in the Modern West, 800-2000', *The International History Review*, 18:3 (August 1996), pp.505–545.
2   Christopher Duffy, *The Military Experience in the Age of Reason* (New York: Hippocrene Books, 1987), p.277.

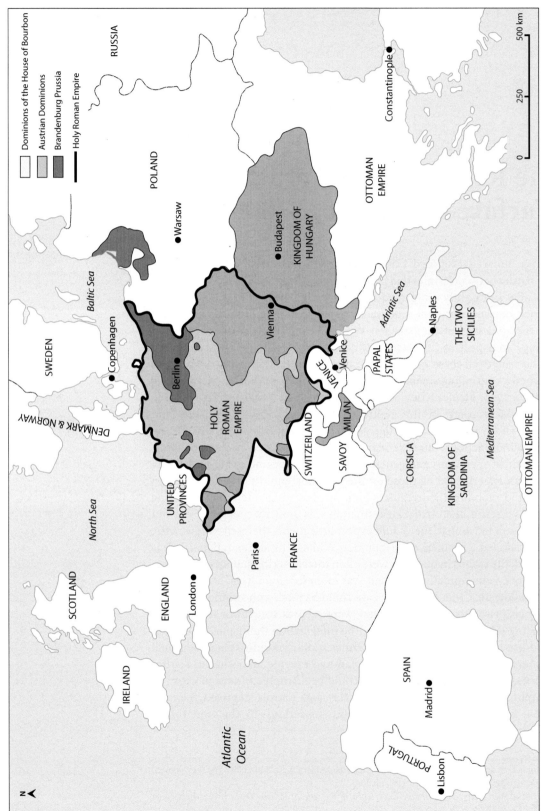

Europe at the time of the Seven Years War.

when light troops launched raids far behind enemy lines, they could force an opponent to deter troops from their intended positions in order to guard rear areas or lines of communications. Often times, these raids targeted enemy supply lines as well. Interdicting supply lines could put a halt to operations further forward.

When it came to taking provisions, only what could be carried away easily was carried off. Wagons laden with supplies were often burned on the spot. Horses were hamstrung or driven off, depending on how much time the raiders had to accomplish their task.[3] Another aspect of inflicting damage on the enemy's logistics often manifested in the form of contributions.

Contributions usually included a combination of money and goods taken from a town, the implicit threat being that if the town did not comply it would be given over to the sack.[4] Light troops exacting contributions from towns often contributed to their reputation for excess, which will be discussed below. At times the allegations of brutality were unfounded, at others, they were all-too accurate. In either case, contributions stood as another way for war to feed war. The exactions received constituted something of a double win for the recipient as they added to his logistics while at the same time decreasing those of his opponent. Finally, the tools of the military trade in irregular warfare were the musket, the sabre, the rifle and, at times, the lance. The most useful attributes a soldier or commander could possess were stealth and a keen sense of when to engage and when to withdraw.

The smoothbore musket, of varying calibres, stood as the standard infantry weapons of the militaries both in Europe and North America.[5] While it was woefully inaccurate at ranges beyond 80 yards, in the hands of an accomplished marksman, it could still be relatively effective. By the early eighteenth century, the French had introduced the socket bayonet, a triangular pointed projection, roughly 18 inches in length, which allowed the musket to work as both a fire and a shock weapon. Generally, units discussed in the following pages who carried muskets tended to be equipped with bayonets as well. Rifled weapons, their assets and liabilities will receive detailed discussion below. For the moment, suffice it to say that while generally armed with smoothbore muskets, some records make mention of 'Croat Rifles,' which may indicate some sharpshooter companies among the irregulars from eastern Europe.[6] Martin Rink offers additional support to the preceding possibility, 'The process of fighting from cover and aimed fire was not unknown on the Habsburg frontier.'[7] Jäger were always armed with rifles,

---

3   Duffy, *Military Experience*, p.277.
4   John W. Wright, 'Military Contributions during the Eighteenth Century', *The Journal of the American Military Institute*, 3:1 (Spring 1939), pp.3–13.
5   The following discussion of muskets is derived from Anthony D. Darling, *Red Coat and Brown Bess* (Alexandria Bay, NY: Museum Restoration Service, 1971), Torsten Lenk, G.A. Urquhart (trans.) and J.F. Hayward (ed.), *The Flintlock: Its Origin and Development* (New York: J.F. Bramwell House, 1965).
6   Jim Purky, 'Light Infantry Forces in the Austrian-Prussian Theaters of the SYW', *Seven Years War Association Journal*, 8:4 (1996), p.40.
7   Martin Rink, 'Der kleine Krieg: Entwicklung und Teens asymmetrischer Gewalt bis 1740 bis 1815', *Militärgeschichte Zeitschrift*, 65:2 (2006), p.363.

as they were part of their peacetime equipage. The Pandours and the Croats often carried one or more brace of pistols as well, usually tucked into a belt worn around the waist.

Additional weapons carried by irregular troops included sabres and lances. Sabres, while generally seen as carried only by mounted troops were often carried by irregular infantry as well. Only mounted irregulars, specifically uhlans recruited in Saxony and Poland were equipped with the lance. Now that the various tactics and weapons employed by the irregular forces in Europe have been described, it is possible to turn to the re-emergence of these troops in the late seventeenth century.

Irregular warfare reached what one historian dubbed its 'silver age' during the wars of Louis XIV of France.[8] Alongside the sieges and occasional battles that marked this period in European warfare there occurred the constant back and forth of raids, counter-raids, ambushes and patrols. These actions, however, occurred essentially on an ad hoc basis, with troops detached from their parent units. In the French case much of this work was carried out by what were referred to as compagnies franches, or free companies. George Satterfield notes 17 of these units were in existence by 1707.[9] Prior to raising the compagnies franches, there existed no regular formations that specialized in or were dedicated to Small War in the French service. Likewise, following the War of the Spanish Succession (1700–1714) the light troops were among the first to be demobilized in the general reductions in strength that usually accompany militaries transitioning to peacetime. As one historian notes, 'most of the compagnies franches were eliminated in 1715, and those that survived were assigned to garrison duty.'[10] Consequently, there did not develop a formal body of understanding on how to conduct this type of fighting, nor did there develop any sort of institutional memory on the subject, much of the experience of irregular warfare in western Europe passed from the scene as the soldiers and officers experienced in the conduct of these operations passed from the scene following the War of the Spanish Succession (1701–1715). While there were always a few who possessed experience in the tactics of Small War, much of the work that went into creating an effective force of irregulars had to be repeated with the outbreak of each successive conflict.

The next conflict to involve much of the continent was the War of the Polish Succession. While this conflict was generally uneventful, it did serve as a training ground for many of the leaders who would emerge across the remainder of the century down to the Wars of the French Revolution.[11] During this conflict, new light units were raised and they conducted fairly successful operations. Likewise, the leaders of some of these units, partizans as they were then referred to, achieved some level of recognition and status.

---

8   George Satterfield, 'The Fate of Petite Guerre in Early Modern Europe', in *Revue Historique des Armées*, 286:1 (2017), pp.48–59.

9   Satterfield, 'Fate of Petite Guerre', p.54.

10   Brent Nosworthy, *The Anatomy of Victory: Battle Tactics, 1689-1763* (New York: Hippocrene Books, 1990), p.213.

11   On the War of the Polish Succession, see John L. Sutton, *The King's Honor and the King's Cardinal: The War of the Polish Succession* (Lexington: University Press of Kentucky, 1980), Maha Vajiravudh, *The War of the Polish Succession* (Oxford: Blackwell, 1901).

This was especially so of leaders such as Jacob Pasteur, La Croix, Dumoulin, and Kleinholds.[12]

The situation was vastly different in eastern Europe. Here, in the region where the Hapsburg domains bordered those of the Ottoman empire, there existed a constant state of low-intensity conflict. These border marches served as the training ground of the Croats, Grenzer and Pandours for whom clashes with their Ottoman neighbours stood as a part of life, and there a particular style of irregular warfare developed. It is worth noting that the term Grenz literally means border in German, so these troops were seen essentially as borderers or border security. Raids and counterraids between those facing one another across a hostile frontier stood as the norm. Stealth and speed in operations were necessary for success as whenever one group left home to attack another, they left their own kith and kin exposed to the possibility of enemy depredations. These troops would eventually be called forth from their native eastern marches to fight in the centre of Europe.

It was during the War of the Austrian Succession (1740–1748) that irregular warfare truly returned to the centre stage in western Europe.[13] Maria Theresa, hard pressed in her war to retain her birth right, called on the troops of her eastern marches, the Pandours and Croats. These men were experts at irregular warfare, especially since for many of them, it stood as a part of their life and livelihood. The Pandours and Croats developed and honed their skills in the constant back and forth conflicts with their Ottoman neighbours to the south. Now, when their empress called, they took their particular form of warfare to the areas around the battlefields of central and western Europe.

In transporting their tactics to the main arena of the conflict, the irregulars from the eastern marches performed several important functions for the Hapsburg armies. As the noted historian Gunther Rothenberg observed, 'They screened the Austrian main body from surprise attacks and, constantly hovering around the flanks and rear of the enemy, forced him to devote a considerable part of his forces to defending his depots and lines of communication.'[14] The units often consisted of both mounted troops and infantry. The mounted troops provided the irregulars with mobility which aided in their tactics, while the infantry provided valuable fire support to their mounted brethren. It is worth noting that until this point, the Hapsburg monarchy had encountered a significant degree of difficulty in managing these subjects. Still, they encouraged their Slav and Magyar nobles to raise their own forces for the purposes of border security as it consequently reduced the strain on the central monarchy.[15] The empress's call resulted in a massive outpouring of manpower from the borders of her empire, such that by 1741,

---

12 Nosworthy, *Anatomy of Victory*, p.213.

13 This conflict is sometimes referred to as the First and Second Silesian Wars. The First Silesian War lasted 1740–1742 while the Second Silesian War lasted 1744–1745.

14 Gunther E. Rothenberg, *The Military Border in Croatia, 1740-1881: A Study of an Imperial Institution* (Chicago: University of Chicago Press, 1966), p.19.

15 John Grenier, *The First Way of War: American War Making on the Frontier* (Cambridge: Cambridge University Press, 2005), p.94.

'A Wallachian Tolpatch with his Arms. A Croat with his Arms Standing Sentry. A Morlachian soldier with his Arms', by Johann Sebastian Müller. (Anne S.K. Brown Military Collection)

upwards of 20,000 Grenzer fought against the Prussian invaders in Silesia.[16] The preceding did not the represent full capacity of the border either, which some place as high as 39,000 infantry and 6,000 cavalry, as to mobilize all of the troops would leave the area open to Ottoman depredations.[17] As a result, only about half of the of the military strength of the region could be brought to bear in other theatres at any given time.[18]

Among these early irregular fighters was Franciscus von der Trenck. Trenck stands out as a colourful figure in his own right. Born in Reggio, Italy in 1711, his father served as an Austrian officer but was of Prussian descent. Trenck grew up Slavonia, Hungary and Italy as his father's career entailed frequent relocation. He joined the Hapsburg Imperial Army in 1728 but resigned soon thereafter. On the death of his wife, he took service in the Russian army fighting against the Turks. It was in this service that Trenck met Ernst Gideon von Laudon, who served as a powerful patron to the Pandour leader. He returned to the Austrian army, where Prince Charles Alexander of Lorraine took an interest in him.[19]

---

16   Rothenberg, *Military Border*, p.19.
17   Stephen Summerfield, *Austrian Light Cavalry and Staff, 1740-1765* (Huntingdon: Ken Trotman Publishing, 2021), p.62.
18   Summerfield, *Austrian Light Cavalry*, p.62.
19   Biographical information on Trenck is derived from Kurt Sonntag, *Trenck, der Pandur und die Brandschatzung Bayerns* (Munchen: Nusser, 1976), and Oscar Teichman, *Pandour Trenck: An Account of the Life of Franciscus von der Trenck, 1710-1749* (London: John Murray, 1927).

On 27 February 1741, responding to the call for aid from Maria Theresa, Trenck raised a unit of 1,000 men, many of whom were volunteers, though the unit included some pardoned prisoners as well. All of the men were ethnic Croats and Serbs from Slavonia.[20] Over the course of its existence Trenck's unit expanded until it eventually reached a peak of 5,000 infantry and light cavalry.[21] Wherever these troops campaigned, whether it was Slavonia, Bohemia, Bavaria or France, they earned a reputation for audacity and effectiveness.[22] Pandour Trenck could be quite successful as a leader of small unit operations, however, he alienated many of his peers through is reputation for bad manners, and worse still, his penchant for brutality and looting while on campaign.

Initially, Trenck's misdeeds tended to be overlooked. In 1745, his unit was raised to the status of a Pandour regiment in response to a petition by the commander to the empress.[23] While he could be quite effective in planning and executing various raids as well as other operations, his excesses of violence and pillaging eventually ran him afoul of the Austrian military establishment and he was relieved of his command in 1746 and sentenced to confinement in one of the imperial fortresses at Brno. The charge was simply 'acts of violence.'[24] During his imprisonment, Trenck composed a memoir which, while certainly self-aggrandizing, offered numerous detailed accounts of his exploits. It would not require too much perusal of the work to gain significant insight into how to conduct irregular operations. Trenck's memoire therefore stands as one of the first attempts to set down how to conduct the various operations of Small War from an actual practitioner. One example of his exploits from the campaign of 1742 went as follows,

> The 26th of February, I was sent to attack the enemy at Reichenhall. I arrived there the 29th, and commencing the attack at five in the afternoon, I took post within twenty paces of the wall, by a smith's shop. I broke down the back part of the smith's house and planted there two pieces of cannon. In the night I received a reinforcement of two companies of grenadiers of old Konigseck's whereupon I redoubled my attack, and kept firing at them and they at me, with great vivacity. At length the garrison, consisting of three hundred men, regular troops besides seven hundred archers, under the command of a colonel Mercy, consented to capitulate, and accordingly surrendered themselves prisoners of war the 30th of March.[25]

The preceding represents something of an atypical activity for irregular troops, as it appears that Trenck and his Pandours were taking part in a siege.

For a brief, English-language description of Trenck's life and exploits, see James R. Mc Intyre, 'A Scoundrel's Scoundrel: The Life and Exploits of Baron Franciscus von der Trenck, Pandour Leader', in *The Journal of the Seven Years War Association*, 19:1 (Winter 2014), pp.27–42.
20 Summerfield, *Austrian Light Cavalry*, p.66.
21 Summerfield, *Austrian Light Cavalry*, p.66.
22 Summerfield, *Austrian Light Cavalry*, p.66.
23 Summerfield, *Austrian Light Cavalry*, p.66.
24 Summerfield, *Austrian Light Cavalry*, p.66.
25 Francis Baron Trenck, James J. Mitchell (ed. and illus.), *Memoirs of the Life of the Illustrious Francis Baron Trenck* (London: W. Owen, 1747), pp.72–73.

Usually, they would be detached from the army during a siege to work at interdicting relief efforts on the part of the enemy. Operating between the besieging force and the garrison they would cut communications between the fortress and any relief force in the vicinity, thus depriving the leaders of both forces of any intelligence concerning one another. In the above example, the action seems to have been against more of a small, fortified village as opposed to a major town as he notes literally breaking into a smith's house, which implies that the walls were not very strongly constructed. Another point of interest is that the defenders, likely local militia, were archers as opposed to musketeers.

In another undertaking shortly thereafter, Trenck's forces marched off in pursuit of enemy irregulars. Trenck noted,

Tidings were brought that the Bavarian huntsmen, who were posted in the windings of the river Iser, had plundered general Hermerstein's baggage, robbed the escort, consisting of forty men, and murdered the captain, together with six common soldiers; I was commanded away forthwith, with sixty-four Pandours and four hundred Croats, to reduce those hunters, who were now 1200 strong, and obtain satisfaction for the damage done to general Hermerstein, which amounted to fifteen thousand florins. This was a very dangerous expedition, having desperate fellows to deal with, whom even our regular troops were afraid of. However, I undertook the job, and ordered my matters as follows. I marched in the dead of the night with my detachment from Munich to Wolfershausen: from whence I might reach with no great difficulty the next day Tilk and Lengries, places situated on the windings of the Iser. Here I sent for intelligence, which happened to be far from favourable, tidings being brought that the hunters were increased to eighteen hundred men. This notwithstanding, I gave orders to my men to hold themselves in readiness to march the next day, intending to give the enemy no further time to grow stronger. The Croatian officers … upon advice received of the enemy's strength, entered into a conspiracy with their four hundred men, that instead of marching to Tilk, they should wheel about and take the road to Vilshoven. They did accordingly as they had agreed upon, and in the morning early, as they passed under my window, they all fired off their pieces, and left me behind in the lurch.

What would any other person have done in my situation with sixty-four men only, and almost within sight of Tilk, and surrounded by, eighteen hundred of the enemy? I called all my men together, and putting on an air of courage and spirit, I told them, that as the other cowardly fellows had deserted us, the booty we should get of those wretches (so I called the hunstmen) would now be all our own; that they were only a parcel of raw undisciplined peasants. I knew the contrary of this very well in my own mind, and was fully sensible of the danger I was exposed to. But I thought it was more advisable to put on a good face before my men, in order to encourage them to the attack; for had I resolved to retire, I should have had a whole swarm of these locusts upon my back. I put myself therefore at the head of my troops, and leading them along side of a new road, I fell suddenly upon the hunters, who had intrenched themselves in the village of Lengries. The attack was so furious and desperate, that at the very first onset I had two men killed and six wounded. Finding the enemy's fire superior to ours, we fell upon them sword in hand, and after a short resistance intirely [sic] routed them. In the pursuit we put fifty-two huntsmen to the sword, set fire to thirty-six houses, and blew up twenty-six wagons of powder into the air, which the garrison of Straubingen had sent them for their defence; and all this was done with a very trifling loss on our side. In this action I cleaved four fellows' skulls myself, and shot another dead… This defeat threw the hunters into such as consternation, that upon my summoning them the day following, they sent me all their arms picked up in the wagons, together with the thieves that had plundered count Hermerstein's baggage, with part of the baggage itself, and all petitioned for mercy. I accepted of their submission, but obliged them to pay fifteen thousand florins ready money, and to deliver a large quantity of forage and wood, and beside I sent away five hundred and seventy-two fine horses to the army, which came in good time, being very much wanted. This expedition being finished, I was recalled to Munich …[26]

The most distinguishing feature of the above account is certainly Trenck's proclivity for self-promotion. Still, several factors in the above operation stand out. One of these was Trenck's decision to travel only at night. Movement at night reduced the chance of discovery of his force's numbers and location by their opponents. As will be seen, the same practice was often followed by irregulars in North America.

Another point of interest that deserves attention involved Trenck's use of plunder as a means to motivate his troops. As will be seen, plunder stood as a common inducement to irregular troops in both theatres under investigation, and to an extent occupied similar roles in both as well. At the most basic level, for the side taking the plunder, it stood as a double win. As in the case above, Trenck's forces took horses much needed for transport by his own side while at the same time depriving the enemy of their use and thus reducing their mobility and consequently their freedom of action.

It is notable that Trenck's pursuit was launched against 'hunters', the literal translation of jäger. Since the jäger were often employed as light troops by the various German states of the Holy Roman Empire, it seems reasonable to surmise, then, that the men under Trenck's command were operating against other irregulars. His dismissive comments on the enemy jäger demonstrate an interesting use of deception as well. In this case, the Pandour leader downplayed the seriousness of the threat posed by the enemy troops in order to bolster his own men's morale.

Another common attribute of irregular operations displayed by Trenck was the use of surprise. In the above episode, the Pandour leader utilized surprise as a means to compensate, at least in part, for his own numerical inferiority, it certainly could stand as a force multiplier. Surprise could be used to sow panic in opposing forces, or to disrupt enemy concentrations as well.

Pandour Trenck's career draws out another important aspect of the upcoming generation of irregular fighters during the War of the Austrian Succession. Their tactical acumen could easily be offset by their indiscriminate use of violence. The use of force can only accomplish military objectives when

---

26   Trenck, *Memoirs*, pp.73–75.

focused on the enemy. Trenck never quite seemed to grasp this reality. Still, he was far from the only leader of irregular forces to engage in unwarranted violence. As the Hapsburg field marshal Khevenhuller-Metsch wrote, 'setting fire to houses, pillaging churches, cutting off ears and eyes, murdering citizens and raping women' were the stock in trade of these troops.[27] Likewise, as one historian of irregular warfare observed, 'For the Central and Eastern European irregulars, civilians, not opposing armies, were the objects of armies in times of war.'[28] Trenck's actions often exemplified this darker side of Small War as well, though he was eventually held to account for his actions and died, as noted, in Spillberg Castle in Brno on 4 October 1749.[29]

Thus, the example of the type of war Trenck and his Pandours waged remained the rule rather than the exception. When the Pandours and Croats first arrived on the scene in western Europe, the militaries they came up against were unprepared to respond to their tactics. As previously noted, in the west, the set-piece battle and the siege had come to dominate. As Frederick II (the Great) of Prussia conceded later,

> Because of his superiority in light troops, the enemy had the advantage of knowing all that transpired in the king's camp [that is, because of the intercepted communications]; nor did the Prussians dare send out scouting parties, at least without sacrificing them, due to the superior enemy parties; thus the king's army, entrenched in the Roman style, was confined to its camp.[30]

Frederick's retreats from Bohemia in both 1744 and 1745 were due to his losses to the Austrian irregulars as opposed to losses in battle.[31] As the renowned historian of eighteenth century warfare Christopher Duffy observed of the Prussian army, 'Almost every regiment owned a horror-story of some episode when it had been caught at a disadvantage by the Croats.'[32] This view was echoed by later historians, such as M.S. Anderson, who noted, 'From early in their invasion of Silesia the Prussians found themselves harassed, their communications threatened and their supplies interrupted by Grenzers and Pandours, irregular units originally raised largely in the Hapsburg military frontier areas in Croatia, which soon became known and feared for their mobility and their propensity to plunder and destroy.'[33]

While the Croats of Maria Theresa's realm were the first irregular troops mobilized in the conduct of petite guerre, they were soon followed by others, such as the Cossacks of the Russian Empire, the compagnie franches of France, the Freikorps of Prussia and the jäger of many of the smaller German states.

---

27   Khevenhuller-Metsch quoted in Grenier, *First Way of War*, p.93.
28   Grenier, *First Way of War*, p.93.
29   Summerfield, *Austrian Light Cavalry*, p.66.
30   Frederick II quoted in Aspery, *War in the Shadows*, p.53.
31   Johannes Kunnisch, *Der Kleinen Krieg: Studien zum Heerwesen des Absolutismus.* (Weisbaden: Steiner, 1973), p.13.
32   Christopher Duffy, *The Army of Frederick the Great* (Chicago: The Emperor's Press, 1996), p.131.
33   M.S. Anderson, *War of the Austrian Succession* 1740-1748 (London: Longman, 1995), p.221.

The freikorps require some explanation, as they formed an intermediary step between the practices common in raising armies that hearkened back the medieval period and the developing bureaucratic state. Initially, the term freikorps was applied to any formation that was not attached to a standing regiment. At first, they found their main employment as garrison forces for the various fortresses, as this would in turn free up troops from the line regiments for service in the field.[34] Essentially, the freikorps were recruited by an individual, usually but not necessarily a nobleman, at their own expense, and not by any government.[35] They were then taken into the service of the respective sovereign. At this time, the recruiter would receive a cash payment from the state to cover the costs they incurred in raising the unit. Often the contract between the government and the recruiter appointed the latter as the unit's commander. In many cases, the commander was allowed fair amount of latitude in choosing their subordinates as well. Once accepted into service by the state, the unit would be fed and clothed at its expense. The advantage of freikorps was that they allowed a sovereign to raise a number of units of light troops fairly quickly and inexpensively. The troops could be raised without dramatically expanding the government bureaucracy as well.

While they served as an effective expedient to raising new formations quickly, the freikorps possessed some significant drawbacks. Chief among these was the fact that the government held very little control over the unit as it remained essentially the property of its commander. Consequently, the relative autonomy of the freikorps prevented the authorities from verifying that the unit remained worth the money paid for it. Furthermore, the lack of official oversight made it difficult to determine if the commander was simply embezzling funds paid for the maintenance of his troops as well. At the same time, these units were not entitled to the same amount of support from the state accorded to the regular line regiments. They could be recruited at the beginning of a conflict and just as easily disbanded at its conclusion. Those who served in the ranks were not entitled to any support should they be wounded and unable to return to a civilian occupation. Freikorps consisted of a variety of troops including dragoons, hussars, infantry, jäger, lancers, and at times possessed their own artillery as well.[36] A unit composed of any one of the preceding types of troops would be designated accordingly. For instance, a company of jäger raised as described above would be known as Frei-jäger. If, however, a squadron of hussars were added to the jäger, it would then become a freikorps. While freikorps were an expedient to raising units for service quickly, their ad hoc nature undermined their unit cohesion and could serve as an impediment to their effectiveness.

---

34   Peter Wilson, 'Glassenapp's Freikorps', *Seven Years War Association Journal*, 10:4 (Summer 1999), p.10

35   Wilson, 'Glassenapp's Freikorps', p.10.

36   Stephen Summerfield, *Prussian Freikorps and Jager of the Seven Years War* (Huntingdon: Ken Trotman Publishing, 2018), p.5. See also James R. McIntyre, 'Pandours, Partisans and Freikorps: The Development of Irregular Warfare and Light Troops across the Eighteenth Century', in Alexander S. Burns (ed.), *The Changing Face of Old Regime Warfare Essays in Honour of Christopher Duffy* (Warwick: Helion and Company, 2022), p.170.

An obvious choice to raise light troops and one already available to many of the leaders in central Europe were the jäger. These were the game wardens on the royal demesne of the various estates across the heartland of the Holy Roman Empire. Their role was to protect the game on the landed nobility's preserve from poachers. They hunted as well to keep the game population down on the royal estates. The activities of their profession, and it was considered a profession with its own guild, ensured that the jäger were skilled at hunting and woodcraft. They carried rifles which were fairly short as compared to the musket, and fired a shot that ranged between .32 and .40 calibre.[37] The jäger, therefore came to their military role 'through natural habits of life.'[38] Their ability to move quietly through densely wooded areas would aid them significantly in scouting as well as staging ambushes or defending against those set up by their Pandour and Croat adversaries.[39]

Among the first to grasp their possible military uses was Frederick of Prussia, who formed a unit of 60 guides from the Prussian game wardens in 1740. They fulfilled the dual role of protecting reconnaissance parties from ambush and guiding the regulars through difficult terrain.[40] Still, there were liabilities for the jäger. They were very vulnerable to cavalry as their rifles possessed no fittings for bayonets and their weapons took up to a minute to reload. During this reloading cycle the jäger were most vulnerable to enemy mounted troops, and to an extent to infantry as well who would take advantage of their vulnerability by charging them with the bayonet.[41]

While Prussia and several of the other German states called up their game wardens, other militaries responded in a more ad hoc fashion with men being detached from existing units and simply being ordered to act as light troops. The results of this approach left much to be desired, and there quickly occurred a shift to the raising of units that either specialized in irregular warfare, or troops were raised from elements of the population that were perceived as possessing specific qualities which suited them to serve as irregulars. As the noted military historian Christopher Duffy observed, 'Though in the beginning, light troops were simply regular line infantry made to perform a new set of tasks and duties, quickly new recruiting and training practices developed.'[42]

Several units raised during the War of the Austrian Succession established a reputation for their proficiency in irregular tactics. One example of such a unit was the Arquebusiers de Grassin, founded by Simon Claude de Grassin

---

37   George Shumway, *Jaeger Rifles* (York, PA: George Shumway Publisher, 2003), pp.14–20.

38   Duffy, *Military Experience*, p.269.

39   Rory M. Cory, *British Light Infantry in North America in the Seven Years War*, MA Thesis, (Simon Fraser University, 1993), p.39; Thomas M. Barker and Paul R. Huey, 'Military Jägers: Their Civilian Background and Weaponry.' in *The Hessians: The Journal of the Johannes Schwalm Historical Association*, 15 (2012), pp.1–15.

40   Duffy, *Army of Frederick*, p.131.

41   Duffy, *Army of Frederick*, p.133.

42   Duffy, *Army of Frederick*, p.212.

'Feld-jägercorps zu Fuss', by
Ludwig Scharf. (Anne S.K.
Brown Military Collection)

based on a royal permit issued 1 January 1744.[43] This unit eventually included a combination of both infantry and cavalry.

Probably the most well-known performance of the Grassins came at the battle of Fontenoy, where, posted in the Bois de Barry they inflicted heavy casualties on the attacking British and Allied infantry, breaking up their advance and pursuing them on their retreat.[44] The Grassins served in *Maréchal* Maurice de Saxe's 1745 campaign in Belgium as well.[45]

During Saxe's campaign in Belgium the Grassins provide an example of how the activities of light troops could sometimes spark larger engagements. Shortly after the battle at Fontenoy, the French army marched toward Rebets. During the march, the Grassins engaged a force of roughly 400 Allied hussars initially driving them out of Lessins. The hussars returned with some 2,000 infantry and cavalry. The Grassins then held out until they were reinforced. In essence, their actions generated an encounter battle that grew in proportions until the Allied troops were driven off the field again.[46]

There were reasons for the ready French acceptance of irregular formations and petite guerre. As historian Brent Nosworthy observes, 'The methods of irregular troops appealed to the French, whose own tactics were offensively oriented and left the soldier to his own initiative much more than in either British or German military traditions.'[47] To be fair, the French possessed some experience of this type of warfare going back to the wars of Louis XIV. Further, they previously experimented with light troops in the form of the compagnes franches. It seems that some memory of these troops persisted with the royal military establishment, since France already had 14 compagnes franches available at the outbreak of the War of the Austrian Succession, each one regulated by royal ordnance dated 1 December 1738.[48] Based on this background, they were quick to perceive the applicability of these formations to the Small War and to grasp the potential for deploying light troops in the more broken sections of the battlefield. It could be argued, then, that the French were quick to develop a military culture with a propensity for irregular tactics. Interestingly, as the French rapidly expanded the number of light troops during the War of the Austrian Succession, they initially focused their recruiting efforts on younger men. They soon discovered, however, that younger recruits generally 'lacked the long-term stamina needed for this very demanding type of work and veterans in their thirties were much preferred.'[49]

It is necessary to address one other example of irregular developing contemporaneously with the War of the Austrian Succession. It is often

---

43   Information on the Grassins is drawn from Brent Nosworthy, 'The Arquebusiers de Grassin', *Seven Years War Association Journal*, 13:1 (Winter 2003), pp.22–23. See also Sandrine Picaud-Monnerat, *La Petite Guerre au XVIIIe Siecle* (Paris: Economica, 2010), pp.345–361.

44   James Falkner, *The Battle of Fontenoy 1745: Saxe against Cumberland in the War of the Austrian Succession* (Barnsley: Pen and Sword, 2019), pp.106–107.

45   Henry Pichat, *Maurice de Saxe's 1745 Campaign in Belgium* (Paris: Librarie Militaire R. Chapelot, 1909), trans. George Nafziger, The Nafziger Collection, 2011.

46   Abbé Rousseau, *The King of France's 1744-1745 Campaign* (Amsterdam: Westein in the Kalverstaat, 1755), trans. George Nafziger, The Nafziger Collection, 2012, p.20.

47   Nosworthy, *Anatomy of Victory*, p.211.

48   Satterfield, 'Fate of Petite Guerre', p.54.

49   Nosworthy, *Anatomy of Victory*, p.212.

'Arquebusiers de Grassin, 1745', unsigned watercolour, 1849. (Anne S.K. Brown Military Collection)

asserted that Great Britain did not possess any irregular forces until their involvement in the North American theatre during the Seven Years War. This conclusion is only partially accurate. While the British Army did not field any light formations officially until the Seven Years War, they were both interacting with and learning from irregulars during the War of the Austrian Succession. On the Continent, figures such as George Augustus, Lord Howe, gained experiences of troops such as the Pandours first-hand while fighting with the Allied army in the low countries. At the same time, in July of 1745, Charles Edward Stuart (popularly known as Bonnie Prince Charlie) sailed for Scotland in a bid to regain the British throne for his father, James Francis Edward Stuart. Charles Edward initiated his campaign by raising the Stuart standard at Glenfinnan on 19 August 1745. While a full recounting of the 1745 Jacobite Uprising is beyond the scope of the present work, a brief overview will highlight some significant connections concerning irregular forces and Small War.[50]

Initially, Charles Edward's forces enjoyed some success, capturing Edinburgh and winning the battle of Prestonpans on 21 September. Many of the clan leaders viewed French aid, and even troops as a necessary prerequisite to joining the uprising. While the French did send some regular troops,

---

50   For a more thorough discussion of the uprising, popularly known as 'the '45', see Christopher Duffy, *Fight for a Throne: The Jacobite '45 Reconsidered* (Warwick: Helion and Company, 2015); Jacqueline Riding, *Jacobites: A New History of the '45 Rebellion* (London: Bloomsbury, 2016).

their numbers were small, and many of those dispatched did not succeed in making the channel crossing.[51] When French military and economic aid did not materialize in the quantities they expected, many remained publicly neutral. Charles Edward responded by launching an invasion of England. Poor logistics and squabbles among the leadership undermined the campaign, and the support of English Jacobites failed to materialize. Consequently, the decision was made to retreat back into Scotland. The retreat was poorly conducted. Still, the Scots managed to elude the slower moving English forces, crossing back into Scotland on 20 December. The Jacobites won a tactical victory against the English at Falkirk Muir on 17 January 1746, however, their main army suffered a severe defeat at Culloden on 16 April 1746 and the rebellion was effectively broken.

Through the course of the fighting, the Scots routinely moved more quickly and outmanoeuvred their English opponents. Realizing the potential of utilizing these qualities for the benefit of the throne, the Crown began to raise Scottish contingents to serve as irregulars. The recruiting of the Scots formed a part of a near-fixation for irregular formations which began sweeping across Europe in the aftermath of the War of the Austrian Succession. Along with the enthusiasm for various light units, numerous veterans and military thinkers began to put down on paper their experiences, as well as their prescriptions for the most effective use of these troops.

---

51   On the French troops, see Andrew Bamford, *The Lilies and the Thistle French Troops in the Jacobite '45* (Warwick: Helion and Company, 2018).

2

Codifying the Experience of Small War

Historian and military analyst J.F.C. Fuller aptly summed up the reaction of many military leaders of the time when he stated, 'By the time the War of the Austrian Succession had been concluded, light infantry, chiefly on account of the Croats and Pandours, forced themselves, willy-nilly, into recognition.'[1] Among those who perceived the potential for light troops was the famed *Maréchal de France*, Maurice de Saxe.

Saxe was born in 1696 in Goslar, then part of the Holy Roman Empire. He was rumoured to be one of the illegitimate children of Augustus the Strong of Poland. He began his military career at age 12, serving in the army of prince Eugene of Savoy during the War of the Spanish Succession after which he served briefly in the Russian army of Peter the Great in the Great Northern War (1700–1721). Saxe next served for one campaign (1717) under Charles VI in his war against the Ottoman Empire. He then returned to France, later serving in the War of the Polish Succession (1733–1735) and finally the War of the Austrian Succession.[2] Considering his background, by the 1730s, Saxe possessed a wealth of experience on warfare in a variety of settings across Europe.

Saxe discussed light troops in his famous, *Mes Reveries*, a work often dismissed by some later authors due to the circumstances under which it was composed. The work was supposedly written 'over the course of thirteen sleepless nights in 1732.'[3] For some time the book circulated only in manuscript form. It was only published in 1757.[4] Once published, however, it exerted a significant impact among military professionals of the day.

Saxe developed a combined force which he dubbed a legion, in recognition of its Roman forebears. Light troops formed an essential part of Saxe's legion. He described the recruiting and composition of his legion as follows,

---

1   J.F.C. Fuller, *British Light Infantry in the Eighteenth Century* (London: Hutchinson & Co., 1925), pp.56–57.
2   For more on Saxe see, Jean-Pierre Bois, *Maurice de Saxe* (Lille: Fayard, 1992); Jon Manchip White, *Marshal of France: The Life and Times of Maurice, Comte de Saxe, 1696-1750* (Chicago: Rand McNally, 1962).
3   Duffy, *Military Experience*, p.viii.
4   Duffy, *Military Experience*, p.55.

The light armed foot are … to be chosen in their regiments, the centurions selecting the younger and most active. Their arms must consist of nothing more than a very light fowling-piece and bayonet with a handle to it. The fowling piece is to be made so as to receive the charge at the breech, so that it will not need to be rammed.[5]

This would enhance the men's rate of fire and allow them to fire from a prone position as well. Saxe continued setting out the light troops in his legion, 'All the equipment must be as light as possible. Their officers will be chosen in the same manner without regard to seniority. They must be drilled frequently and must practice jumping and running, but, above all, firing at a mark at three hundred paces distance.'[6]

Further, the troops of the legion would be placed in the advance guard when the body moved to the attack. Moving out some 100 to 200 paces from the line in dispersed order, these troops would be the first to engage the enemy. Beginning when they reached a distance of 300 paces from the enemy, the light troops were to commence firing at will. They were to maintain their fire until they narrowed the distance to roughly 50 paces. Their commander would then order the light troops to retreat and the men would retire slowly firing as they did so. Their retreat would, in turn, allow the men to rejoin the main body of the legion and fill in the intervals between the regiments. Saxe calculated that his light infantry would fire on the enemy for seven to eight minutes during the course of the above attack. Interestingly, while in theory the men should be able to get off six shots per minute, if they adhered to the standard expectations placed on them, Saxe calculated the rate of fire of his light troops on the basis of only four shots per minute.[7] More significantly, it seems that the role of the light troops was to lure enemy forces forward to confront the main body of the legion.

Others, in addition to Saxe, sought to codify their experiences with irregular warfare in the conflict just past. The works these veterans produced included Armand François De La Croix's *Traité de la Petite Guerre Pour la Compagnies Franches*, Thomas Le Roy de Grandmaison's *A Treatise on Military Service* and Mihály de Jeney's *The Partisan*. Even Frederick II set down his thoughts on light troops, how they should be led and how their tactics could be applied most effectively and countered.[8] It should be

---

5   Maurice de Saxe, *Mes Reveries*, quoted in Thomas R. Phillips (ed.), *The Roots of Strategy: A Collection of Military Classics* (London: John Lane, 1943), p.214.

6   Saxe in Phillips, *Roots of Strategy*, p.214.

7   Robert S. Quimby, *The Background of Napoleonic Warfare: The Theory of Military Tactics in Eighteenth-Century France* (New York: Columbia University Press, 1957), p.48.

8   Armand François De La Croix, *Traité de la Petite Guerre pour les Compagnies Franches, Dans lequel on voit utilité, la difference de leur Service d'avec celui des autres Corps, la manière la plus avantageuse de les condiuré, de les équiper, de les commandeur & les discipliner; & les ruses de Guerre qui leur sont propres* (Paris: Antoine Boudet, 1759); Thomas Le Roy de Grandmaison, *La Petit Guerre ou Traité de Service les Toupes Legeres en Campagne* (Paris, n.p., 1756) translated by Lewis Nicola as *A Treatise on the Military Service, of Light Horse, and Light Infantry, and in the Fortified Places. By Major General de Grandmaison, Formerly a Captain, With the Rank of Lieutenant Colonel of Cavalry* (Philadelphia: Robert Bell, 1777); Louis Michel de Jeney, *The Partisan: Or the Art of Making War in Detachments* (London: n.p.,

clear from the preceding chapter that there developed in the French army something of a preoccupation for irregular formations and the type of war they conducted. To some extent this is explained by the notion that irregulars fit in with the French vision of how they fought wars, their military culture. It should come as no surprise then, that the first authors to attempt to analyze the raising, training and employment of light troops were French.

De la Croix's was the first to be published, coming out in 1752. The work addressed a number of significant points concerning the use of light troops. His main themes included such topics as the discipline that should be observed when marching, and more interestingly, the manner of making night attacks.[9]

Writing soon thereafter, Thomas Auguste Le Roy de Grandmaison composed his *La Petite Guerre, ou Traité du Service des Troupes Légères en Campagne*. Thomas Le Roy de Grandmaison was born in 1715 to a family of the provincial nobility and showed an early aptitude for the military profession. He joined the French army and became a gentleman volunteer. Grandmaison experienced his first major taste of combat during the War of the Austrian Succession. His career did not start auspiciously. He was captured. 'Taken from Bertholds in Austria in November 1741, he spent seven months in Hungary as a prisoner.'[10]

The young soldier did not waste his time in captivity, however. Instead, he considered the superiority of the Hungarians in petite guerre, especially their mounted troops. He was fascinated by the cunning of their horsemen, the composition of the Hungarian saddles, and the exoticism of their dress. The dress of the Croats clearly impacted the later uniforms of the French mounted troops, as well as others, in the form of pelisses and caps. He was further captivated by their language and swordsmanship.[11]

On his return from captivity, Grandmaison left Dumoulin's free company in 1743. In January of 1744, he took advantage of the creation of the new formation of light troops discussed above, the Arquebusiers de Grassin, to raise one of six companies of 50 horsemen for the regiment.[12] Raising the company allowed Grandmaison to skirt the often tedious and expensive process for becoming a captain. At the same time, it offered him some chance at remuneration. In addition to the purely monetary incentives, there was perhaps the greater incentive of serving under Simon Claude de Grassin, whom he likely knew by reputation.

Grassin was first a *capitaine* in the grenadiers in the regiment of Picardy. He had distinguished himself in Bohemia and Bavaria by his practice in Small War. His successful efforts bolstered his request to raise his own unit.

1760); Frederick II von Hohenzollern, anon. trans., *Military Instructions, written by the King of Prussia, for the Generals of his Army* (London: n.p., 1762).

9   M. De la Croix, *Traité de la Petite Guerre pour la Compagnies Franches* (Paris: n.p., 1752), pp.25–26, 31–33, respectively.

10   Sandrine Picaud-Monnerat, 'Thomas-Auguste Le Roy de Grandmaison (1715–1801) un officier au service de la petite guerre', *Revue Internationale de Histoire Militaire*, 81 (2001), p.102.

11   Picaud-Monnerat, 'Grandmaison', p.102.

12   The Arquebussier likewise possessed 900 riflemen in nine companies.

Recruiting the Arquebusiers was a slow process. A list of officers, compiled between 1 January 1744 and 31 December 1746 yields 73 names. Many of the men in the unit were very young as well.[13] The Grassins were very active in the latter half of the War of the Austrian Succession, between 1744 and 1748.[14] Probably the most significant years for the Grassins were 1745 and 1746. As noted in the previous chapter, the Grassins played an integral role in the French victory at Fontenoy. Likewise, their accomplishments during 1746 led Grandmaison to receive the Cross of Saint-Louis for his role in the battle of Rocoux.[15] By this point, he had been wounded in combat several times as well.[16] This activity provided Grandmaison with numerous examples to draw from when he wrote his treatise. Interestingly, he attributed the unit's failures to the practice then prevalent of recruiting enemy prisoners into the ranks.

In January 1748, Grandmaison achieved the rank of *lieutenant colonel*. He appears to have passed over the rank of *major* or spent a very short period in that rank. His promotion was supported by Simon de Grassin, as well as the Comte de Estrees and the Marquis de Breze.[17]

Following the Peace of Aix-la-Chapelle, Grandmaison set down his reflections on his experiences.[18] An early commentator on the use of light troops, Grandmaison remarked on a number of issues connected with their recruitment, training and deployment. Early in the *Treatise* he discusses the issue of recruiting, beginning with the officers. He cautioned, 'The first business of a Colonel commissioned to raise a body of light troops is to appoint his officers. If self-interest prevails with him, employments are given to those who offer most, and not to those of most capacity; if, on the other hand, merit is preferred, he seeks only for men of reputation, experience and conduct.'[19] Thus he advocated for positions being awarded on the basis of merit rather than wealth, a concept that would become prevalent in France only with the Revolution. At the same time, the focus on the ability of a partisan officer was something often commented on by various authorities. Likewise, as will be seen below, leadership in an irregular unit could serve as a vehicle to social advancement.

Grandmaison next described the qualifications for the commander of light troops, 'It is absolutely necessary that a Colonel of light troops should be a man who has seen service, is well acquainted with the petite guerre; as he is answerable for the corps entrusted to him by the King, and by his advanced position near the enemy, is in constant danger of being carried

---

13   Picaud-Monnerat, 'Grandmaison', p.103.
14   Picaud-Monnerat, 'Grandmaison', p.103.
15   Picaud-Monnerat, 'Grandmaison', p.106.
16   Picaud-Monnerat, 'Grandmaison', p.106.
17   Picaud-Monnerat, 'Grandmaison', p.107.
18   Lewis Nicola produced an English translation of Grandmaison's *La Petite Guerre* in Philadelphia in 1776 which has been generally accepted. It is from this translation that subsequent materials from Grandmaison will be taken.
19   Thomas Le Roy de Grandmaison, Lewis Nicola, (trans.), *A Treatise on the Military Service, of Light Horse, and Light Infantry, and in the Fortified Places. By Major General de Grandmaison, Formerly a Captain, With the Rank of Lieutenant Colonel of Cavalry* (Philadelphia: Robert Bell, 1777), p.20.

off by them.'[20] Grandmaison's admonition that the officer commanding light troops be experienced in Small War seems obvious enough, however, in the context of the times, when commissions were often up for purchase, it served as an important injunction.

Regarding the proper employment of light troops, in a section titled *Of Parties, of Attacks, of Ambuscades, and of Surprises by Night and Day*, Grandmaison set out the responsibilities of a commander when entering a foreign territory,

> He interrogates every person he meets, to learn what is done or said in the country. If he hears that some party has been in the neighborhood, he must always suppose but half the number told him; for it is well known, that fifty men, either foot or horses, who file along a road appear much more numerous to the country people, then they really are; therefore his resolution, to seek or avoid the enemy must not entirely depend on their reports.[21]

Several points of interest emerge in the preceding. First is Grandmaison's concern with gathering information as a means of ensuring the security of the detachment. Along with the concern over security is a healthy caution to scepticism concerning the information gleaned from civilians.

Shortly thereafter Grandmaison provides very clear instruction on how to attack an enemy post,

> The most favourable time for an attack, is an hour before day, at which time men are generally in the deepest sleep; but as it may happen, that the enemys [*sic*] continuance in the village will not be longer, than what necessary for resting the men, who are then immediately to march, you must take the opportunity of defeating them while lodged in the houses, which you may be informed of by the country people, or by spies.[22]

Grandmaison continued, stressing 'Never, out of choice, defer the attack longer, especially if, after striking the blow, you have a long and dangerous retreat to make; as you may by this means employ the remainder of the night in getting at a distance.'[23] Clearly, Grandmaison offered much of practical value to the officer leading a force of light troops. His directions on when to launch an attack on an enemy post focused on the period when their guard was likely to be the least observant. Further, he enjoined the commander of light troops to be quick and aggressive in order to facilitate the retreat of his own force under cover of darkness. The use of the night for cover resembles the actions that Trenck discussed above. Grandmaison's injunction on the timing of an attack bear a strong resemblance to the preferences of Native American as will be discussed below.

---

20   Grandmaison, *Treatise on the Military Service*, pp.21–22
21   Grandmaison, *Treatise on the Military Service*, p.73.
22   Grandmaison, *Treatise on the Military Service*, p.75.
23   Grandmaison, *Treatise on the Military Service*, p.75.

Grandmaison aptly summed up the issue of supply in Small War, stating, 'The petite guerre, is a trade very fatiguing, often it requires Lacedemonian frugality and hardship, at other times everything is in profusion, this depends on the circumstances.'[24] While there is a fair amount of information on Grandmaison's career to provide context for his writing, the same is not the case with the next author.

For some time, establishing certain biographical information regarding the third author, Lajos Mihály de Jeney (1723–1797) presented some difficulty. Much of this was due to the fact that his work, like that of Grandmaison, first appeared in French, but was soon translated in English. Consequently, most subsequent historians assumed he was a French officer. Jeney in fact hailed from a Transylvanian noble family[25] and began his service as a hussar to the Austrian Empire in 1737 during the Austro-Turkish War of 1737–1739.[26] During the War of the Austrian Succession he served in the Baranyay Hussars as a non-commissioned officer. From there, he switched over to the French service beginning in 1747, being promoted to *lieutenant*. He spent the period between 1747 and 1753 with the Berchény Hussar Regiment. The following year, Jeney transferred to the geographic engineering department of the French army, where he served until 1755. It was likely during his service as a cartographer that Jeney wrote his treatise.

Clearly, Jeney meant his *The Partisan: Or the Art of Making War in Detachments* to serve as a sort of introductory text on the practice of Small War. Likewise, he saw it as a particularly challenging form of combat. For instance, he states at the outset of his work, 'There is no military Employment that requires more extraordinary Talents than that of a Partisan.' He continued, observing, 'He should be blessed with an Imagination fruitful in Projects, Stratagems and Resources.'[27] These were in Jeney's estimation the factors which went into making the successful partisan.

One aspect of Small War which seemed of particular importance for Jeney was finding the proper officers and men with the proper personal and physical attributes to conduct partisan operations. Concerning the personal qualities of the officers, he noted, 'There is nothing more dangerous than for a Partisan to be, in the least degree, attached to Women, Wine, or Wealth: The first will make him neglect his Duty, and will frequently expose him to Treachery and Destruction, the second is the cause of perilous Indiscretions...'[28]

Jeney discussed what he perceived as the key attributes of the common soldier in Small War as well. He, like many contemporaries, spent significant time discussing the physical attributes of the partisan. Given the nature of the service these men would undertake, such concern was only sensible. The

---

24   Grandmaison, *Treatise on the Military Service*, p.227.
25   Biographical information on Jeney is derived from Picaud-Monnerat, *Petite Guerre*, p.578 and Annamária Jankó, 'An Outstanding Person of the First Military Survey: Mihály Lajos Jeney.' *Cartographic Studies*, 13. Studies in honor of Professor István Klinghammer's 65th birthday. ELTE Department of Cartography and Geoinformatics. (2006) pp.201–207.
26   On the Austro-Turkish War of 1737–1739, see Virginia H. Aksan, *Ottoman Wars 1700-1870: An Empire Besieged* (London: Longman, 2007), pp.102–117.
27   Jeney, *The Partisan*, p.6.
28   Jeney, *The Partisan*, p.9.

issue of the proper height for a partisan was important among several of these authors, and Jeney was no exception, nor could he resist a barb at one of his contemporaries,

> There are others who, for the same Service, chuse [sic] to have their Infantry of a moderate Size, namely, about Five Foot, and their Cavalry Five Foot Five Inches. Mr. de Grand-Maison, in his Traité de la Petite Guerre is of this Opinion. I am not in the least surprised at it, since it corresponds exactly with the size of his own Person. A Man of Five Foot, says he, square built, is stronger and more able to bear Fatigue than one that is much taller, and consequently much fitter for a Foot Soldier. [29]

When it came to Jeney's own opinion as to the proper height of the partisan, he began with a general observation, '…Infantry should consist of the tallest Men we can meet with. As their Legs are longer, they will naturally make longer Paces when expedition is required, and, in an Action they will pierce with greater ease, and more certainty.'[30]

He continued, with a more specific prescription, 'It is my opinion therefore, that every Foot Soldier, for this Service, should measure at least Five Foot Six Inches (Royal Standard) and that Men of a larger size should be no means be rejected; but it is highly necessary that they should be perfectly well Limbed, not too Fat, and without any bodily Complaint whatsoever.'[31]

Not only did he list and discuss the physical attributes which he believed went into making a successful partisan, Jeney defined a number of key concepts of Small War as well. For instance, he explained that 'An Ambuscade is a body of Men concealed in a Wood, or otherwise with an Intention to surprise the Enemy. There are no Stratagems of War which afford a partisan better Opportunities of displaying his Genius and Resolution.'[32]

Yet another commentator, Frederick II of Prussia, set down his prescriptions for dealing with enemy light troops following on the conclusion of the War of the Austrian Succession as well. His Military Instructions, written in the late 1740s, contained a section titled Maxims and Instructions for the Light Troops, and all Officers Commanding in Detachment. While both the larger work and the particular section were initially kept secret, a copy was smuggled out of Prussia and translated into English by an anonymous British officer. In the opening to his section on light troops, Frederick leads off with an injunction to any officer commanding an advanced guard, 'His first care must be, to surround his post with a chain of sentries, or Videtts [sic], in such a manner that nothing can possibly approach him without his knowledge.'[33] The reason for this focus on the security of the post at the outset lay in the bitter experience of having so many of his units surprised

---

29   Jeney, The Partisan, p.11.
30   Jeney, The Partisan, p.12.
31   Jeney, The Partisan, p.12.
32   Jeney, The Partisan, p.106.
33   Frederick II, Military Instructions, Written by the King of Prussia, for the Generals of his Army: Being His majesty's own Commentaries on his Former Campaigns. Together with Short Instructions for the use of Light Troops (London: T. Becket and P.A. De Hondt, 1762), p.176.

by Austrian irregulars in the war just ended. The concern with security continued through the first chapter. Another section soon thereafter declared, 'No Detachment, or Relief, must be suffered to pass the Guard, before they have been regularly examined by a Non-commission'd Officer, even tho' they should give the Word, and tho' they should give a wrong Watch-word, you are not to fire, provided they halt, but if they continue to advance, you are to charge them immediately.'[34] The preceding was given in order to protect against enemy light troops using captured uniforms in order to infiltrate a Prussian camp.

A few pages later, Frederick set out very specific guidelines for the officer of a detachment of light troops on the march at night, of which Trenck himself may have approved. First, he asserted 'During the night, the officer will preserve his communications with his advanced guard, by causing a few men to march between them at a distance of thirty or forty paces from each other.'[35] He then added, 'It is very necessary, during the night, to be attentive that the men do not sleep, lest those in the rear should be left behind.'[36]

Gaining intelligence was of great importance to Frederick. He observed, 'When you come near the enemy, without being discovered, you must send some of your Hussars disguised, who are to learn, from the peasants, the situation of the enemy, but, to prevent suspicion, they are not to take the direct road.'[37] Next, the warrior-king turned to provisions for the protecting the detachment's camp, 'Whilst in the day time, you conceal yourself in the woods, you are to fix sentries in the tops of the highest trees.'[38]

Concerning the treatment of civilians, Frederick wrote, 'In case he should be in want of forage, or provisions, he must send, to the nearest village, a non-commissioned officer, and three or four disguised Hussars, with orders to collect what is wanted, to pay for the provisions, and give receipts for the forage, that you may be supposed to then be friends. The peasants are to be discharged as soon as they have delivered the forage … at the place where you halted.'[39]

Finally, in 1754, Lancelot Turpin de Crissé published his *Essai sur l'art de la Guerre*. The work encompassed two volumes. It was translated into English by a Captain Joseph Otway.[40] The second book of volume one contained sections dealing with the use of spies as well as ambushes.[41] Similarly, all of the fifth book of second volume addresses the necessity of having light troops and their proper usage.[42]

---

34 Frederick, *Military Instructions*, p.179.
35 Frederick, *Military Instructions*, pp.191–192.
36 Frederick, *Military Instructions*, p.192.
37 Frederick, *Military Instructions*, p.193.
38 Frederick, *Military Instructions*, p.193.
39 Frederick, *Military Instructions*, p.193.
40 Lancelot Turpin de Crissé, *Essai sur l'art de la Guerre* (Paris: Prault, 1754), Lancelot Turpin de Crissé, Captain Joseph Otway (trans.), *Essay on the Art of War* (London: A. Hamilton, 1761).
41 Crissé, *Essay on the Art of War*, vol.1, pp.155–162, 163–174.
42 Crissé, *Essay on the Art of War*, vol.2, pp.109–138.

From the preceding, it should be clear that each of these authors saw themselves as developing the parameters of this method of warfare. In this, he fell into what is referred to as the Military Enlightenment. As one of the historians of this aspect of the broader Enlightenment noted, 'The scientific model was perceived by them as a general method for the foundation of human knowledge and activity on an enduring basis of critical empiricism and reason.'[43] What other thinkers noted as the chains of tradition that bound other fields of human inquiry in outdated modes of thought and action the philosophes of the Military Enlightenment saw as holding back improvements in the conduct of war. Their answer to this was to take the concepts of the broader intellectual movement and apply them in the military sphere:

> Indeed, the military thinkers of the Enlightenment maintained that the art of war was also susceptible to systematic formulation, based on rules and principles of universal validity which had been revealed in the campaigning of great military leaders of history. At the same time, it escaped formalization in part, while the rules and principles themselves always required circumstantial application by the creative genius of the general.[44]

In essence, then, war encompassed elements of both art and science and for the authors currently under examination, nowhere was this assessment more valid than in the conduct of Small War. It should be kept in mind that the works discussed above were disseminated across the continent as well. Editions were available in Britain, first in French and later in translations beginning in the 1750s.[45] Consequently, these ideas were at least available to numerous military leaders of various ranks should they be interested in perusing the treatise being produced.

The use of light troops had grown significantly during the War of the Austrian Succession. As the American military historian Russell F. Weigley aptly summarized, 'much of the impetus toward employing light infantry in skirmishing tactics rolled across Europe not eastward from North America but westward from the Ottoman Empire.'[46] For the first time, as well, various practitioners of Small War sat down following the conclusion of the fighting in order to codify their experiences. Their writings would in many ways serve as the basis for the conduct of petite guerre in the coming clash.

These writings were not the only activity related to irregular warfare which took place during the period of peace following the Treaty of Aix-la-Chapelle. The French utilized camps of instruction to test various methods of employing light infantry, including merging their open tactics with the

---

43   Azar Gat, *The Origins of Military Thought: From the Enlightenment to Clausewitz* (Oxford: Clarendon Press, 1989), p.27.

44   Gat, *Origins*, p.29.

45   Samuel James Dodson, *Battle of Vellinghausen: Lessons Learnt? A study of the British army in the closing Stages of the Seven Years War in Western Europe as studies through the Battle Vellinghausen*, MA Thesis (University of Leeds, 2019), p.43.

46   Russell F. Weigley, *The Age of Battles: The Quest for Decisive Warfare from Breitenfeld to Waterloo* (Bloomington: Indiana University Press, 1991), p.269.

closed tactics of the regulars. The French attempted these hybrid tactics by forming platoon-sized piquets in each battalion who would provide a screen for an advance, occupying any 'advantageous terrain such as a hedge, mill, or the border of woods.'[47]

By the same token, there existed some detractors of the growing popularity of light troops. Some contemporaries feared that troops allowed the additional freedom of serving in light units would desert as soon as they were out of sight of their superiors.[48] As Sir Michael Howard noted Maria Theresa's adversaries complained that the light troops operated at such distances from the main Imperial armies that they were 'no more than brigands and murderers.'[49] Howard's point is echoed by Ilya Berkovich who notes that 'Low regard was also reserved for the free battalions operating on the periphery of regular armies, not least because of their disregard of accepted honourable conventions.'[50] The renowned French historian André Corvisier summed up the sentiments aptly in his classic study of early modern armies. While speaking in general terms, his comments seem particularly applicable the sentiments of those who shunned the use of irregular troops, 'Commentaries on the moral behavior of the troops are on the whole very critical...Violence, licentious behavior, and looting were the factors most often mentioned.'[51]

---

47 Nosworthy, *Anatomy of Victory*, p.214.
48 Ilya Berkovich, *Motivation in War: The Experience of Common Soldiers in Old Regime Europe* (Cambridge: Cambridge University Press, 2017), p.56.
49 Sir Michael Howard, *War in European History* (Oxford: Oxford University Press, 1976), p.77.
50 Berkovich, *Motivation in War*, p.169.
51 André Corvisier, Abigail T. Siddal (trans.), *Armies and Societies in Europe, 1494-1789* (Bloomington: Indiana University Press, 1979), p.179.

3

Raising the Light Infantry for the Seven Years War in Europe

The War of the Austrian Succession clearly produced a fixation with light troops in Europe, however, the conflict failed to produce an acceptable result for any of the belligerents with the exception of Brandenburg Prussia. The Treaty of Aix-la-Chapelle clearly supports Clausewitz's dictum that peace is never final.[1] The period after 1748 seemed more one of preparation for a renewal of conflict in Europe than a true time of peace. The major European powers worked to prepare for the next confrontation. This fact made all the more interesting in that the spark that would light the next conflagration among the great powers did not strike on the European continent on this occasion.

Where the previous conflicts of the eighteenth century had started in Europe among the great powers and then spread to their respective colonies, this one followed the reverse track. The war began in North America, when George Washington of Virginia got into a skirmish with French troops near Fort Duquesne (modern Pittsburgh) in what was known as the Ohio country. Word of the clash quickly spread to the European metropole. As the word of Washington's encounter disseminated across the continent, the various powers braced for another showdown between the houses of Bourbon and Hanover.

The preparations of the various states touched off a reshuffling of alliances which stood through the previous conflict suddenly shifted – the so-called diplomatic revolution. Now France allied with their long-time continental rival Austria along with Russia and Sweden. Seeking a continental partner to tie down the French forces and defend George II's patrimony of Hanover, Britain allied with Prussia.

Along with the diplomatic manoeuvring, the states sought to rapidly expand their respective militaries for the coming conflagration. Light troops were to play a significant role in the armed forces of all the belligerents. The following pages will highlight how the light troops were raised by the various states as well as present some examples of the Small War actions in which

---

1   Carl von Clausewitz, Michael Howard and Peter Paret (trans.), *On War* (Princeton: Princeton University Press, 1976), p.80.

they took part. At the same time, the light forces, as Martin Rink points out, began to come under greater control of the state. In essence, the irregulars became more regular or at least regulated.[2] An unforeseen consequence of this enhanced state control was that in many cases, these troops became 'jägers in name only,' as David Gates observed.[3] Not all of the units fielded by the belligerents will receive attention, only those that stood among the more significant players will be discussed.

Heading the list of belligerents to raise light troops for the coming conflagration was the Austrian Empire. Once again, Maria Theresa called upon her Pandours and Croats to come to the defence of her throne. There existed good reason for the empress to turn to the troops of her eastern marches once again. As her minister Wenzel Anton Count von Kaunitz-Rietberg noted,

> The Croats do not receive the credit which is their due. These men are the ones who are in the closest and most immediate contact with the enemy. They keep them in a state of constant unrest, they have put up with more hardship and danger than the other troops … and they have to run rather than march. They are given the most exacting tasks as a matter of routine, and their losses are treated as being of no account.[4]

Kaunitz's words of praise were echoed and given amplification by one of the early historians of the Seven Years War, Johann von Archenholz, who observed concerning these border troops,

> The Croats make the best light troops in Europe. The nature of the soil of their country, sandy and not very fruitful, the quantity of wooded land, a chain of mountains, and a rough climate are the causes of inuring the naturally powerful frame of the Croats, of accustoming them to all the hardships and privations of life, and of making them good soldiers. Hunting to which they are forced to have recourse for their support in their native land, makes them careless [of] all danger and they bear hunger and thirst, heat and cold, the most excruciating pain with the greatest equanimity, added to this they have no fear of death. In their love of their country and of their prince they are surpassed by no people, and with them desertion is never heard of; their arms in the use of which they are very expert, are a musket with a bayonet and a sabre.[5]

The Croats that would fight in the Seven Years War were not the same as those who participated in the War of the Austrian Succession. Responding to the excesses of soldiers such as Trenck and his ilk, the military establishment sought to bring the Croats under greater military discipline. The reasons for these efforts lay in the excesses committed by the irregulars in the preceding

---

2   Martin Rink, 'The Partisan's Metamorphosis: From Freelance Military Entrepreneur to German Freedom Fighter, 1740-1815', *War in History*, 17:1 (January 2010), p.14.

3   David Gates, *The British Light Infantry Arm c. 1790-1815* (London: B.T. Batsford Ltd. 1987), pp.18–19.

4   Kaunitz, Military Conference of 1 November 1757, quoted in Duffy, *Instrument of War*, p.396.

5   Johann von Archenholz, F.A. Catz (trans.), *The History of the Seven Years War in Germany* (Frankfurt am Main: C. Jugel, 1843), p.497.

conflict. As the preeminent military historian of the period, Christopher Duffy, observed,

> Although the Croats were supposed to receive pay and rations on the same scales as the 'German' forces, there were lengthy periods when they were left without any support, which encouraged them to take what they needed—and sometimes a little more—from the local population. It was never easy to distinguish between the bands which plundered out of necessity and those which plundered for criminal gain.[6]

He continued, noting that regular officers tended to take the negative view of all irregulars, and tended to see them 'as an infection which corrupted all the regular troops with whom they came in contact.'[7] After the reforms were implemented the resulting formations encompassed a corps that was more governable by the officers but in ways less effective. The Austrians resorted to raising greater numbers of light troops as well. By the outbreak of the Seven Years War, the Austrians possessed some 46,740 Croats who were liable to service. These could be called up in batches of roughly one-third at a time.[8] Christopher Duffy observed, '…the availability of light troops of their own would give the Austrians the means to answer the Prussian free battalions in kind and help to bolster the flagging efforts of the Croats.'[9] Clearly, the Austrians sought to make up for a decline in quality with additional quantity. He goes on to trace part of this decline in the effectiveness of the irregulars to changes made in their armaments. Whereas in the War of the Austrian Succession, the Croats were armed with their long Dalmatian muskets, which were accurate up to between three and four hundred paces, they were now armed with the standard Austrian infantry weapons, the use of which they never mastered.[10]

In addition, the Croats of the Seven Years War were instructed to dispense with their preferred tactic of the charge with the cold steel. The charge had served them well in the previous conflict as they brandished their long Turkish-style sabres. Now they were indoctrinated to rely on their musketry.[11] Both approaches seemed at odds with the Croats' natural habits of life.

The propensity of many commanders in the European theatre has been mentioned on several occasions in the preceding pages. At times, such as when the Austrian war council, the Hofkriegsrath, reprimanded the Prince of Zweibrücken, it was thought that this propensity stemmed from indecision. There was significant displeasure with the use of light troops to launch minor raids on enemy posts as well.[12] No less a figure than the empress Maria Theresa opposed this activity on two grounds, 'On the one side these operations exhaust the troops and horses to the point of ruin, and

---

6   Duffy, *Instrument of War*, p.396.
7   Duffy, *Instrument of War*, p.396.
8   Duffy, *Force of Arms*, p.14.
9   Duffy, *Instrument of War*, p.240.
10   Duffy, *Instrument of War*, p.397.
11   Duffy, *Instrument of War*, p.397.
12   Duffy, *Instrument of War*, p.396.

'A Pandour Collonel. A Pandour Ensign. A Pandour Collonel watch master', by Johann Sebastian Müller. (Anne S.K. Brown Military Collection)

cost the lives of many brave soldiers … whose loss we deplore. At the same time these undertakings do nothing of consequence to promote our main objectives, or dislodge the enemy from their positions.'[13]

It is clear that by this point, the Austrians possessed the best light forces in Europe. As one prominent historian of the eighteenth century noted, 'In the period extending from the Silesian Wars and the War of the Austrian Succession until the middle of the 1750s the ascendancy of the Austrian light troops at "*der kleine Krieg*" was assumed to be absolute.'[14] Likewise, some attempt had been made to rein in their actions and make them more disciplined. As one historian notes, 'The changes as they affected the Croatian light infantry were a unsatisfactory compromise, for they had deprived the Croats of something of their warrior virtues, without endowing them with the solidity of the 'German' infantry.'[15] The Austrians raised freikorps as well to participate in the coming conflict, however, these were not as effective as the formations recruited from the Ottoman frontier.[16] Consequently, 'the Austrians were in danger of losing

13   Maria Theresa to Serbelloni, 7 June 1762, quoted in Duffy, *Instrument of War*, p.396.
14   Duffy, *Instrument of War*, p.395. Italics in original.
15   Duffy, *By Force of Arms*, p.12
16   Jim Purky, 'Light Infantry Forces in the Austrian-Prussian Theaters of the SYW', *Seven Years War Association* Journal, 8:4 (Winter 1996), p.41.

the edge in irregular warfare they had enjoyed as recently as the 1740s.'[17] The decline in effectiveness of Austrian light troops posed its own threat as the opponents of the Hapsburgs saw the value of such forces and raised their own accordingly. The focus on light forces encompassed all of the belligerents, including Austria's primary foe.

In Prussia, Frederick II took a significantly different approach which has led some to conclude that they never developed an adequate response to enemy light troops. For instance, a recent popular history of the Seven Years War notes 'The major failing of Frederick and his army was their inability to deal with the Austrian light troops, the *Grenzer*.'[18] This assertion is false, as will be shown below. This view is reinforced by the late Christopher Duffy, who observed that Frederick II 'believed the enemy would always hold the advantage' in light troops.[19] Duffy continued, asserting, 'In the Seven Years War the Prussian regulars could still venture only at their peril into broken and unfamiliar country.'[20] What will emerge in the following pages is that while this may have been true at the outset of the conflict, the Prussians did develop countermeasures to address the threat posed by the Austrian light forces.

The Prussian warrior-king did, to a limited extent, utilize freikorps, however, these could be seen as more of a temporary solution in that they provided troops that could go into the field and counter the irregular forces of Prussia's opponents while he prepared more thoroughgoing countermeasures.

A number of frei units were raised at the outset of the war. Two examples demonstrate their recruiting and employment of these formations. Both of the examples given are from frei infantry battalions. The king of Prussia gave his ascent to the marquis Ludwig de Malverzpi d'Angelelli for the creation of the Frei-Infanterie d'Angelelli on 5 December 1756, and the unit began to recruit. Among those who joined the newly-formed unit was Johann Jakob von Wunsch, who would later raise his own frei company and rise to the rank of *general der infanterie* in the Prussian army.[21] Angelelli hailed from a northern Italian noble family of military adventurers who provided their services to a number of European states over the course of the seventeenth and eighteenth centuries. The marquis d'Angelelli remained in command of the unit until his retirement in March of 1760.[22] The unit was up to strength and ready to enter the field by the spring of 1757 and joined the main Prussian army in the vicinity of Prague. At that time, the unit consisted of five musketeer companies and possessed two 1-pounder amusettes.[23] The concept for the amusette, which literally translates as 'play-thing', is usually

17   Duffy, *By Force of Arms*, p.12

18   Daniel Marston, *The Seven Years War* (Oxford: Osprey Publishing, 2001), p.20.

19   Duffy, *Instrument of War*, p.395.

20   Duffy, *Instrument of War*, p.395.

21   'Johann Jakob von Wunsch, *Kronoskaf*, <http://www.kronoskaf.com/syw/index.php?title= Wunsch,_Johann_Jakob_von>, accessed 1 July 2023.

22   Stephen Summerfield, *Prussian Frei-Infantrie, Militia and Navy of the Seven Years War* (Huntingdon, England: Ken Trotman, 2018), p.21.

23   Summerfield, *Prussian Frei-Infanterie*, p.21.

credited to Maurice de Saxe. Essentially, it appeared similar to a large musket, with a very long barrel and could fire a one-pound ball. Consequently, it was designated as artillery. These weapons were sometimes called wall-guns as they could be balanced and fired from a fortress wall. In the field, one soldier often balanced the barrel on their shoulder while the other fired. The purpose of the weapon is unclear, though some believe it was used to take down individual personnel.[24]

The Frei-Infanterie d'Angelelli began its active military service on Monday, 2 May 1757 when it arrived in Pirna and served as part of the escort for a military convoy bound for Prague. Later, on 22 November 1757, the unit took part in the battle of Breslau, being used to defend the village of Kleinburg. They initially held the village against determined attacks by 16 grenadier battalions under Austrian *Generalfeldwachtmeister* Wolffersdorf. Eventually, Angelelli's infantry were forced to withdrawal, but not before they set the village on fire. The battalion fell back a short distance and drew up behind a ditch where they held out until reinforced by a battalion under August Wilhelm, Prince of Bevern.[25]

Soon thereafter, the Frei-Infanterie d'Angelelli took part in the battle of Leuthen on 5 December 1757. In this engagement, it was posted along with several other frei battalions in the front line, in the centre of the Prussian forces, occupying the village of Borne and thus threatening the Austrian right wing. It further contributed to the Prussian victory by helping to defeat the Austrian cavalry on the right wing.[26]

The following year, 1758, saw the Frei-Infanterie d'Angelelli serving as part of the main Prussian army under Frederick and taking part in the invasion of Moravia. During the campaign in Moravia, the corps was surprised on the night of 20 April by Austrian light troops under the command of an *Oberst* Brentano. The battalion lost four officers and 47 men in the attack as well as its two artillery pieces.[27] The preceding demonstrates that the Austrian light troops continued to constitute a formidable foe. During the retreat from Moravia, the battalion served in the rearguard of the army. Likewise, it formed a part of the vanguard during the fighting to drive off the Austrian invasion of Saxony. On 14 October, the battalion was posted at the foot of the Birkenbusch near Hochkirch. At 5:00 a.m., when the Austrian attack jumped off, the Frei-Infanterie d'Angelelli stood among the first units to be hit. Consequently, it fled to the rear along with the Frei-Infanterie du Verger.[28] The unit wintered in Silesia over 1758–1759 as a part of Zieten's corps.

Prior to the opening of the 1759 campaign, the Frei-Infanterie d'Angelelli received an augmentation of several 3-pounder artillery pieces and had

---

24   James R. McIntyre 'Eighteenth Century Heavy Metal: The Amusette and the Musketoon', *Eighteenth Century Warfare* (August 2022), <https://18thcenturywarfare.wordpress.com/articles-2/>, accessed 4 July 2023.

25   'Frei-Infanterie de Angelelli', *Kronoskaf*, < http://www.kronoskaf.com/syw/index.php?title= Frei-Infanterie_de_Angelelli>, accessed 1 July 2023.

26   'Frei-Infanterie de Angelelli', *Kronoskaf.*

27   'Frei-Infanterie de Angelelli', *Kronoskaf.*

28   'Frei-Infanterie de Angelelli', *Kronoskaf.*

their amusettes taken away. The campaign of 1759 saw the unit once again serving with Frederick's main army, though nothing eventful occurred that directly effected the battalion. During the winter of 1758–1759, the unit was augmented with a second battalion.[29]

As noted above, in 1760, *Oberst* Angelelli retired and was succeeded by Johann Franz Collignon.[30] Consequently, the name of the battalion changed in order to reflect the new leadership. On 23 June most of the first battalion of the unit were captured by the Austrians at the battle of Landeshut. The remnants of the first battalion were then combined with those of several other frei infantry battalions to form the Chaumont Battalion and sent to relieve the garrison of Colberg as part of Werner's corps.[31]

Following the successful relief of the Russian siege of Colberg (27 August–18 September), the unit returned to the main Prussian army under Frederick. The frei battalion was now attached to Goltz's corps. Over the winter of 1760–1761, the first battalion was reconstituted at Wittenberg and the converged battalion of Chaumont disbanded.[32]

Through 1761 and 1762 the battalion served under Prince Henry in Thuringia. On 27 March 1761, the French attacked and nearly wiped out the battalion near Nordhausen. It was disbanded at the conclusion of hostilities.

A second example of a frei battalion raised as a contingency at the outset of the conflict which better fits the standard view of such formations comes in the Frei-Infanterie von Kalben. Raised on 21 September 1756 at Reichenbach and Zwickau in Saxony by its commander Heinrich Detlev von Kalben. Much like Angelelli's unit, the Frei-Infanterie von Kalben consisted of five musketeer companies as well and possessed two 1-pounder amusettes.[33]

Once completed, the battalion was attached briefly to Bevern's Corps, then joined the main army under Frederick. The battalion took part in the capture of Pilsen on 19 May and Hersback on 23 May 1757 respectively. On 1 June, it helped to exact a contribution from the town of Furth in Anspach for the Prussian army. On 2 June the battalion marched on the castle of Fahrenbach. Through the summer, the unit proceeded to exact additional contributions from the surrounding area.[34]

The only major action the battalion fought in during the campaign of 1757 was the battle of Breslau, 22 November 1757. During this engagement, von Kalben's battalion served in Kleist's brigade, and was therefore in the first line on the right wing of the army. *Oberst* von Klaben was mortally wounded in the fighting and replaced by Konstantin Nathanael von Salenmon and the unit renamed the battalion von Salenmon, a designation it retained through the remainder of the war.[35]

29 'Frei-Infanterie de Angelelli', *Kronoskaf*.
30 Summerfield, *Prussian Frei-Infanterie*, p.21.
31 'Frei-Infanterie de Angelelli', *Kronoskaf*.
32 'Frei-Infanterie de Angelelli', *Kronoskaf*.
33 Summerfield, *Prussian Frei-Infanterie*, p.18.
34 'Frei-Infanterie von Kalben', *Kronoskaf*, <http://www.kronoskaf.com/syw/index.php?title=Frei-Infanterie_von_Kalben>, accessed 1 July 2023.
35 'Frei-Infanterie von Kalben', *Kronoskaf*.

As the Frei-Infanterie von Salenmon, the unit's history is similar to that of Angelelli's. It took part in the battle of Leuthen on 5 December. It seems that during the winter of 1757–1758, the battalion made up its losses from the previous season's campaign by recruiting enemy prisoners. The following year, the Frei-Infanterie von Salenmon served in Frederick's invasion of Moravia. On 8 June, while marching past Liebenhausen, the unit was attacked by Austrian light troops and the prisoners recruited into the frei battalion deserted. The Austrians took some 300 prisoners from the weakened corps. The survivors of the preceding engagement, some 200 men, were added to an ad hoc force tasked with escorting a crucial ammunition convoy from Troppau to Olmütz. As a result, they were caught up in the fighting around Domstadtl, detailed in a subsequent chapter.[36]

The success of the raid on Domstadtl forced Frederick to lift the siege of Olmütz and retreat out of Moravia to Silesia. The Frei-Infanterie von Salenmon served as part of the rear guard during the withdrawal.[37] Later that same year, on 6 October, the battalion was serving as the vanguard when it was surprised by a large Austrian cavalry corps while moving out of the forest at Bischofswerda. In the fighting that ensued the battalion sustained a loss of some 400 men and three artillery pieces. Eight days later, the battalion fought in the bloody battle of Hochkirch where it was attached to Retzow's corps. Following the Prussian defeat at Hochkirch, the Frei-Infanterie von Salenmon served as part of the vanguard during the march that led to the camp at Ullersdorf.[38]

As with the Frei-Infanterie d'Angelelli, the Salenmon wintered in Silesia as part of Zieten's corps. Similarly, they had their amusettes replaced with 3-pounder cannon prior to embarking on the 1759 campaign.

From 24 February to 4 March, the battalion served in a small Prussian corps under the command of *General-Major* Mortiz Fraz Kasimir von Wobersnow which raided into Poland to disrupt the Russian magazines there. The incursion succeeded in destroying enough food to sustain 50,000 men for three months.[39]

Later in 1759, the battalion was transferred to Prince Henry's command with which it took part in the combat at Sorau on 2 September. During the retreat that followed the Austrian victory at Sorau, the frei battalion formed a part of the vanguard, however, it remained behind to defend a bridge at Bruschmuhle and held off a major Austrian attack, forming square to prevent the enemy calvary from catching up to the last Prussian units as they retreated.[40]

The last major action the Frei-Infanterie von Salenmon took part in during the 1759 campaign was the battle at Maxen, fought on 20 November. Here it served as part of then *General-Major* Johann Jakob von Wunsch's brigade and surrendered with the rest of the Prussian forces.

36 'Frei-Infanterie von Kalben', *Kronoskaf*.
37 'Frei-Infanterie von Kalben', *Kronoskaf*.
38 'Frei-Infanterie von Kalben', *Kronoskaf*.
39 'Frei-Infanterie von Kalben', *Kronoskaf*.
40 'Frei-Infanterie von Kalben', *Kronoskaf*.

Over the winter of 1759–1760, a new battalion was raised in Leipzig to replace the captured first battalion. It was therefore designated the second battalion. In 1760, it served as part of the king's army in Saxony, where it took part in the battle of Torgau on 3 November. The battalion remained with the main Prussian field army under Frederick for the remainder of the war and was disbanded at the conclusion of hostilities.[41]

The experiences of the two units described above reinforce several common conceptions concerning the freikorps. One of these was their lack of reliability, which in turn stemmed from the expedient of recruiting from enemy prisoners of war. Witness the experience of the Frei-Infanterie von Salenmon while fighting in Moravia in 1758. In addition, there was the propensity to utilize these forces wherever troops were needed, sending them to act as irregulars on some occasions and then placing them in the line of battle on others. The histories of both the Angelelli and Salenmon battalions attest to the practice.

Freikorps could be raised as temporary units to plug the gaps in that developed in the Prussian Army due to hard campaigning as well. The Freikorps von Kleist presents an example of a unit raised for the latter purpose, which grew into one of the largest irregular units fielded by the Prussians during the Seven Years War. This unit was raised by Friedrich Wilhelm Gottfried Arnd von Kleist beginning in 1759. Kleist was a favourite of Frederick's and had previously commanded a unit of hussars who were clad mainly in green. Thus, they were known as the 'green hussars', and their commander gained the nomme de guerre Green Kleist.[42] The unit began when Frederick ordered that a squadron of volunteer hussars be raised and attached to Hussar Regiment Number 1. He designated von Kleist to recruit and then command the unit. Kleist recruited his squadron around Dresden. Initially, it consisted predominantly of Hungarian deserters. Likewise, it was led by a *Leutnant* Johann Michael von Kovacs who would later emigrate to North American where he aided in the development of the Continental Army's mounted arm during the American War of Independence.[43]

When it came to raising his freikorps, Kleist began with a battalion of infantry known as the Green Croats. This included a contingent of jäger that reached three companies in strength by 1762.[44] In September of 1761 Kleist added an additional battalion of infantry. Consequently, by 1763, the foot contingent of the corps, including musicians and staff numbered some 1,692 officers and men.[45]

From its inception, Kleist's freikorps included mounted troops as well. Beginning with an initial contingent of one squadron of hussars, raised late

41 Summerfield, *Prussian Frei-Infanterie*, p.18.

42 Stephen Summerfield, *Prussian Freikorps and jäger of the Seven Years War* (Huntingdon: Ken Trotman, 2018), p.11

43 'Freikorps von Kleist', <http://www.kronoskaf.com/syw/index.php?title=Freikorps_von_Kleist#Uniforms_of_the_J.C3.A4gers>, accessed 1 July 2023. On Maichael Kovacs, sometimes given as Kovats, see Jim Piecuch (ed), *Cavalry of the American Revolution* (Yardley: Westhome Press, 2014), pp.43–48.

44 Summerfield, *Prussian Freikorps and jäger*, p.11.

45 Summerfield, *Prussian Freikorps and jäger*, p.11.

in 1760, the mounted contingent was augmented by an additional squadron later that same year and eventually reached a peak strength of five squadrons by 1762, at which time it was redesignated as a regiment. The troops for this unit were recruited in the areas of Leipzig and Zerbst.[46] The least well documented formation in Kleist's freikorps were his Uhlans. All that is known is that they reached a peak strength of some 10 squadrons and were clothed in Polish style dress.[47]

Soon after it was raised, Kleist's freikorps went into action, raiding into Bohemia at the end of November in 1759. The raiders, composed of Kleist's hussars, penetrated as far as Dux, Aussig and Töplitz. During the raid, the unit plundered the monastery at Osseg following the monks' refusal to pay a contribution. Kleist and his hussars then returned to Freiberg.[48]

The following year, Kleist again raided into Bohemia. His freikorps then joined the forces under *General-Lieutenant* Hülsen who were operating in Saxony. In an engagement fought at Strehla on 20 August 1760, Kleist's two frei-hussar squadrons and four frei-dragoon squadrons distinguished themselves by besting the Barany Hussars and Zweibrücken Chevaulegers, capturing three standards in the process.[49] Given the Austrians reputation for light troops at the outset of the conflict, this stood as a significant accomplishment for the Prussians. Later, just prior to the battle of Torgau, on 2 November, Kleist led the vanguard of the Prussia army towards Staupitz where he captured five officers and 312 Austrian troopers.[50] The following day, 3 November, at the conclusion of the Battle of Torgau, Kleist's frei-hussars and frei-dragoons took part in the pursuit of the retreating Austrian forces.

The unit saw limited action through the first part of the 1761 campaign. In mid-September of that year, it joined Platen's corps and took part in the relief of the siege of Colberg (24 August–16 December 1761). Following the relief of Colberg, the unit went into winter quarters.

During 1762, elements of the frei-corps took part in the fighting at Teplitz on 2 August. Likewise, at Freiberg on 29 October 10 hussar squadrons, 10 squadrons of Uhlans and two Croat battalions, along with two jäger companies from Kelist's freikorps, were present.[51] The unit was disbanded on the conclusion of hostilities.

The preceding short unit histories demonstrate several significant points concerning the frei battalions and freikorps as utilized by the Prussians. In the case of the Angelelli and von Kalben/Salenmon battalions, while both were recruited at the outset of hostilities, they were repeatedly reformed and reinforced. This leads to the conclusion that they possessed some inherent value as military formations. A significant part of that value likely stemmed from the flexibility of these formations. Both served in the line in various

---

46   Summerfield, *Prussian Freikorps and jäger*, p.15.
47   Summerfield, *Prussian Freikorps and jäger*, pp.17–18.
48   Summerfield, *Prussian Freikorps and jäger*, p.23.
49   Summerfield, *Prussian Freikorps and jäger*, p.23.
50   Summerfield, *Prussian Freikorps and jäger*, p.23.
51   Summerfield, *Prussian Freikorps and jäger*, p.23.

engagements. By the same token, both could easily act as light troops as well, a function they performed when they served as part of either the vanguard or rearguard for the army on the march. Jim Purky notes that there were 12 Freikorps in the Prussian service at various times during the Seven Years War. He describes them as being 'composed of mercenaries, thieves and other soldiers of fortune raised and equipped by private individuals.'[52] His assessment is borne out by the evidence presented above to some extent. An additional reason for the use of frei-battalions and freikorps lay in the simple fact that they were composed of personnel deemed disposable by the state.

All of these points serve to reinforce the notion that formations such as Kleist's freikorps and the frei battalions discussed above were considered expedients. While they served well enough as a stop gap measure, the Prussians still needed a more consistent and disciplined countermeasure to the tactics of enemy irregulars.

Frederick, for the most part relied upon his regular line troops to counter the Austrian light troops. As Katrin and Sascha Mobius point out in their outstanding study of motivation in the Prussian army during the Seven Years War, it was not that the men in his regular forces lacked training, or that they suffered from some tactical deficiency. Instead, it was the simple fact that the men recruited into the ranks of Maria Theresa's light forces came by so much of their training from the natural habits of life.[53] As Frank Wernitz observed, 'The Prussian kingdom lacked a borderer group from which to raise light troops, which was a disadvantage.'[54] Not only did this mean that the Prussian army lacked a ready reserve from which to draw troops, it meant as well that there existed a general dearth of military experience concerning light troops to draw upon. As Katrin and Sascha Möbius point out 'The Austrian army's "borders" offered a pool of recruits who could be used in the Little War.'[55] Further, they note, 'Moreover, their life in the border regions provided a good part of the training necessary for skirmishing and commando actions.'[56] The problem then was at least in part one of economics. In essence, the Austrians had their troops trained for free based on their location. Prussia possessed no such military border with any power. Instead, the Prussian infantryman did in fact receive a significant amount of training from the state, making him more expensive to replace than one of Austria's Croats.[57]

Given these realities, Frederick determined to utilize his hussars as the main troops with which to prosecute Small War. Beginning in 1742, the hussars were used as scouts and light mounted forces.[58] By the time of the

---

52   Purky, 'Light Infantry Forces', p.42.

53   Katrin and Sascha Möbius, *Prussian Army Soldiers and the Seven Years War: The Psychology of Honour* (New York: Bloomsbury Academic, 2020), p.125.

54   Frank Wernitz, *Die Preussischen Freitruppen im Siebenjährigen Krieg 1756-1763* (n.p.: Podzun-Pallas, 1994), p.12.

55   Möbius, *Prussian Army*, p.125.

56   Möbius, *Prussian Army*, p.125.

57   Möbius, *Prussian Army*, p.125.

58   Alexander Querengässer, 'Prussia's Army on the Eve of the Battle of Rossbach', in Alexander Querengässer (ed.), Rick Sanders (trans.), *The Battle of Rossbach 1757: New Perspectives on the Battle and Campaign.* (Warwick: Helion and Company, 2022), p.35.

'Prussian (?) hussar officer charging in the Seven Years War', by Herbert Knötel, (1955). (Anne S.K. Brown Military Collection)

Seven Years War, these troops were consistently employed as scouts and as the advanced guard of the main army. Dragoons, were utilized as light troops as well, backing up the hussars.[59] Still, in the end it was the regular line infantry, the musketeers, fusiliers and grenadiers, especially the last group, who did the bulk of the fighting in the Small War for the Prussians. The Möbiuses give the statistic of the grenadiers' participation in skirmishes outnumbering their actions in major battles by a factor of nine to one.[60] They further note that the men's routine use in Small War amounted to a daily training regime all its own and that this regimen consisted of all sorts of martial activities.[61]

The Möbiuses further note that the men raised in the fusilier units following after Frederick's ascension to the throne in 1740 'were not light troops in the strict sense of the word—their men and muskets were smaller than those of the musketeers, but their training was similar to them.'[62] The approach described here reinforces the notion that the Prussian response to the threat posed by Austrian irregulars was to strive for greater aptitude in drill by implementing, as Brent Nosworthy describes, 'a number of systematic precautions to counter this threat.'[63] The approach of using regular troops to counter opposing irregulars thus involved both the mounted and foot contingents of the Prussian army. Further, this approach resembled developments in the North American theatre which will be discussed in later chapters.

For Katrin and Sascha Möbius the training of both cavalry and infantry to work as light troops and counter the actions of enemy irregulars actually stood out among strengths of the Prussian army in the Seven Years War. They offer a very detailed account of just how the Prussian army operated to counter the efforts of enemy light forces,

> The efficiency of the Prussian army in the Little War was a result of combined arms operations. The outer ring of troops screening the marching columns of the army or of a foraging detachment was formed by hussars. They were also the 'sensors' of the army. They were backed up by squadrons of dragoons, cuirassiers or even larger detachments of hussars, which could come to their aid at any time. These were followed by infantry, mainly grenadiers but also musketeers or fusiliers, who were able to able to attack enemy infantry in terrain unsuited for cavalry.[64]

They conclude noting 'It was exactly this system of mutual support that military experts regarded as the heart of Prussia's successes in the Little War.'[65] Their line of argument runs very much counter to the grain of the reigning assessment of the Prussian army in the Seven Years War, that it never developed an effective counter to Austria's light forces.

---

59   Möbius, *Prussian Army*, p.125.
60   Möbius, *Prussian Army*, p.126.
61   Möbius, *Prussian Army*, p.127.
62   Möbius, *Prussian Army*, p.127.
63   Nosworthy, *Anatomy of Victory*, p.211.
64   Möbius, *Prussian Army*, p.127.
65   Möbius, *Prussian Army*, p.127.

While Prussia approached the problem of Small War from the perspective of greater systematization, many of the small German states once again turned to their game wardens and raised up units of jäger. Hesse-Cassel, which stood among the first states to mobilize their gamekeepers as soldiers, dating back to the Thirty Years' War,[66] raised two companies at the outset of hostilities and they joined the Allied army composed of various contingents first under the command of William, Duke of Cumberland, and later under the leadership of Ferdinand, Duke of Brunswick.[67] The Hessian jäger were initially based at castle Waldau and provided perimeter security for the army.[68] Among the more unique contingents raised to serve in the Small War was the Schaumburg-Lippe-Bückeburg Carabinier and Jäger Corps.[69] The Carabinier were mounted and constituted a specialized unit developed under the personal attention of the count Wilhelm zu Schaumburg-Lippe-Bückeburg. Wilhelm is most well-known as an authority on artillery, and as a mentor of the Prussian military reformer Gerhard Johann David von Scharnhorst (1755–1813).[70] A distinguishing feature of the carabiniers was their black cuirass. While small, the carabiniers and foot-jäger never exceeded 100 men total and usually hovered in the high 80s, they remained highly active through the duration of the fighting in the western European theatre serving in the Allied army under the Ferdinand, Duke of Brunswick. On numerous occasions, the light troops of Ferdinand's army forced the French to retreat by interdicting their supply lines. They often protected supply lines of their Prussian allies in the western theatre as well.[71]

Hanover raised their own light forces as well. The Hanoverian light troops generally fell into two categories, those raised as a part of the Hanoverian army, and those paid for by the British government as subsidy troops. In ways, the Hanoverian army lagged behind many of its neighbours as it fielded no light forces prior to the outbreak of the Seven Years War.[72] The Hanoverian light troops were a mix of mounted and foot. Stephen Summerfield asserts that the foot jäger were mostly armed with muskets and bayonets.[73] This seems unlikely as one of the distinguishing characteristics of the jäger was their use of the short jäger-rifle. It could be, however, that over the course of the war, the attrition which was common among light troops led to depletion

66   Rudolf Witzel *Hessen-Kassels Regimenter in der Alliierten Armee 1762* (Norderstedt: Books on Demand, 2007), p.209.
67   The classic study of this force is Sir Reginald Savory, *His Britannic Majesty's Army in Germany during the Seven Years War* (Oxford: Clarendon Press, 1966).
68   Heinz Wetzel, *Die Hessischen jäger: einer deutche Truppenhistorie in politischen Wandlungsprozess von vier Jahrhunderten (1631-1987)* (Kassel: Verlag George, 1987), pp.17–18.
69   The history of this unit, and its many Small War activities, are detailed in G.W. Düring, *Geschichte des Schaumburg-Lippe-Bückebourgischen Karabinier und Jäger-Corps* (Berlin: Ernst Siegfried Mittler, 1828).
70   Charles E. White, 'Scharnhorst's Mentor: Count Wilhelm zu Schaumburg-Lippe and the Origins of the Modern National Army', *War in History*, 24:3 (March 2017), pp.258–285.
71   Cory, 'British Light Infantry', p.47.
72   Stephen Summerfield, *Hanoverian Army of the Seven Years War: Uniforms, Organization and Equipment* (Huntingdon: Ken Trotman Publishers, 2019), p.219.
73   Summerfield, *Hanoverian Army*, p.219.

of the true jäger and led to their replacement by troops not drawn from the actual game warden's guild.

One of the Hanoverian light contingents was Luckner's Corps, the creation of one Count Nikolaus Luckner. His background demonstrates some of the opportunities offered through proficiency in irregular warfare, and thus warrants some attention. Born in Cham, Bavaria on 22 January 1722, he hailed from humble origins. Luckner's grandfather was an innkeeper and hops merchant in Cham, while his father served as the city treasurer of the town in the 1730s. Nikolaus received his early education from Jesuits in Passau and went on to attend the University of Ingolstadt.[74]

In 1741, early in the War of the Austrian Succession, the young man, not quite 20, joined the Bavarian army, enlisting in a troop of mounted grenadiers. Two years later, Luckner transferred to Gschray's Freikorps as a *leutnant*. Soon, he rose to the rank of *kapitän*. When the Elector of Bavaria leased his forces to the Dutch Republic, Luckner switched to the Frangipani Hussars and fought in the Netherlands. Shortly after the end of hostilities in 1748, Luckner resigned his commission in the Bavarian army and moved to an estate he had purchased in Holstein.[75]

With the outbreak of the Seven Years War, Luckner once again sought to engage in military service. In 1757, he spent 70,000 Thalers to raise and equip a unit of hussars, the Luckner Freikorps. With this meagre formation of some 54 hussars drawn from the Dutch service,[76] Luckner entered the Hanoverian service with the rank of *kapitän* beginning his operations on 6 December of that year.[77]

Later in the year, he seized a French supply train composed of 24 heavily loaded wagons on 9 December, and on the 31st, he and his unit dispersed a force of some 200 French hussars and 60 dismounted troopers, capturing 66 of them in the process.[78]

By the following year, he held the rank of *oberstleutnant*, leading a unit of eight officers and 178 hussars organized into two squadrons.[79] The expansion of Luckner's unit as well as their exploits led to his being promoted to full *oberst* in 1759. In 1760, he was raised to *generalmajor* and became a *generalleutnant* in 1761 at the age of 39.

Throughout the war Luckner continued to demonstrate a profound ability as a partisan leader and a generally solid officer. So much so, that on 19 January 1760, as the Allied army went into winter quarters after a long a gruelling campaign, Luckner was placed in overall command of a series of advanced posts running from Dillenburg through Homberg on the Ohm and

---

74   'Count Nikolaus Luckner', *Kronoskaf* <http://www. http://www.kronoskaf.com/syw/index. php?title=Luckner,_Count_Nikolaus> , accessed 31 May 2023. On Luckner's Corps, see also Joachim Niemeyer, *The Hanoverian Army during the Seven Years War 'Gmundener Prachtwerk.'* (Copenhagen: Bent Carlsens Forlag, 1977), pp.70–71 and Summerfield, *Hanoverian Army*, pp.220–223.
75   'Count Nikolaus Luckner', *Kronoskaf.*
76   Summerfield, *Hanoverian Army*, p.220.
77   'Count Nikolaus Luckner', *Kronoskaf.*
78   'Count Nikolaus Luckner', *Kronoskaf.*
79   Summerfield, *Hanoverian Army*, p.220.

including Marburg and Hartzfeld.[80] A command such as the preceding meant that his troops would stand as the first line against any enemy incursions. It also meant that they were likely to see significant action while the remainder of the army took advantage of the break from active operations to rest, refit and begin the training of new recruits.

Luckner continued to be active in the western theatre through the remainder of the conflict, amassing an impressive combat record.[81] While a full accounting of his exploits falls beyond the scope of the present narrative, it is worth including that Luckner eventually rose to the rank of *generalleutnant* in the Hanoverian service. Following the conclusion of the Seven Years War, he switched to the French Army, where he rose to the rank of *maréchal*, a rank he held from 1791 to 1792.[82]

Luckner's career thus illustrates another factor in the experience of a number of officers of irregular formations in the Seven Years War in particular and across the eighteenth century more generally. Leadership in an irregular formation stood as a path to social mobility. One commentator noted that Luckner's was 'A truly meteoric progress.'[83] Certainly, part of his rapid rise derived from the fact that on his first campaign in 1757 his troops captured the French advocate of Small War, Grandmaison. Still, it demonstrates the possibilities for social climbing which accompanied a commission in the light troops, as these same billets were often frowned upon by officers hailing from the established nobility. That the son of a city treasurer could rise to attain a title of nobility, and albeit briefly, serve as a *maréchal* of France would certainly spawn numerous imitators seeking to follow his example. While Hanover struggled, at least initially, to raise continents of light troops, other European states, such as France, resorted to methods proven in previous conflicts.

The French, for their part, began raising numerous contingents of compagnes franches at the outbreak of the Seven Years War, and they raised numerous other formations as well.[84] There existed within the army of Louis XV considerable difference of opinion on the best tactical formations. Much of the debate centered on which formations should be employed.[85] Official guidance on the matter proved somewhat lacking in the Ordinance of 1755, which was in force during the conflict and which permitted a wide variety of tactical arrangements: thin line, double line, and closed column, as well as skirmishers.[86]

Still, the French raised numerous light formations. The histories of many of these are detailed in comte Charles Pajol's *Les Guerre sous Louis*

---

80   'Count Nikolaus Luckner', *Kronoskaf.*
81   'Count Nikolaus Luckner', *Kronoskaf.*
82   'Count Nikolaus Luckner', *Kronoskaf.*
83   Joachim Neimeyer, *The Hanoverian Army during the Seven Years War 'Gmundener Prachtwerk'* (Copenhagen: Bent Carlsens Forlag, 1977), p.71.
84   Comte Charles Paul Victory Pajol, *Les Guerres sous Louis XV* (Paris: Librarie de Fernin-Dioderot et Cie, Imprimeurs de l'Institut, 1891), Tome VII.
85   For a thorough discussion of these debates, see Quimby, *Background to Napoleonic Warfare.* See also, Nosworthy, *Anatomy of Victory*, pp.329–342.
86   Quimby, *Background to Napoleonic Warfare*, p.91.

XV, Tome VII. One unit worth particular attention, given its overall history, was the Chasseurs de Fischer. Fischer's chasseurs were an exception that helped reinforce the rule. Johann Christian Fischer, an officer of German descent who served with distinction during the siege of Prague raised the unit beginning in November 1743. While Fischer's chasseurs possessed an initial strength of some 400 men, they quickly grew to some 600.[87] At the end of the campaign in 1748, the unit was reduced to a cadre of some 60 troopers. Still, the Chasseurs de Fischer, along with the Volontaires Royaux and the Volontaires de Geschray were retained at the end of the War of the Austrian Succession.[88] During the intervening years of peace, the unit remained active in operations suppressing smugglers.[89]

As the clouds of war again gathered over the European continent, Fischer's chasseurs were augmented to 220 men in five foot companies of 40 men each and one mounted company of 20 troopers as of 1 January 1756.[90] The unit continued to be augmented over the course of the war, reaching a peak level of 2,088 officers and men. It was transferred to the command of Louis Gabriel d'Armentière, marquis de Conflans as of 27 April 1761, at which point the designation changed to Chasseurs de Conflans.[91] While under Fischer, the chasseurs earned a reputation as one of the most effective French light units in the western theatre. In part, the effectiveness of Fischer's chasseurs was likely due to continuity, both in leadership and to the fact that at least a cadre of personnel remained with the unit between the wars. When called to service in the Seven Years War, the unit possessed at least some corporate knowledge of how to conduct the operations that constituted the mainstay of Small War. In fact, the Chasseurs de Conflans were likewise retained following the end of hostilities and were only disbanded in 1776.[92]

Learning from the experience of the conflict, in his *Instruction pour l'infanterie*, *Maréchal* Victor François, duc de Broglie introduced the chasseurs or light infantry company to the French infantry. According to his *Instruction*, each company consisted of a captain, a lieutenant, two sergeants, four corporals, a hornist and 50 soldiers.[93]

Broglie's chasseur company became the second elite company in each regiment, after the grenadiers. Consequently, it would be stationed on the left of the regimental line when encamped as well as on the battlefield. When marching the chasseurs were to be assigned to the rear guard, thus replacing

87 'Chasseurs de Fischer', *Kronoskaf*, <http://www.kronoskaf.com/syw/index.php?title=Chasseurs_de_Fischer>, accessed 10 July 2023.

88 Terry Crowdy, *French Light Infantry 1784–1815; From the Chasseurs of Louis XVI to Napoleon's Grande Armée* (Warwick: Helion and Company, 2021), pp.16–17.

89 E. de Ribaucourt, *The Military Life and Exploits of J.-C. Fischer Brigadier of the Armies of King Louis XV Founder and Commander of the Corps of Chasseurs (1743-1761)* (Paris: Librairie Universelle, n.d.), G.F. Nafziger, (trans.), The Nafziger Collection, 2022, pp.37–38.

90 'Chasseurs de Fischer', *Kronoskaf*, <http://www.kronoskaf.com/syw/index.php?title=Chasseurs_de_Fischer>, accessed 10 July 2023.

91 'Chasseurs de Fischer', *Kronoskaf*.

92 'Chasseurs de Fischer', *Kronoskaf*.

93 Digby Smith, *A New History of the Seven Years War* (Huntingdon: Ken Trotman Publishers, 2016), vol.1, pp.39–40.

the previously employed picquet.[94] Broglie's inclusion of light companies in his instructions can be seen as another instance of trying to bring irregular troops under stricter control. By the same token, it demonstrated their growing significance to the military organizations of the European states as well. They were only introduced in 1760 and therefore exerted little influence on the poor French performance in the conflict. While the French reforms to their light infantry came late in the war, the development of light troops by the British overall is often categorized as behind the development of those forces on the continent.

The British lagged behind the other nations of Europe in the development of light troops. Likewise, the British case is fairly unique as the light formations were developed in two separate theatres, Europe and North America. The North American experience will be discussed in the chapters relating to that theatre. In Europe, Great Britain dispatched a force to the continent beginning in 1757, however, these were regular infantry units. Corporal William Todd noted the difficulties caused by the troops. Todd's remarks on the light troops of the enemy merit quoting at some length as they offer a contemporary's perspective on many of the themes already discussed concerning the irregulars:

> [They] are call'd unregular troops as they seldom or never Joyn with the army but keeps on the out skirts, either in front or upon the flanks & is under no command but their own officers...if pandores[sic] or Yaegers be overcom'd by the enemy ... they seldom will give them any quarter upon either side, for both armies has a great aversion to them as they are counted no more on them a company of Banditti or Robbers, although there is plenty of them both in our army & theirs. It is those sort of people that mostly plunders the wounded or slain after a battle... so that they are despised by all Soldiers & their officers is the same as the men.[95]

Todd noted the independent nature of their service, something that many later theorists would comment on in a positive light. Likewise, he observed how the light troops seldom granted or were granted quarter, and how their activities were often seen in the same light as simple criminality. Especially poignant is his mention of the light troops scouring the battlefield to rob the dead and wounded, something that any member of a regular formation would likely find odious.

The issue remained, however, how to respond to the the threat posed by these light troops. To some extent, the British forces relied on the light troops raised by their German allies to address the threat of Small War. Eventually, however, they British were forced to field their own light troops as well. Todd describes how this was accomplished, 'Prince Ferdinand gave orders for a detachment of 50 men per battalion to be appointed, with the officers in proportion, for Chasseurs, under the command of General Luckner.'[96] The

---

94   Smith, *New History of the Seven Years War*, p.40.
95   William Todd, Andrew Cormack and Alan Jones (eds), *The Journal of Corporal Todd, 1745–62* (Thrupp: Sutton Publishing for the Army Records Society, 2001), pp.196–197.
96   Todd, *Journal of Corporal Todd*, p.193.

choice of Luckner to lead the light troops is intriguing in itself, since, as noted above, he already possessed significant experience leading light troops. The decision to appoint Luckner to command resembles the manner in which Robert Rogers Rangers, and more particularly, his school of ranging, was employed by British officers in North America.

If any country truly trailed in the raising of light troops, it was the Russian Empire. At the outset of the conflict, the Russians tended to rely upon their traditional irregular forces, the various Cossack formations. By the middle of eighteenth century the Cossacks concentrated in three main groups. From west to east, these consisted of the Little Russian Cossacks of the Ukraine, the Zaphorozhians, and the Don Cossacks.[97] Like the Croats and Pandours of Maria Theresa's realm, these troops came by much of the military acumen through their natural habits of life, as they fought regularly against the Ottoman Turks to the southward. The Little Russian Cossacks were becoming less wild than previously and therefore were perceived as losing some of their military edge. Still, they could field roughly 22,000 mounted troops by the middle of the century.[98] The Zaphorozhian Cossacks continued to range more freely over the steppes and could provide an additional 15,000 troops to the military of Tsarina Elizabeth.[99] The Don Cossacks, meanwhile, could be counted on for some 15,700 troops.[100] A German General Staff History discusses the Cossacks as roughly organized into units of 1,000 men each across the regions listed above.[101]

Each Cossack was expected to provide their own mounts and equipment. The weapons carried by individual Cossacks served to distinguish the relative wealth of the warriors. A chieftain, for example, might carry, in addition to his lance, a sabre of Persian or Turkish manufacture, a well-crafted musket or a brace of pistols, while a humble warrior would come with his lance, a fairly basic sword and perhaps a dagger. Still, the primary weapon of the Cossacks remained the lance. The shaft of the weapon was generally of pine, and ranged from 12 to 18 feet in length, and one-and-a-half-inches thick. At the butt, there was a loop to facilitate carrying, and at the other end a three-sided iron head. A plume of black horsehair or silk was used to decorate where the shaft entered the tip. The quality of these weapons declined over the course of the century, and some ended in only a wooden tip. Consequently, many Cossacks switched to bows and arrows as projectile weapons.[102]

The preferred tactic of the Cossack was to hang on the wings of an enemy army, especially their cavalry. They would fall back in the face of an organized charge. If a solitary rider broke ranks, however, a Cossack would engage them

---

97 Christopher Duffy, *Russia's Military Way to the West: Origins and Nature of Russian Military Power 1700-1800* (London: Routledge, 1981), pp.157–158.

98 Duffy, *Russia's Military Way to the West*, p.158.

99 Duffy, *Russia's Military Way to the West*, p.158.

100 Duffy, *Russia's Military Way to the West*, pp.158–159.

101 Großen Generalstabe, *Die Kriege Friedrichs des Großen, Dritter Theil: der Siebenjährige Krieg 1756-1763*. (Berlin: Ernst Siegfried Mittler und Sohn, 1902), pp.20–22.

102 Duffy, *Russia's Military Way to the West*, p.162.

ПРУСКОЙ ДРАГУНЪ РОСИСКО И КАЗАКЪ

КАЗАКЪ

ДРАГУНА ПРУСКОГО РУБИТЪ

'Pruskoi dragun, Rosiskoi kazak', 1757. (Anne S.K. Brown Military Collection)

in individual combat with his lance.[103] The principle aim of the Cossacks in combat, then, stood in disrupting the cohesion of their opponents.

The Cossacks often presented something of a hinderance for Russian commanders due to their treatment of civilians while on campaign. Their proclivity to loot and engage in other excesses led to the mere mention of them generating fear in the likes of enemy soldiers and civilians alike.

While they earned a reputation for bravery as well as savagery, the Cossacks only became effective light cavalry late in the Seven Years War.[104]

Even with their general lack of effectiveness as light troops, the Russian empire relied on the services of the Cossacks for much of the conflict. It was only during the campaign of 1761 that Lieutenant-General Pyotr Alexandrovich Rumyanstev introduced the first two jäger battalions to the Russian army.[105] Rumyanstev was the commander in the Russian army of the period most likely to introduce an innovation such as the jäger. Born in 1725 in Moscow he hailed from a well-connected family of Russian court nobility.

103 Duffy, *Russia's Military Way to the West*, pp.162–163.
104 Duffy, *Russia's Military Way to the West*, p.162.
105 Duffy, *Russia's Military Way to the West*, p.120.

In his youth, he was part of the Noble Cadet Corps, a unit for instruction of promising young men of the boyar class.[106]

According to the most recent scholar of the Russian Army in the later eighteenth century, 'Rumyanstev expressed very clear ideas about the role of merit, ideas that aligned with the broader world of the Military Enlightenment.'[107] At the same time, he could be territorial, viewing the Russian general staff as challengers to his personal power and authority.[108] Overall, however, he is viewed a 'One of the foremost Russian generals of the 18th century.'[109]

It would come as only natural, then, that following several years of experience of the Prussian freikorps and jäger and their ability to make operations difficult for their opponents, Rumyanstev should contemplate a countermeasure. According to Christopher Duffy, as the Russian general prepared to launch his 1761 siege of Colberg, he sought a to raise a corps which would provide some defence against the Prussian irregulars. Likewise, he had previously considered raising his own unit of jäger for some time, even discussing the issue with his adviser, a Captain Lambert.[110]

On 18 August, Rumyanstev informed a Major Ivan Ivanovich Meller-Zakomelski he had decided to raise a unit of 1,040 light infantry.[111] Interestingly, the unit was clad in the red of the Russian artillery as opposed to the standard green of the infantry, or of the other jäger for that matter. This may reflect the fact that the unit was raised late in the war, and that there was not the time to devise a distinctive uniform. It may have contributed to David Gates' dubbing the Russian troops as jägers [sic] in name only'[112] as well. Regardless of how the decisions concerning the clothing of the new unit were made, the men were organized into two battalions of five companies each.[113] In keeping with the current practices in the West as described above, 'The troops were to be drawn as far as possible from men who had been hunters in civilian life, and who had lived together in the same regiments.'[114] Such a practice would help to insure several things: first, that the men possessed the requisite skills Rumyanstev sought to include in the new formation, and second, that the men of the new unit would develop some form of group cohesion more quickly than if they were simply thrown together without any consideration of their previous service. The men were to be lightly equipped, carrying three days rations with them in their knapsacks at all times.[115]

---

106 Eugene Miakinkov, *War and Enlightenment in Russia: Military Culture in the Age of Catherine II* (Toronto: University of Toronto Press 2020), p.56.
107 Miakinkov, *War and Enlightenment in Russia*, p.78.
108 Miakinkov, *War and Enlightenment in Russia*, p.34.
109 'Count Pyotr Alexandrovich Rumyanstev', *Kronoskaf*, <http://www.kronoskaf.com/syw/index.php?title=Rumyanstev_Count_Pyotr_Alexandrovich>, accessed 6 July 2023.
110 Duffy, *Russia's Military Way to the West*, p.120.
111 Duffy, *Russia's Military Way to the West*, p.120.
112 Gates, *The British Light Infantry Arm*, p.11.
113 Duffy, *Russia's Military Way to the West*, p.120.
114 Duffy, *Russia's Military Way to the West*, pp.120–121.
115 Duffy, *Russia's Military Way to the West*, p.121.

The men of the new formation seemed to adapt very quickly to their new roles, serving to good effect in the siege of Colberg.[116] Instead, it was the officers who seemed to encounter greater difficulty in understanding and implementing the tactics they were now expected to employ. Professor Duffy notes, '… Rumyanstev had to spell out the tactics very specifically, instructing Meller-Zakomelski that he was to employ the men in woods, villages, ravines and similar broken terrain where they could take advantage of the ground.'[117]

As indicated by the preceding, by the outbreak of the Seven Years War, the trend toward the use of light troops was in full swing. Even powers on the periphery of Europe such as Sweden were raising light troops.[118] The only state that did not raise any substantial light formations was Saxony, however, the rapid invasion and occupation by Prussian forces at the outset of the conflict likely precluded the Saxon army from raising any such units.[119] Most commanders understood that light troops' primary role was in the Small War. Still, there existed a number of problems. For instance, it remained unclear to the military professionals across the continent how best to utilize light forces in the battle line. While it was clear that light troops could be useful in battle, it remained uncertain as to how best to deploy them to achieve results.[120] In part this was due to the lack of formations held over from the previous conflict. While there were certainly formations such as the Chasseurs de Fischer and men such as Luckner, who possessed prior experience with light troops, they were in the minority. Lacking officers possessing experience in the Small War, the leaders of new formations had to develop tactics for their troops once again. To some extent, this was offset by the publications discussed in the previous chapter, however, it is necessary to keep in mind that many of these were not available until the latter 1750s. Only La Cointe published his work prior to the outbreak of the Seven Years War, in 1752. Still, once hostilities commenced officers were not long in learning how to utilize the light troops under their command.

---

116 Duffy, *Russia's Military Way to the West*, p.117.
117 Duffy, *Russia's Military Way to the West*, p.121.
118 Jeff Leach, 'Swedish Jäger Units of the Seven Years War', *Seven Years War Association Journal*, 10:1 (Winter1997), pp.33–42.
119 On the Saxon Army in the Seven Years War, see Stephen Summerfield, *Saxon Army of the War of the Austrian Succession and the Seven Years War: Uniforms, Organization and Equipment* (Huntingdon: Ken Trotman Publishers, 2018).
120 Duffy, *Military Experience*, p.277.

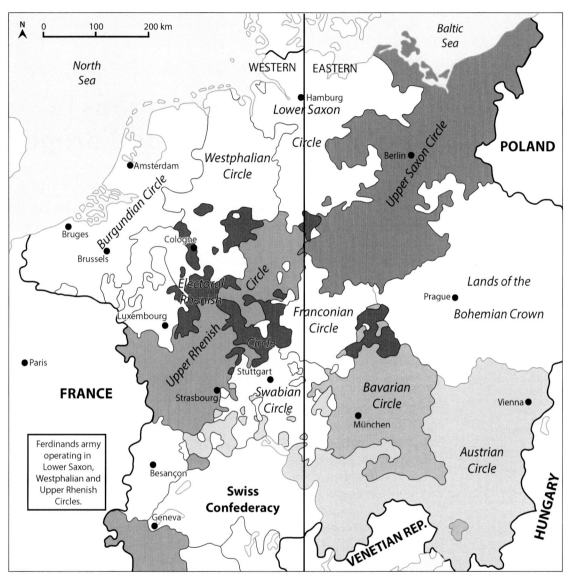

Europe at the time of at the start of the Seven Years War. The line down the center delineates the two theatres, eastern and western.

4

Light Infantry Operations in the Seven Years War in Europe

As the spectre of war once again loomed on the European horizon, across the continent, states summoned their armed forces into being. Recruiters fanned out, employing various means to lure men to the colours. Companies and regiments that had been merely cadres quickly expanded up to something near their full establishment. Units formed, trained, and began moving into the field. The beginning of active combat operations in the Seven Years War in Europe is usually marked from Frederick II of Prussia's invasion of Saxony on 29 August 1756. The beginning of the various actions that composed the Small War could be marked from the same day. The following pages will highlight numerous examples of these operations. For the most part, the focus will fall on the western theatre as the succeeding chapter will be dedicated to the raids on Gundersdorf and Domstadtl in the eastern theatre. Still, the 1757 raid on Berlin will receive attention as it served as an example of Small War writ large as well.

Several themes will emerge: first, all of the tactics described in the preceding discussion of eighteenth century Small War were applied equally in both the eastern and western European theatres. The division between the theatres being defined by a line running from north to south through the Lower Saxon Circle, through the Franconian, Swabian and Austrian Circles to Venice (see the map following the end of the previous chapter). The division is based on both the main combatants and the leadership. In the east, Frederick II of Prussia commanded the main field army of his state against the forces of Austria, Russia and Sweden. In the west, the fighting was primarily between the French and their Saxon contingent, and a British[1] supported Allied army, first under William August, Duke of Cumberland (1757–1758), and then under Ferdinand, Duke of Brunswick (1759–1763). Thus, the light troops remained very active, even when the regulars enjoyed the relative respite of winter quarters. The result being that the Small War exacted a significant toll on its practitioners.

---

1   Since George II of Great Britain supplied troops from both Britain and Hanover, as well as subsidies to support the other components of the force, it is sometimes referred to as His Britannic Majesty's Army.

Second, that the Austrian approach to irregular warfare was losing some of its potency. Meanwhile, the Prussian countermeasures were gaining in effectiveness when it came to blunting the efforts of the Habsburg adversaries.

In the centre Europe, the Austrian light forces managed some early success against their Prussian adversaries. At the same time, there were indications that they were losing their edge in partisan warfare as noted in the previous chapter. One of the first of these setbacks occurred with *Feldmarschall* Maximilian von Browne at Schandau on 14 October 1756. Browne's light troops sustained a costly defeat just after he called off his attempt to rescue the Saxon main army at Pirna.[2]

It seems that during the fighting, a unit of horse attacked a company of the Ottocaner grenadiers who had not fixed their bayonets. The Prussians succeeded in wiping them out. Anton Losy von Losenau used the above incident as an example in writing to *Feldmarschalllieutenant* Count Andreas Hadik von Futak concerning the tactical shortcomings of the Croats.[3] Losy further noted that the Croats were peculiarly vulnerable when fighting against disciplined, unbroken mounted forces as they were often deployed in isolated units to serve as advance or rear guards and consequently had little protection when forced to fight Prussian cavalry. By way of a solution, he offered up the idea that they should be formed in column and prevented from breaking formation in order to engage the enemy.[4] The potential downside of such a formation lay in the fact that it would present an appealing target to any enemy artillery it came in range of.

Losy was correct in his assertion that many Austrian commanders posted their light troops in small units around their main forces. The goal of these deployments involved providing security against enemy irregulars. At the same time, it meant that the light troops were posted 'in such a way that we had, as usual, a little everywhere, but nowhere formed a whole.'[5]

Light troops were employed to provide security for the regulars in the western theatre as well. Often, the light troops on one side were deployed to counter those of the enemy. For example, a French officer noted prior to the Battle of Hastenbeck, 26 July 1757, '...the Marshal sent all light troops to our camp, to prevent it being looted by the enemy'.[6] As in the previous example, the light troops were deployed in order to prevent the camp being looted, which could consequently disrupt the operational options of the main force.

Similar incidents occurred which illustrate how uneven a contest between regulars and light troops could be. For instance, the following example derives from a clash between the Prussians and the light troops of the Reichsarmee on 27 June 1757, for instance:

2   Duffy, *Instrument of War*, p.395.
3   Duffy, *Instrument of War*, p.395.
4   Duffy, *Instrument of War*, p.395.
5   Anton Losy von Losenau, quoted in Duffy, *Instrument of War*, pp.395–396.
6   Ewan Carmichael, *Like a Brazen Wall: The Battle of Minden, 1759, and its Place in the Seven Years War* (Warwick: Helion and Company, 2021), p.72. On the battle of Hastenbeck, the most recent work at the time of the present writing is Olivier Lapray, *Hastenbeck 1757: The French Army and the Opening Campaign of the Seven Years War* (Warwick: Helion and Company, 2021).

> At dawn, a Prussian detachment of 1,500 men attacked our abatis near Welpert. They pushed us as far as Preznitz. The enemy had about thirty killed and wounded; on our side there were five Croats killed, seven wounded and a lieutenant taken prisoner. General Kleefeld assembled a detachment to drive the enemy away, but the Prussians, after having pillaged several small farms, retired to Annaberg.[7]

In this brief action, the Prussians inflicted some damage on their foes in the Imperial army and took an officer prisoner. They also foraged, or as the account describes their actions, 'pillaged'. The topic of the behaviour of light troops is addressed below. It should be noted that all of the belligerents accused the light forces of their respective opponents of failing to adhere to accepted practices in warfare.[8]

While the Prussians were improving at countering their Austrian foes in Small War, the latter still possessed an edge early in the war. The experience of the grenadier battalions of Billerbeck and Waldow will stand for many others. Two days after victory at the battle of Richenberg in Bohemia, on 23 April 1757, the Duke of Bevern's battalions were pushing through some broken country in the direction of an Austrian position. The valley floors were teaming with Croats, hussars and Hungarian infantry, and the two battalions halted until Bevern could come up with the main force. The following recounts what occurred following Bevern's advance:

> When he arrived he ordered the advance guard to occupy the heights facing the hills held by the enemy. Our battalions were still short of the summit when the Croats fired a volley, which killed a number of our men. We stayed on that hilltop for three hours—it was extremely cold and we were buffeted by a violent wind. Towards evening the order came for the battalions to come down and occupy a belt of brushwood at the bottom of the hill … as we neared the bushes we were greeted by a fire which was all the more deadly because the Croats were lying prone and firing point blank at out grenadiers, and the officers in particular, whereas we could see nobody at all and were unable to exact our revenge.
>
> Our battalions stayed in that wood for more than eighteen dangerous hours. At last on 24 April the Duke of Bevern allowed our battalions to fall back a little and pitch their tents. All the same the canvas was riddled with bullets in a matter of hours, and all through the night the camp was on constant alert, with sentries having their throats cut and bullets whistling about our ears.[9]

In the preceding encounter, the Croats demonstrated their continued tactical acumen as they launched one ambush when the battalions attempted to occupy the top of the hill and withdrew, only to reposition themselves and meet the Prussians once again when they came down off the hilltop. Their use of cover and firing from a prone position allowed the Croats to inflict

---

7   Anon., Neil Cogswell (trans and ed.), *Zweybrücken in Command: The Reichsarmee in the Campaign of 1758* (Warwick: Helion and Company, 2019), pp.38–39.

8   James R. McIntyre, 'Atrocity in the Seven Years War in Europe: A Critical Reevaluation', May 10, 2019, 86th Annual Meeting of the Society for Military History, Columbus, Ohio.

9   Quoted in Duffy, *Instrument of War*, p.395.

significant damage on the Prussians while conserving their own forces. It is worth noting as well that these types of engagements exerted a morale toll on the defending force as well as they seemingly could not respond effectively against their assailants.

Another example of a fairly regular action fought by light troops occurred on 23 March, 1758. As reported by one of the earliest historians of the conflict, Sir Charles Hotham-Thompson, 'A party of hussars belonging to the Allies came up with the rear guard of the main body of the French near Soest in the country of Marc; and having attacked them made a considerable number prisoners, took ten pieces of cannon, five 24-pounders, and five 6-pounders, together with a large magazine.'[10] Capturing prisoners deprived the enemy of manpower. Likewise, the prisoners might end up as recruits in a freikorps. Perhaps more significantly, the capture of artillery pieces could bolster the artillery park of the Allied army while at the same time weakening that of the French.

Raids constituted an important part of the work of the light troops as well. An account concerning Marburg in the fall of 1760 provides an excellent example of the form such actions could take. At the time the city was occupied by the French and being used as a depot for supplies. The Hereditary Prince of Brunswick dispatched several forces of light troops to attack the city:

> The Allies therefore, did not seek to raid these depots, but to destroy them, in order thereby to cut off the supply to the enemy. For this purpose they formed their own separate corps of light troops. Colonel Johann Heinrich von Fersen, a Swede by birth, and Major von Bülow commanded two such corps. Both received orders from the Hereditary Prince of Brunswick to take Marburg by surprise and seize the magazines there. Fersen therefore advanced via Brilon and Medebach, and von Bülow from the Diemel area via Corbach and Frankenberg, so that both met in the night of September 9th to 10th, 1760 near Marburg. To cover this enterprise, which dared to be in the rear of the French armies, the hereditary prince himself took up a watchful position on the Eder in Waldeck.
>
> Without firing a shot, the Allies forced their way through the gardens into the city and immediately surprised the main guard in the local town hall, which consisted of 24 to 30 men. Then the work of destruction began. Fourteen ovens belonging to the French field bakery were knocked down. Everything that could not be taken away was destroyed. The flour from the magazines was thrown into the water and the wine was poured into the streets. This destruction was by no means limited to the stores belonging to the French, there was also plunder and destruction among the local inhabitants, so as not to let anything fall into the hands of the French.[11]

---

10 Sir Charles Hotham-Thompson, *Operations of the Allied Army under the Command of His Serene Highness Prince Ferdinand, Duke of Brunswick and Lüneburg, 1757-1762* (Point Pleasant, NJ: Winged Hussar Publishing, 2016, reprint of 1764 original), p.27.

11 Wilhelm Kolbe, *Marburg und der Siebenjährige Krieg: Ein Vortrag gehalten in der Versammlung des Hessischen Geschichtsvereins zu Marburg am 28 Januar 1880* (Marburg: R.G. Elwert Verlagsbuchhandlung, 1880), pp.37–38. The translation is my own.

Several aspects of the above account fit well within the parameters of the Small War discussed throughout. The raiders used night to cover their approach to the town. They surprised the main guard and attacked without firing a shot. Once they had secured possession of the town, they worked to destroy any supplies which could not be carried off by the raiders. The actions of the attackers led to a certain level of indiscipline as well which manifested in the abuse of the civilian population.

For the light troops, even winter quarters offered little respite, as noted by *kapitän*, later *oberstleutnant*, Johann Kasimir von Monkewitz of the Schaumburg-Lippe-Bückeburg Carabinier Corps:

> I must say that the light troops in winter quarters, like those who come to Haltern, almost always have to watch their hats; as in the middle of the campaign, especially when the enemy is a bit distant. The scouts can not always be depended on; the patrols can be caught, or, more often, fail, very often they do not discover anything of the enemy, go back calmly, announce that they have not discovered anything, and the next hour the enemy is on their feet, chasing them, and coming to visit us when we least expect it.[12]

Monkewitz was a skilled partisan commander of Lithuanian descent who first served in a frei-battalion in the Prussian during the War of the Austrian Succession. He joined the army of count Wilhelm of Schaumburg-Lippe-Bückeburg, where he remained for the duration of his service.[13]

A specific example of the sort of activities the light troops undertook in winter occurred in January 1758:

> The 31st, a detachment of Prussians re-entered the city of Halberstadt, and, on February 1st, pushed forward a party to Hornburg, who made there, and in the neighboring village about 500 prisoners and on the 2nd, a party of cavalry and hussars advanced to the gates of Steinfeld before the garrison had received the least notice of their march; killed the sentinel, and immediately entered the city where they made 600 of Turpin's Regiment of hussars prisoners of war and seized all their horses and baggage, the rest of the garrison fled in the greatest confusion towards Schlade...[14]

The light troops, then, continued active operations during the winter months when the soldiers of the regular line regiments enjoyed at least some form of respite. Their continued activity meant that light units had less time to rest, repair equipment and indoctrinate new soldiers. One result of this was that they endured a higher casualty rate. One source places the attrition rate of light forces at 50 percent for the last two years of the conflict.[15] As one

---

12 G. W. von Düring, *Geschichte des Schaumburg-Lippe-Bückeburgeschen Karabinier–und jäger–Korps im Siebenjährigen Kriegs* (Berlin: Graf Sigfried Mittler, 1828), p.96. The translation is my own.

13 See 'The Life of Lieutenant Colonel Joachim Kasimir von Monkewitz,' in my translation of Düring, *History of the Schaumburg-Lippe-Bückeburg Karabinier and jäger Corps* (Point Pleasant, NJ: Winged Hussar Press, forthcoming).

14 Hotham-Thompson, *Operations*, p.20.

15 Neimeyer, *Hanoverian Army*, p.69.

contemporary noted, 'these men who are exposed continually, as if they are a species of humanity whose lives were of less account.'[16]

During the campaign of 1759, the Schaumburg-Lippe Carabiniers participated in the Battle of Lippstadt. 'On the afternoon of June 30,' began von Monkewitz in the Schaumburg-Lippe-Bückeburg Carabinier Corps's diary,

> a strong enemy detachment approached Borke, drove out the workers employed there by the engineer from the Bückeburg contingent, Major von Römer, and drove off some of the garrison's cattle. I had to leave immediately with the corps, and the commanding General von Hardenberg promised to support me through a detachment of volunteers. I set off after the enemy in a strong detachment, that my retreat was in any case assured by the detachment mentioned above, but, with all due caution, on the left the foot-jäger of the corps between Lippstadt and Lipperode were in a good position. The cattle were chased away from the enemy and thrown back to Lipperode. In the meantime, however, a strong division of the enemy between Lipperode and the Lippe had penetrated, and threw back my foot-jäger, together with the detachment that had arrived as a sortie, from the city. Major von Römer was with me when the enemy fire began in our back; I sent a Carabinier to see how it was while we were in the midst of the Haider, Lipperode right in our backs. The Carabinier soon returned with the news that the enemy had thrown the brigades into the fortress and heavily infested the way forward with an infantry detachment. Römer and I resolved to make our way back to Lippstadt with our sabers in our fists. The enemy we had before us seemed to have had enough of it and fled towards Mettinghausen. I let the trumpeter blow and commenced the march into the ordeal in due course; but soon we became aware that 300 grenadiers had already reportedly prepared for our arrival and had thus posted themselves behind some ditches and hedges and that it was considered impossible to get through here. Likewise, a group of enemy hussars and dragoons penetrated from Lipperode towards our left flank. Now the horses had to do their best. Riders went over hedges and ditches in the direction of Sauerlage and Kappeln, and though the enemy's cavalry were rather better than ours, they were not able to jump over the empty ditch we followed to the road that leads from Rhede to Lippstadt. We were happy to reach the fortress again, having lost no more than 2 dead, 4 wounded and 2 horses.[17]

Another example of the difficulties faced by the light troops comes, once again, from the pen of the Schaumburg-Lippe officer, *Major* von Monkewitz, promoted at the beginning of 1760, and dates from the winter quarters of the corps in early 1760. 'I must say that the light troops in winter quarters, like those who come to Haltern, almost always have to watch their hats; as in the middle of the campaign, especially when the enemy is but a bit distant. The scouts can not always be depended on; the patrols can be caught, or, more often, fail, very often they do not discover anything of the enemy, go back calmly, announce that they have not discovered anything, and the next hour

---

16   Quoted in Duffy, *Instrument of War*, p.394.

17   Düring, *Geschichte des Schaumburg-Lippe-Bückeburgeschen*, pp.72–73.

the enemy is on their feet, chasing them, and coming to visit us when we least expect it.'[18]

Later, during the summer of 1760, another incident occurred which is indicative of how a clash between light troops could bring about an encounter battle. As described in the *Geschichte des Schaumburg-Lippe-Bückeburgeschen Karabinier–und Jäger–Korps*:

> On 22 July, at daybreak, a considerable detachment under Major von Bülow attacked the village of Helsen, which the enemy vigorously defended. Although stubbornly growing in numbers as reinforcements were funneled in, the enemy were in the end thrown out. The Carabiniers made 23 of the enemy prisoners and captured 6 horses. The battle, however, grew protracted and became more and more heated, as successive formations of the enemy arrived, so that in the end the fight became too uneven and Major von Bülow ordered a retreat. Major von Monkewitz commanded the rear guard with 300 Hanoverian grenadiers and the foot-jäger of Bückeburg. The enemy troops, the Volontaires Royaux, were attacking fiercely, forcing the rear-guard to make a stand and fight. After fierce rifle fire from both sides, the enemy finally saw itself forced to pursue more slowly; but 16 grenadiers and 3 jäger were killed, and 25 grenadiers were wounded, along with 8 jäger. Major von Monkewitz had his horse shot out from under him. The battle ended only at nightfall, the detachment of the major of Bülow again occupied the post of Külte.[19]

As seen above, an attack on an enemy post, seemingly meant to stand as a raid, grew into a larger engagement as both sides sent more troops into the fray. A significant conclusion to be drawn from the above is that the tactical engagements of Small War could exert an effect on the larger operational picture. Even when not intended to disrupt enemy plans, clashes such as the one described above could derail the foe's intentions by siphoning off troops previously slated for them.

An example that highlights the role of chance and individual initiative in Small War derives again from the history of the Schaumburg-Lippe-Bückeburg contingent. It warrants inclusion as it demonstrates the manner in which light forces could be opportunistic. The instance occurred during the summer of 1760:

> On the morning of 28 August, Monkewitz was dispatched with the Carabinier and 100 Hessian hussars to reconnoitre the road from Marburg to Kassel. In the area of Gudensberg he reached an enemy flour transport and fell so unexpectedly on the covering force, which was composed of Fischer's hussars, that they fled wildly. Some twenty wagons were destroyed, and six men were captured, with these prizes and prisoners, the force returned to Zierenberg during the night.[20]

---

18   Von Monkewitz, quoted in Düring, *Geschichte des Schaumburg-Lippe-Bückeburgeschen*, pp.96.

19   Düring, *Geschichte des Schaumburg-Lippe-Bückeburgeschen*, pp.100–101.

20   Düring, *Geschichte des Schaumburg-Lippe-Bückeburgeschen*, p.107.

Here, a routine patrol led to the discovery of an enemy contingent escorting a supply train. Interestingly, both the patrol and the escort consisted of light troops, demonstrating that by this point in the conflict both sides seemed to appreciate the value of irregulars in such actions. Once again, the attackers destroyed the supplies they could not take with them. While destroying the flour brought no benefit to the Carabinier in the form of additional supplies, it at least worsened the supply situation of the enemy. Consequently, actions such as the destruction of the flour were not simply random destruction. Instead, they did serve a valid military purpose. Even so, both sides tended to depict them as random and wanton acts of unnecessary violence and excess in their respective propaganda.[21]

A final instance of the Small War involving the forces of Schaumburg-Lippe-Bückeburg contingent merits inclusion as it highlights what could occur when a occur when a commander let their guard down, something many of the authors cited in chapter three cautioned against. The action described below took place during the campaign of 1760 and took the form of a raid on the town of Butzbach conducted in mid-September:

> Captain von Hattorf of Freytag's jäger Corps with 100 horses, and Lieutenant von Berk with 30 of the best-behaved Carabinier composed the vanguard which was sent against Butzbach. Here stood two squadrons of hostile cavalry, with the utmost tranquility and cheerfulness, expecting nothing less than an attack from an enemy standing far away in Paderborn. It might have been about 9 o'clock in the morning when Hattorf arrived in front of Butzbach and immediately threw himself into the village at a full-out gallop. Some of the enemy riders sought to get on horseback; The allied troops hit them so hard that not a single one managed to escape. A part of the enemy's army threw themselves into two houses in the market and began a heavy carbine fire against the horsemen engaged in the gathering of the captured horses. Lieutenant von Berk parted with a part of his people attacked the one house, which was done in the same way by Captain von Hattorf against the other. Although the enemy bravely fought back, the attackers still penetrated, and the defenders had to jump over the wall. Hattorf returned with 123 drey horses, a few hundred slaughter cattle and 26 laden wagons with food on the same day to Marburg, after he sold the slaughter cattle – which was not to be carried away – to some Jews he negotiated with on the way. 41 men and 1 officer were brought along as prisoners; von Hattorf had lost 13 men and 9 horses, among them 6 Carabinier and 5 horses from the corps.[22]

The above account contains several details worthy of comment. First, the attacking force utilized surprise and speed to launch an attack on a garrisoned walled town. The attack came later in the morning than usually recommended by contemporary theorists on Small War. To some extent, the timing may have enhanced the surprise of the attack.

---

21   For a more thorough description of the use of incidents such as the one discussed here in the propaganda of the various belligerents in the European theatre, see James R. McIntyre, 'Atrocity in the Seven Years War in Europe: A Critical Reevaluation', unpublished paper.

22   Düring, *Geschichte des Schaumburg-Lippe-Bückeburgeschen*, pp.108–110.

The account continues, giving some idea of the conduct of urban warfare in the eighteenth century, with troops of the garrison falling back through the market, and eventually sheltering in private homes. The assaulting force, then, had no option if they were to press their attack, but to attempt to force their way into these residences, which they did, forcing the remaining members of the garrison to abandon the town.

Following the capture of the town, supplies that could be carried away were organized along with the prisoners taken in the fighting. In this case, however, additional supplies, specifically the cattle, which could not be taken with the raiders were not destroyed, but instead sold to local merchants.

Up to this point, the examples presented have highlighted the activities of light troops in the Small War at which they excelled. None of the actions depicted thus far provided any instances of how the actions of light troops could have bearing on major engagements. The following actions, which occurred before and during the Battle of Vellinghausen on 15/16 July 1761 highlight just these possibilities.[23] Hotham-Thompson noted how a 'Lieutenant Muller being sent with a party of 20 cavalry to meet a column of carriages that was escorted by ten dragoons, two officers, and 50 soldiers were dispersed;' Muller 'then pursued the dragoons to the very gates of Kassel, where they escaped him, his horses being spent with fatigue.'[24] Still, the raid was a success, as 'Above 30 carriages, with bacon and other provisions, going to the French headquarters were burnt for want of time to carry them off, in sight of the garrison of Kassel.'[25] Thus, while the raid was not completely successful, in that it did not take supplies from the enemy and add to the supplies of the Allied army, it at least deprived the enemy of the provisions. Further, as noted at the outset, captured supplies in whatever form were often destroyed for lack of time or transportation to carry them off in the Small War. The burning of supplies within sight of the garrison likely exerted a psychological impact on their morale as well.

The Battle at Vellinghausen was significant in its own right. It demonstrated the ability of Ferdinand of Brunswick to best a combination of two numerically superior French armies and demonstrated the growing proficiency of the British infantry in Small War tactics.[26] In addition, during the night of 15/16 July, the Hessian Regiment von Gilsa was ordered to prevent the French from cutting the road to the town of Hamm. In essence, they were ordered to act as light troops, the reverse of what often occurred, when light troops were pressed into service in the battle line. While the use of regulars as ad hoc light formations remained a standard practice, many authors discussed in the second chapter rejected it. Among the men in the Regiment von Gilsa was a young Johann Ewald, who would go on to be a

---

23   On Vellinghausen, see Savory, *Britannic Majesty's Army*, pp.319–326. See also, Szabo, *Seven Years War*, pp.352–353.

24   Hotham-Thompson, *Operations*, p.154.

25   Hotham-Thompson, *Operations*, p.154.

26   C. T. Atkinson, 'Highlanders in Westphalia, 1760–62: and the Development of Light Infantry', *Journal of the Society for Army Historical Research*, 20:40 (1941), p.218. See also Dodson, 'Vellinghausen', pp.53–54.

major author on Small War.[27] Ewald would later comment on his experience in the battle in his first treatise, *Gedanken eines hessischen Offiziers uber sa, was man bei Fuhrung eines Detachments im Felde zu thun hat.*[28]

Whenever the main forces were encamped and therefore stationary, the Small War tended to expand significantly. William Todd of the British Army observed something of the aforementioned trend on 15 October 1761 'Encamped near Birkhausen, & every thing remains much the same as in several days past, as the Pandores[*sic*] & Advance troops are Constantly Skirmishing with various success, not worth Notice.'[29] Todd's downplaying of the skirmishing between the main forces leaves the reader with the impression that these clashes occurred so routinely that for the light troops, they barely registered as possessing any significance.

As is often the case with units that specialize in a specific activity, many of the light formations acquired a reputation. Certainly, Luckner's Hussars from the Hanoverian army stood out as one such unit. These troops were 'present at almost every action involving light cavalry work, whether outpost duty, raids or skirmishing, and distinguished themselves by a courage bordering on recklessness.'[30] Much the same could be said of the Schaumburg-Lippe-Bückeburg Carabinier Corps,[31] Fischer's Corps, Freytag's Jäger Corps,[32] and Stockhausen's Corps.[33]

While this chapter has thus far focused on Small War actions in the western theatre, there is one encounter fought during the summer of 1757 in the east which was so significant it warrants some discussion. It presents an example of the basic Small War tactic of the raid employed on a large scale.

The Prussians had made a terrible error in their deployments, and the Austrian commander, Prince Charles of Lorraine stood determined to make them pay for their miscalculation.[34] The Austrian dispositions in mid-September 1757 were as follows: On the 13th, the Austrian army passed the Queiss at Lauban (present day Lubun, Poland) and advanced further into Silesia.

Prince Charles left a force of some 15,000 troops under *Feldzeugmeister* Marschall at Lauban to protect Lusatia. Shortly thereafter, on 15 September, an additional Austrian corps of 7,000 men under *Feldmarschalllieutenant* Count Andreas Hadik was posted at Radeburg. Hadik commanded the light troops screening Ernst Dietrich Marschall's corps. Marschall's force stood tasked with remaining in eastern Saxony and keeping a watch for Frederick.

---

27   James R. McIntyre, *Johann Ewald jäger Commander* (New York: Knox Press, 2020), pp.26–27.

28   Johann Ewald, *Gedanken eines hessischen Offiziers uber sa, was man bei Fuhrung eines Detachement im Felde zu thun hat* (Cassel: Johann Jacob Cramer, 1774), p.32.

29   Todd, *Journal of Corpral Todd*, p.207.

30   Neimeyer, *Hanoverian Army*, p.71.

31   See Düring, *Geschichte des Schaumburg-Lippe-Bückeburgeschen* for a complete account of the unit's activities.

32   Neimeyer, *Hanoverian Army*, p.73. On Freytag's Jäger, see also 'The Freytag Jäger Corps in the Seven Years War: Their Organization and Employment', *Journal of the Seven Years War Association*, 22: 4 (Summer 2019), pp.13–21.

33   Neimeyer, *Hanoverian Army*, p.72.

34   Unless otherwise noted, the following account is derived from James R. McIntyre, 'The Raid on Berlin, 1757', *Journal of the Seven Years War Association*, 22:3 (Spring 2019), pp.20–42.

At the same time, they were to maintain contact with the Reichsarmee.[35] They were deployed so as to interdict any possible offensive moves by Frederick. Hadik was placed under Marschall's orders.

Prince Charles asked Hadik what he thought of the possibility of taking advantage of the Prussian situation and launching a raid on Berlin. Hadik supported the venture and the Austrian commander determined on launching the expedition with Hadik in command. It is clear that Vienna placed high expectations on the raid. The Austrian minister Wenzel-Anton Kaunitz told the French ambassador that 'we flatter ourselves that this expedition, although brief in duration, will throw the king of Prussia's civil and military economy into a fair measure of disorder.'[36] In addition, there was the hope that the raid would force Frederick to pull troops from Saxony in order to defend his capital. If successful in this regard, the raid would place the operational initiative clearly in the hands of the Austrians in the eastern theatre. Thus, from the outset, the raid on Berlin was conceived as an operation with clear strategic effects.

Preparations for the raid began immediately. Marschall detached 1,200 foot and 800 horse from his corps and sent them under *Oberst* Count Gourcy of the Prince Savoyen Dragoons to bolster Hadik's force. The rendezvous point was Elsterwerda. On 25 September, the first detachment from Marshall's corps set off from Lusatia to the assigned rendezvous point. In order to ensure the safety of the left flank of the raiding force, *Generalfeldwachtmeister* Kleefeld, a reliable officer, was sent with a force of some 1,800 troops to line the Röder and the Schwarze Elster.[37] On the 30th, Marschall marched to Görlitz with his entire corps to act as a covering force for Hadik.

About that same time, chance intervened, as it often does in warfare. Hadik fell ill, and the raid had to be postponed into October. His illness and recuperation rendered Hadik motionless until 9 October. At that point, the partisan commander marched from Radeburg and Grosshain on Elsterwerda. The following day, after detaching 1,000 Grenzer and 300 Hussars between Schandau and Meissen, Hadik assembled the remainder of his Corps at the designated rendezvous at Elsterwerda, north of Dresden. Hadik's subordinates included Baron von Babocsay, Count Mitrovsky and von Kleefeld.

The detachment assembled at Elsterwerda consisted of about 1,000 men from various cuirassier regiments, 1,100 men of the Baranyay Hussars under the command of *Oberst* Ferdinand Franz von Ujházy. In addition, Hadik possessed an infantry force composed of some 2,100 Grenzer and about 900 regular infantry. The artillery consisted of a modest two 3-pounder and four 6-pounder guns.

Once his force was in motion, Hadik provided the following directives to his men should they encounter a Prussian force while on the march. These orders are worth quoting at some length as they provide insights into Hadik's thinking concerning the raid. He instructed:

---

35 Duffy, *By Force of Arms*, p.67.
36 Wenzel-Anton Kaunitz to the French ambassador, quoted in Duffy, *By Force of Arms*, p.67.
37 Duffy, *By Force of Arms*, p.67.

If we encounter the enemy, the cavalry is to act with determination, and not allow itself to receive the charge. During the combat the cavalry will station small parties out on the flanks of the two wings, and, if circumstances allow, detach the third rank so as to work around the enemy flanks and rear. The other two ranks continue to act in close order, and we must always retain a reserve. The infantry will advance boldly, and not open fire unless it finds itself in an advantageous position to do so, in which case it must keep up a continuous fire at will. After the Croats have fired, their third rank will go over to the attack with drawn swords, while observing the proper intervals.[38]

The preceding is an excellent example of raiding tactics. Hadik's focus, at all times, was to maintain the speed and secrecy of his movements. Thus, his injunction for the cavalry to fall back, likewise, for the infantry to refrain from firing. If drawn into a firefight, the men were to maintain a constant fire, which would likely end the engagement quickly. In many ways, Hadik's orders to his men echo the practices employed by Pandour Trenck in his actions.

One liability contained in Hadik's orders to his troops was the continuing deployment of troops in small detachments. This approach was problematic for the Austrians, especially with regards to their light troops, on which more later.

As his troops began moving into Brandenburg, Hadik, for his part, drew up a list of targets. The locations he noted were to be targeted for destruction or at least disruption. For instance, Hadik planned to attack the arms works at Alt-Schadow on the upper Spree as well as the arsenal, factories, depots, and records in Berlin.[39] In addition, he composed a list of important civil leaders he hoped to seize as hostages. One of these major figures was the Prussian minister Heinrich Podewils.[40] Likewise, prominent members of the merchant community were to be taken as hostages as well.[41]

Reacting to the news of the threat to his capital, Frederick began moving forces to defend the city. He set out with his own troops camped around Buttstädt in Thuringia to Ekartsberga and Lißdorf. Likewise, he dispatched his artillery towards Naumburg. In addition, Frederick sent orders to Prince Moritz to immediately cross the Elbe near Torgau in order to forestall Hadik.

The following day, 12 October Hadik reached Luckau with his forces. At Luckau, he detached his subordinate, *Oberst* Ujházy, with some hussars in order to cover his flank and to raise contributions in Golssen, Baruth and Mittenwalde counties. Raising contributions has already been discussed above, and its effects need no restating here aside from pointing out that the lack of the supply in an area stripped by contributions could seriously inhibit Prussian forces attempting to intervene and disrupt Hadik's force.[42]

---

38 Hadik quoted in Duffy, *By Force of Arms*, p.69.
39 Duffy, *By Force of Arms*, p.69.
40 Szabo, *Seven Years War*, p.101.
41 Duffy, *By Force of Arms*, p.69.
42 Wright 'Military Contributions', pp.3–13.

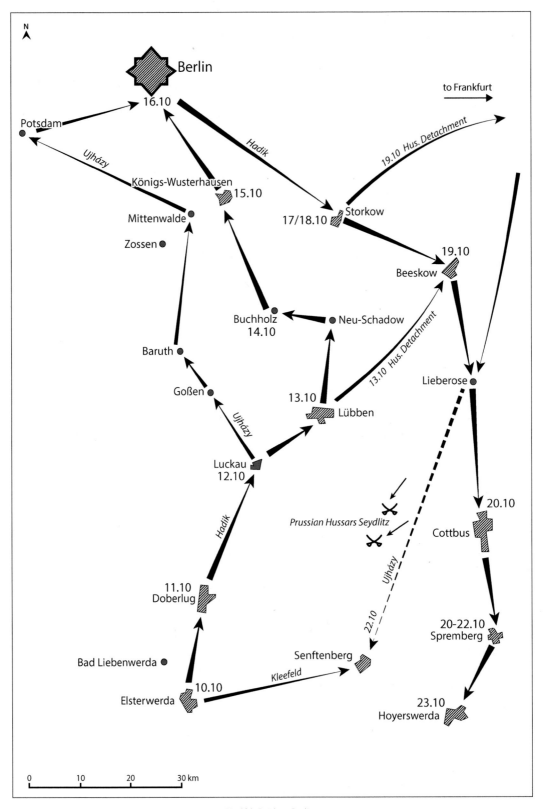

Hadik's Raid on Berlin.

Meanwhile, the Prussians under Frederick moved out from their camp in Thuringia in Saxony and began marching to defend Berlin. Given Hadik's head start, on the following day, 13 October, the Austrian commander reached Lübben, the hope that he could somehow prevent his opponent from reaching the Prussian capital before him would appear to be a bit of wishful thinking on Frederick's part.

By the 14th, Hadik's forces had arrived at Wendnish-Buchholtz (present day Märkish-Buchholz). Once there, he sent forward a detachment of hussars towards Beeskow on the banks of the Spree River. They were to reconnoitre and seize the bridge at Beeskow. Hadik sent another detachment to Alt-Schadow to destroy the local ammunition foundry located in the town. The men 'spent a busy day smashing foundry moulds, commandeering 1,211 rounds of mortar bombs, howitzer shells and cannon shot, and breaking up nearly 19,000 more.'[43]

The Austrian commander utilized the cover of night on 15–16 October to conceal his final approach to the Prussian capital.[44] Further, he broke from the roads and made his approach via the royal forest near Schmöckwitz. This last move helped to conceal Hadik's numbers from the Prussians.[45] The suburbs of the city were defended by a 4.4-metre-high wall. All the environs of Berlin including the sections of the inner city, were enclosed within the walls. These included Berlin, Kolin, Friedrickswerder, Dorotheensrtadt (Neustadt), and Friedrichstadt. The suburbs of the city, those areas outside the older walls, included Kolin Köpenick, Stralau, and Spandau.

At the time of Hadik's raid, the garrison defending the city amounted to no more than 5,521 men or six battalions. The troops were of debatable fighting capacity. Specifically, they included two battalions of the Leon Fusiliers, 1,390 men. There was a small contingent of Saxons made up of only 42 officers and 197 men. These were troops who had been dragooned into the Prussian service earlier in the war, and as the weakness of their formation demonstrates, were highly prone to desertion. An attempt had been made to fill out the ranks of the unit with recruits from Anhalt and militia from the Kurmark Landmiliz. Still, the unit had not had time to coalesce as a fighting force, and the undermining influence of the Saxon contingent on morale should be kept in mind. In addition, there were five companies of the garrison regiment VII Lange, which totalled another 699 men. This unit was commanded by one *oberst* von Sydow but had been filled out with militiamen the previous month. Next was the Land Regiment Lüderitz composed of some seven companies totalling 1,536 men. Finally, there were the depot troops contained in the city who made up some 1,197 men. The artillery defences of the city amounted to only eight artillerists with two guns. The arsenal contained additional guns, which included one 12-pounder and nine

---

43   Duffy, *By Force of Arms*, p.69.

44   It is worth noting that Hadik's actions here were in keeping with the ideas put out by the leading writers on irregular warfare of the day. On this point see Jeney, *The Partisan*, p.41; See also, M de la Croix quoted in M. la Cointe, *The Science of Military Posts, for the use of Regimental Officers, who Frequently Command Detached Parties, in which is shewn the manner of Attacking and Defending Posts* (Nîmes: Royal Academy, 1761), p.209.

45   Duffy, *By Force of Arms*, p.69.

3-pounders, however, it is not clear whether these were even mounted on carriages. Twenty-two additional 3-pounders destined for Magdeburg may still have resided in the city as well. Likewise, there existed a manpower pool of some 110 militia who had been trained in servicing the guns by the invalid corps. In an effort to provide himself with some cavalry for scouting and reconnaissance, the military commander of the city, von Rochow, tried, unsuccessfully, to equip some recruits destined for the Bayreuth Dragoons with horses drafted from the city's breweries.

As the day dawned on 16 October, the Austrians reached Berlin. Rochow, bereft of cavalry, dispatched a detachment of 500 of the Loen Fusiliers under an *Oberstleutnant* von Zitzewitz to locate the raiders. As the troops made their way out of the city, they found Austrian hussars deployed by the Silesian and Kottbus Gates. Zitzewitz moved to engage them, but the hussars withdrew into the forest before the Prussian infantry could close with them. Coming up empty-handed, Zitzewitz returned to the city to reinforce the men defending the gates.

Around 11:00 a.m. Hadik emerged from the Silesian Gate into Berlin at the head of some 3,000 men and four guns and demanded the ransom of 300,000 thalers from the city. The Prussian garrison refused to accede to his demand. While the negotiations over the fate of the Prussian capital were getting off on the wrong foot, rumours spread through streets of the city like the fires of a Mongol horde. One story running through the capital was that Hadik's troops were merely the vanguard of an Austrian army under Marschall pegged by the rumourmongers at 15,000 strong.

Following his initial rebuff, Hadik developed a contingency plan. He set *Oberst* Ujházy the task of launching a diversionary attack on the Potsdam Gate. Simultaneous with Ujházy's attack, Hadik would lead the main assault on the town.

Delivering his attack on the weakly defended capital, Hadik launched his four Grenzer companies under *Oberst* Reid against the Silesian Gate and the bridge over the Spree River. Reid was supported by two 6-pounder guns deployed between the walls and the wet ditch at the gate. Ujházy for his part remained with his troops in the woods near the Academy. Seeing the danger of his attack being thrown back, and all of his meticulous planning coming to naught, Hadik funnelled in two additional companies of Grenzers, specifically the grenadiers of the Slavonisch-Gradiskaners and the Karlstäder-Szlumiers.

The defence of the city had so far cost the Prussians five officers and 93 men killed, including *Oberst* von Lange and a *Major* von Tesmar, as well as 143 men and 12 officers wounded. 427 men had been taken prisoner. The all-important measure of morale in eighteenth century armies, desertion, claimed an additional 200 Prussians. Clearly, this was not a force of modern Spartans willing to stand against all challengers. By the same token, they had no Leonidas to stand with them. Outside of Babocsay, only 28 other 'Austrians' were killed in the attack, an impressively small number.[46]

---

46   Christopher Duffy, *Prussia's Glory: Rossbach and Leuthen, 1757* (Chicago: The Emperor's Press, 2003), p.107. In his more recent work, Duffy gives the Austrian losses as under 40, still, and impressively low number for the enterprise undertaken. See Duffy, *By Force of Arms*, p.70.

Here was the decisive moment of the raid. While Hadik controlled much of the suburbs, the Prussians could still, theoretically, have held out within the walls. By the same token, Hadik was under no illusions as to his movements thus far going undetected. He had only so much time to achieve what he could in the capital and be off, or risk being crushed against the same walls he currently surrounded. In order to successfully accomplish his mission, to the extent he still could, Hadik had to keep the Berliners under the impression that he possessed a full corps of some 15,000 men. Likewise, he had to restrain his own men from rampaging through the areas of the city they occupied and in doing so throw away all unit cohesion. The Austrian commander certainly realized by this point that his carefully planned program of demolitions and confiscations had to be thrown to the wind.[47] Hadick now called on the residents of Berlin to pay him a ransom of 500,000 thaler in order to spare the city.

Some parlaying ensued. Eventually, Hadik exacted 235,000 thalers from the leaders of Berlin, 25,000 of which was paid directly to the troops to prevent them plundering the city.[48] In order to be certain Berlin was not plundered, Hadik kept his men outside the Excise Wall and placed the gates under guard.[49] Hadik enhanced this rich contribution with some gifts for his sovereign as well. There is the story that once the major terms had been agreed to Hadik made one additional request of the city leaders, two-dozen ladies' gloves, stamped with the coat of arms of Berlin which he could present to the empress Maria Theresa. Christopher Duffy lends some support to this tale noting that 'Hadik used to go to great lengths to secure agreeable presents for his wife, on occasion from as far away as Paris, which lends some credibility to the story of the Empress's gloves.'[50]

As Hadik took this tribute, he sent word to *Feldmarschall* Count Leopold von Daun, then operating in Silesia, of his successful occupation of the Berlin suburbs. Count Olivieri of the Prinz Savoyen Dragoons carried the report to Daun. At the same time that Hadik reached and occupied the suburbs, Prince Moritz arrived at Jüterborgk, and Prince Henry moved off from Lutzen to rendezvous with Frederick.

Successful in his mission so far, Hadik now had to withdrawal before the Prussian net closed around him and his force. Beginning at 5:00 a.m. on 17 October, he abandoned Berlin, hastened by the news that Prince Moritz had reached Storkow. His tribute from the city filled 14 confiscated coaches loaded with cash and bills of credit for the city's ransom.[51]

Even while making good his retreat, Hadik sought to expand on the damage he inflicted on Prussia. He chose a route to the east of the Spreewald in order to lay new areas of Brandenburg under contribution and place some distance between himself and the advancing Prussians.[52] In addition, he

---

47   Duffy, *Prussia's Glory*, p.107.
48   Duffy, *By Force of Arms*, p.70, gives the numbers 500,000 thalers and 10,000 respectively.
49   Duffy, *By Force of Arms*, p.70.
50   Duffy, *By Force of Arms*, p.70.
51   Duffy, *By Force of Arms*, p.70.
52   Duffy, *By Force of Arms*, p.70.

dispatched a smaller force against Frankfurt-an-Oder to exact a ransom of 30,000 thalers from that city. Hadik began his move in the nick of time, as by 8:00 p.m. on the same day, Seydlitz entered the city at the head of some 3,000 men. While on his way into the town, Seydlitz even engaged Hadik's rear guard under Ujházy at Thyrow. Now it was the Prussians' turn, Seydlitz troops captured one officer and 27 hussars.

The above represents only a small sampling of the skirmishes, raids, counterraids and ambushes. that went to make up the Small War within the Seven Years War. Activity on the part of the light units was fairly constant, so much so that soldiers such as William Todd found it barely worth mentioning by the latter years of the conflict. At the same time, the activities commonly associated with Small War could grow to larger proportions. The raid on Berlin was certainly ostentatious. Likewise, it forced both Frederick and Prince Henry to redirect their efforts. While the action involved more troops than many of the others detailed above, it did utilize many of the same tactics. At the same time, because the raid on Berlin occurred on a larger scale than other episodes of Small War, the scale magnified the effects. In each of the case described in the preceding pages, efforts by light troops disrupted the enemy's plans and stymied their efforts. An even more profound example of what light troops and their tactics could do presented itself in the raid on Domstadtl.

5

The Raid on Gundersdorf and Domstadtl

While Andreas Hadik's 1757 raid on Berlin was singular in its audacity, the ambushes at Gundersdorf and Domstadtl represent the apex of what Small War could achieve. These engagements serve as examples of a moderate investment of resources on the part of the Austrians which yielded significant strategic results. The damage the Austrians inflicted on the major supply convoy forced Frederick to give up his siege operations around the city of Olmütz, and to break off his entire campaign in Moravia. Consequently, they served to disrupt Frederick's entire plan for the 1758 campaign.

In order to emphasize the significance of the raids on Gundersdorf and Domstadtl, really two rounds of a general attack, it is first necessary to outline the overall strategic situation as it stood in the eastern European theatre in the spring of 1758. Following the twin victories of Rossbach and Leuthen in 1757, which saved Prussia from the coalition arrayed against it, Frederick sought to return to Silesia and retake the important city of Schweidnitz. From there he turned his attention to Moravia, which he invaded and pointed his forces toward the fortified city of Olmütz. The Prussians opened their formal siege of the city on the night of 27–28 May.

In besieging Olmütz, Frederick hoped to draw the Austrian *Feldmarschall* Leopold Josef von Daun into an open field confrontation. The Austrian commander refused to take the bait, however. As one contemporary source summarized, 'The king of Prussia endeavoured by every art in his power to provoke Daun to a battle; but that able general knew too well the advantage of the game he was playing, to throw it out of his hands.'[1]

Essentially, Daun seemed to realize that while he refused to confront Frederick in an open field engagement, he retained the choice of when and how to act, what modern students of war refer to as the operational initiative.

Daun was the son of *Feldmarschall* Wirich Philipp von Daun, who successfully defended Turin in 1706. Leopold von Daun was one of the leading figures in the reform moment within the Austrian army during the late 1740s and 1750s and authored the Daun'sche Reglement of 1749. Further, he was

---

1   Anon., *A Complete History of the Present War, from its Commencement in 1756, to the End of the Campaign, 1760* (London: Owen, Davis & Reymers, 1761), p.263.

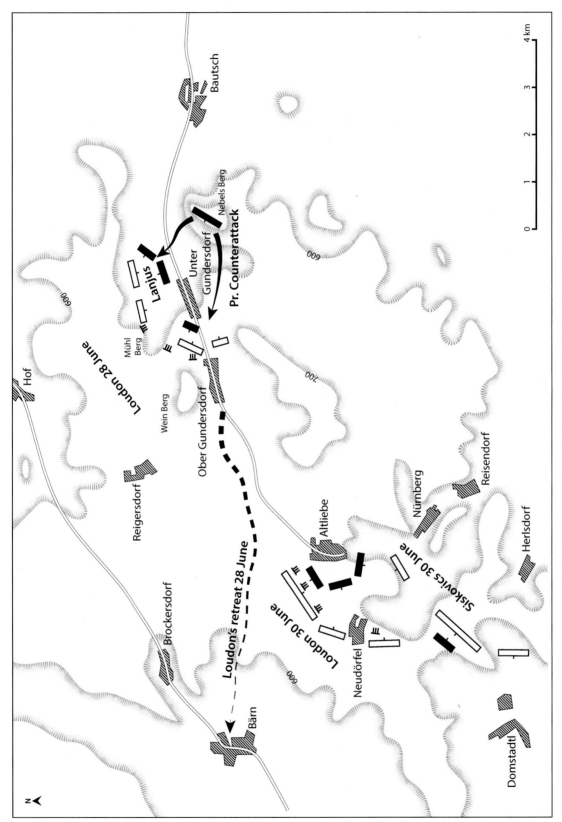

Map of the engagements of Gundersdorf and Domstadtl from 28 to 30 June 1758.

the founder and first director of the military Academy at Wiener Neustadt.[2] He possessed a preference for manoeuvre and defensive tactics as opposed to giving battle and therefore was an able foe of Frederick's.

Further, as Christopher Duffy noted concerning Frederick's position at this time, 'He had known that Olmütz was strong, but he had not expected that the Austrian army would hang back and deny him his battle.'[3] In refusing battle, the Austrians, in turn, dictated Frederick's actions in laying siege to the city.

The siege of Olmütz progressed slowly through the months of May and June. Consequently, it began to consume more resources than Frederick planned. Many thought the fortress was nearing the end of its ability to resist the Prussian attackers. Still, the efforts cost significant supplies not only of bombs and solid shot for the artillery, but thousands of rounds of musket-shot for the infantry who constantly engaged in small-unit actions with the Austrian light forces defending the city.[4]

Supply therefore stood as a constant worry for the Prussians from the opening of operations.[5] The concern on Frederick's part came down to would his own supplies be exhausted before those of his opponent?[6] By mid-June, three convoys had already made the difficult journey from Neisse to resupply the Prussian forces. The first of these encompassed 800 wagons and included the entire siege train for the army. It arrived safely on 20 May, approximately two weeks after Frederick had taken up his position at Olmütz. The comparatively easy passage of the earlier convoys seems to have lulled Frederick into a false sense of security concerning his communications with Neisse.[7] Even so, the experience of the second convoy should have alerted the soldier-king to possible dangers.

While *General-Major* Nicolaus Lorenz Puttkamer managed to bring the convoy under his command safely through to Olmütz on 1 June, he was not so lucky on the return march. On 8 June, the escort of two frei battalions was ambushed and virtually wiped out, one of them being the frei battalion Salenmon detailed above.[8] The loss of this force underscored, or should have for Frederick, the significance of guarding his lines of communication.

Likewise, the French author and expert on Small War Thomas Le Roy de Grandmaison gave some important instructions moving a convoy through a defile, 'When you have crossed the plain, you make your carriages file off alternately, one from each column to file through the defile, taking care always to make those in the rear advance, so as not to leave any interval, and

---

2   Duffy, *By Force of Arms*, p.422.

3   Duffy, *By Force of Arms*, p.105.

4   Duffy, *By Force of Arms*, p.105.

5   Peter Wilson, 'The Ambush of the Olmütz Convoy at Domstadtl, June 28-30, 1758', *Seven Years War Association Journal*, 8:4 (Winter, 1996), p.11.

6   Franz A.J. Szabo, *The Seven Years War in Europe 1756-1763* (New York: Longman, 2008), p.148.

7   Wilson, 'Ambush', pp.11–12.

8   Wilson, 'Ambush', p.12.

to reinforce your rear guard, to resist the last efforts of the enemy on the rear of the convoy.'[9]

Still, in order to complete the capture of Olmütz, additional supplies were necessary. Frederick ordered additional supplies brought up in a massive fourth convoy which included some 4,000 wagons; 818 of these would transport the ammunition necessary to complete the siege.[10] The trip from Troppau, where the convoy assembled, to Olmütz usually took about six days. It should be emphasized that many of the horses owned by local farmers that were conscripted for the convoy were in poor condition as well. The General Staff History reports that they were 'lying down from exhaustion.'[11] At this time, the roads stood in deplorable condition as well, which adversely effected the distance possible to cover on any given day.

The convoy itself stretched over some 32 kilometres. To provide cover to the long line of wagons, a force consisting of six battalions of fusiliers, and two of grenadiers, with three battalions of recruits and convalescents, along with 1,000 horsemen, was cobbled together to provide an escort. An *Oberst* Mosel, described as 'a man of determination and experience,' commanded the force.[12] Aside from the garrison battalions, which were drawn from Brieg and Breslau, all the units that composed escort force were recruits or convalescents still recovering from wounds received in the heavy fighting of the previous campaign but able to perform light duties. Swelling the oversized column even further were the 4,000 civilian baggage attendants.[13] Mosel divided the convoy into 10 sub-detachments, each of which was covered by a battalion and a few cavalrymen. In doing so, however, he further weakened both the advanced and rear guards.[14] It was the age-old problem of 'he who tries to defend everything defends nothing.' In attempting to provide some cover for the entire column, Mosel stretched his defenders too thin to be effective.

No plan, and certainly none involving a force of this magnitude, is implemented in a vacuum. Moravian peasants kept the long column under observation and passed the information they gleaned on to Austrian detachments in the region. The efforts of these civilians kept *General der Cavallerie* Adolph Nicolaus Buccow, the Austrian commander in the area, apprised of every detail relating to the convoy.[15]

Buccow dutifully passed along the information to *Feldmarschall* von Daun, with the suggestion that some effort be made against the convoy. Daun developed a plan to do just that.

---

9   Grandmaison, *Treatise*, p.212.

10   'Combat at Domstadtl', *Kronoskaf*, <http://www.kronoskaf.com/syw/index.php?title=1758-06-30_-_Combat_of_Domstadl>, accessed 22 May 2023.

11   Großen Generalstabe, *Die Krieges Friedrichs des Großen, der Siebenjährige Krieg 1756-1763*, Siebenter Bande: Olmütz und Crefeld (Berlin: Ernst Siegfried Mittler und Sohn, 1909), p.93. Unless otherwise noted, all translations from the General Staff History are my own.

12   Duffy, *By Force of Arms*, p.105.

13   Wilson, 'Ambush,' p.12.

14   Großen Generalstabe, *Krieges Friedrichs*, p.93.

15   Duffy, *By Force of Arms*, p.105.

A private of Pandour Kleist, part of the Freikorps von Kleist, commanded by *Oberst* Friedrich Wilhelm von Kleist (Green Kleist) 1759.
(Original artwork by Alexandr Chernushkin © Helion & Company 2023)

An infantryman of the Joseph Philipp Graf von Guicciardi Liccaner Grenz-Infanterie-Regiment, circa 1762. (Original artwork by Alexandr Chernushkin © Helion & Company 2023)

An infantryman of the Chasseurs de Fischer, 1761. (Original artwork by Alexandr Chernushkin © Helion & Company 2023)

A ranger of Rogers' Rangers, 1758. (Original artwork by Alexandr Chernushkin © Helion & Company 2023)

A private of the 80th Regiment of Foot, 'Gage's Light Infantry', 1759. (Original artwork by Alexandr Chernushkin © Helion & Company 2023)

A jäger of Schaumburg-Lippe-Bückeburg Jäger Corps, 1760. (Original artwork by Alexandr Chernushkin © Helion & Company 2023)

A Canadian Iroquois Warrior, 1756. About the time of the raid on Fort Bull. (Original artwork
by Alexandr Chernushkin © Helion & Company 2023)

An officer of the Canadian Militia, circa 1760. (Original artwork by Alexandr Chernushkin © Helion & Company 2023)

Aware of the Prussian supply situation through their scouts and the peasantry of the region, and likewise realizing that a successful interdiction effort could help to raise the siege of Olmütz the Austrians began to plan an attack on the Prussian supply column as soon as they learned of its existence. Daun arrayed his 45,000 troops in a wide arc from his main position 40 kilometres (about 24 miles) southeast of Olmütz to Dobramillitz. There they faced Frederick's forces south of the city. The Austrians were deployed as follows: *Generalfeldwachtmeister* Joseph Count Siskovics and *Generalfeldwachtmeister* Josef Saint-Ignon occupied Prerau southeast of Olmütz with 4,000 men. Meanwhile, Buccow commanded a force of 12,000 troops with which he advanced on Littau to the northeast. *Feldmarschalllieutenant* DeWille screened the main army with 5,000 Austrian and Saxon cavalry which he kept in close proximity to the Prussian positions at Prossnitz. Finally, general Bieberstein held Olmütz itself with a mixed force of 10,000 Austrian and Bavarian infantry.[16]

Buccow's role would be to march his main force southwest to Ptin and Pumgenau and there take a position on the right flank of the Prussian field army.[17] This manoeuvre would have the effect of fixing the latter force in place so that they would be unable to come to the aid of the convoy when Daun sprang his trap. Buccow received the final approval to go ahead with the attempt on the evening of 25/26 June.[18]

Two detachments were tasked with launching the actual attack on the convoy. The first was a western force under the command of *Generalfeldwachtmeister* Loudon. The force would be composed of four battalions, one dragoon regiment, one regiment of hussars, and 600 Croats. They had orders to join the command of *Oberst* Louis Lanjus which had moved ahead to Reigersdorf. Lanjus had under him 280 grenadiers, 340 hussars, and 600 Croats as well.[19] Loudon's force would be detached from Buccow's.

The eastern force, then, under *Generalfeldwachtmeister* Siskovics was comprised of a detachment from Daun's army. Siskovics's command included one grenadier battalion, two battalions of fusiliers and four companies of carabiniers.[20] Siskovics's corps would have the longer march as they were to move counter-clockwise to Prerau, where they would receive a reinforcement of 1,200 horse and 1,000 Croats under Saint-Ignon. They would then make their approach to the convoy from the east.[21]

The Prussians for their part were not completely unaware of the Austrian movements, and *Feldmarschall* James Keith ordered *General der Cavallerie* Hans Joachim von Zeiten to make contact with the convoy. Zeiten, acting on these orders, dispatched an *Oberst* Paul Werner with a force of roughly 1,000 men to the village of Giebau which lay between Zieten and Domstadtl.[22]

16   Wilson, 'Ambush', p.14.
17   Wilson, 'Ambush', p.14.
18   Großen Generalstabe, *Krieges Friedrichs*, p.95.
19   Wilson, 'Ambush', p.14.
20   Wilson, 'Ambush', p.14.
21   Wilson, 'Ambush', p.14.
22   Wilson, 'Ambush', p.12.

Zieten decided on resting his troops as his infantry were exhausted from their exertions.[23]

Meanwhile, Mosel's column moved at a ponderous pace, with the advanced guard, such as it was, arriving at Bautsch only on 25 June. There Werner penned a letter to Zieten informing the latter that he planned to reach Giebau on the 27th.[24]

Loudon began moving his force into position on the evening of 26 June. He marched his troops through the night, employing a classic partisan tactic, to reach Sternberg at the foot of the border plateau the next morning. His target began to make its way up the opposite side of the watershed on the 26th, however due to its incredible length, the column moved at a staggeringly slow pace. Christopher Duffy estimates the length of the column as 'something like thirty miles of route in ideal conditions.'[25] He is quick to add, however, the conditions were far from ideal. The weather was rainy, and the road was already churned up by passage of Prussian military transports.[26] Recall as well the condition of many of the draft horses. As a result, at the end of the first day's march, only a third of the column managed to reach the first planned overnight position at Bautsch. The remainder of the convoy continued trying to move out from their starting point at Troppau.

Still, when Loudon received intelligence that the head of the column had reached Bautsch he grew alarmed, as he had further information that Prussian *General-Lieutenant* Markgraf Karl von Brandenburg-Schwendt was approaching the column with an additional 4,000 troops to provide extra security. In the end this intelligence proved false.[27] The Austrians had planned the ambush since the convoy left Troppau, and Loudon did not want to see these efforts come to naught.[28]

The reported relief force was in reality merely a reinforcement consisting of one grenadier battalion, 300 hussars and 200 dragoons under the command of an *Oberst* Werner. This was the same Werner *General der Cavallerie* Zieten had sent with a detachment to Giebau. Loudon receiving no updates from Siskovics, determined on a forced march over the plateau. In part, Loudon's rapid movements were spurred on by the false intelligence concerning the relief force.[29] This movement placed his corps in the vicinity of Domstadtl by the evening of the 27th. On establishing himself in this new position, Loudon planned to launch his attack on the convoy while it remained well short of Olmütz. Hitting the convoy in this region would obviate the possibility of Loudon being caught between the convoy's escort troops and the reinforcements approaching from the plain.[30]

In order to prevent his own force from being surprised while he ambushed the Prussians, Loudon held back a reserve at Domstadtl consisting of 300

23   Großen Generalstabe, *Krieges Friedrichs*, p.97.
24   Großen Generalstabe, *Krieges Friedrichs*, p.93.
25   Wilson, 'Ambush', p.12.
26   Wilson, 'Ambush', p.12.
27   Duffy, *By Force of Arms*, p.107.
28   Wilson, 'Ambush', p.14.
29   Großen Generalstabe, *Krieges Friedrichs*, p.95.
30   Duffy, *By Force of Arms*, p.107.

hussars and 300 Croats under a *Major* Goes. Loudon then ordered the remainder of his troops to rise at midnight. This would be their third forced march in as many days.[31] Likewise, Siskovics and St Ignon moved northwards from Prerau with their column so that they could be in position to attack the Prussian column from the east.[32]

Meanwhile, Mosel, having himself received intelligence of the Austrian movements on the 27th, drew the convoy up into a defensive *Wagenberg* at the town of Bautsch.[33] The Wagenberg was essentially a defensive encirclement of the wagons to use them as an ad hoc field fortification. As the forecast attack did not materialize, he set out once again at 2:00 a.m. on 28 June in the hopes of arriving at Domstadtl by midnight.[34] His flank parties were marching alongside the column in 'peletons' or platoons.[35]

Loudon followed the road through the valley to the village, which comprised of a collection of long huts. There was still no sign of Siskovics on the far side, but Loudon could not delay. On receiving word of the convoy's movements, he performed a personal reconnaissance.[36] His scouts reported that the head of the Prussian column had already entered Unter-Gundersdorf. As he later reported, 'I rode forward and came into contact with the enemy, taking three prisoners.'[37] These were likely scouts out ahead of the main column.[38] In doing so, he likely disclosed his presence as well.

Loudon had previously deployed his forces to the north of Unter-Gundersdorf. Likewise, he had placed the troops of *Oberst* Lanjus, who had moved up from Riegersdorf on his left wing.[39]

Rather than break off now that his presence was known, Loudon went immediately over to the attack, trying to capitalize on what element of surprise he still possessed. Again, a classic partisan tactic. His battery north of the road began to fire on the advance guard of the Prussian column.[40] At the same time, a *Kapitän* Rouvroy placed three batteries of artillery in the hills which dominated the western exit of the village. As his guns began to play upon the Prussians, they forced the leading escorts, the first battalion of Jung-Kreytzen, to retreat and fall back on a battalion of the Alt-Billerbeck Grenadiers. These troops were already positioned to the south of the road.[41]

Coming under cannon fire and the more accurate fire of the Croats, the Prussians on the right flank fell back. It should be kept in mind that the troops defending this portion of the column were mere recruits from the Prince Ferdinand Regiment and for many this was their first experience of combat.[42] Mosel attempted to rally his escort on the Nebels-Berg when

---

31   Duffy, *By Force of Arms*, p.107.
32   Wilson, 'Ambush', p.14.
33   Großen Generalstabe, *Krieges Friedrichs*, p.93.
34   Wilson, 'Ambush', p.12.
35   Großen Generalstabe, *Krieges Friedrichs*, p.96.
36   Großen Generalstabe, *Krieges Friedrichs*, p.96.
37   Loudon quoted in Duffy, *By Force of Arms*, p.107.
38   Großen Generalstabe, *Krieges Friedrichs*, p.96.
39   Großen Generalstabe, *Krieges Friedrichs*, p.96.
40   Wilson, 'Ambush', p.12.
41   Duffy, *By Force of Arms*, p.107.
42   Großen Generalstabe, *Krieges Friedrichs*, pp.96–97.

the Croats discovered something of greater interest to themselves in the village. The ambush scared off many of the civilian drivers who cut the traces of their horses and fled back to Troppau with their teams. As a result, numerous wagons stood motionless and unguarded in the village, ripe for the plucking. Among the wagons 'there were a large number of barrels bearing the inscription "Flinkensteine", musket flints.'[43] Some of the Croats broke four of the barrels open with their swords, discovering that they were in fact loaded with four and eight-groschen pieces.[44] The discipline of the troops, nominally commanded by a *Kapitän* Anton Kovatshovits of the Warasdiner St George Croats, gave way and the men succumbed to their proclivity to loot.[45] The men's desire for booty was another facet of the behaviour of light troops, especially those who were not thoroughly indoctrinated in the military institutions of the state. Kovatshovits tried to restore some discipline amongst his men. Failing in the attempt, he allowed them their bounty. This eventually redounded on him as he was looked over for promotion years later, essentially on the grounds of unseemly conduct.[46]

Despite the looting by some Croats, the battle raged all around. Loudon ordered the troops of *Oberst* Lanjus to take up a position on his eastern flank. Lanjus's position immediately fell under a determined attack from three Prussian battalions. The Prussians advanced north from the Nebels-Berg. Two of the battalions were summoned up from the rear guard by *Oberst* Mosel. These men had a greater distance to traverse. Still, they succeeded in driving Lanjus and his men from the Mühl-Berg at bayonet point.[47] Once the Prussians secured the high ground, they planted their artillery and managed to beat back no less than five assaults by Loudon's infantry.[48] The Prussian success on the Mühl-Berg was compounded when the battalion of Alt-Billerbeck, to their left, seized one of Rouvroy's batteries, sword in hand, as it were.[49] The General Staff History notes that the Prussian cavalry units present could not organize themselves quickly enough to play a role in this part of the fighting.[50]

After fighting for more than three hours, Loudon's force sustained more than 450 casualties with 52 killed, 104 wounded and 339 missing or captured.[51] His situation grew even more complicated in the afternoon, with the arrival of fresh Prussian reinforcements. This was Zieten who moved up with five battalions and 12 squadrons to come to the aid of the column.[52]

In reality, on this first attempt against the column Loudon defeated himself. A fact to which he later admitted. He believed he would have won

---

43   Duffy, *By Force of Arms*, p.107.
44   Duffy, *By Force of Arms*, p.107.
45   Duffy, *By Force of Arms*, p.107.
46   Duffy, *By Force of Arms*, p.107.
47   Großen Generalstabe, *Krieges Friedrichs*, p.97.
48   Duffy, *By Force of Arms*, p.107.
49   Duffy, *By Force of Arms*, p.107.
50   Großen Generalstabe, *Krieges Friedrichs*, p.97.
51   Duffy, *By Force of Arms*, p.107.
52   Duffy, *By Force of Arms*, pp.107–108.

the day, 'if I did not also fear coming under attack from the rear.'[53] Still, one setback, no matter how significant, did not amount to enough to squelch an aggressive spirit such as Loudon's.[54] He fell back on Bärn, where he remained a danger to the Prussian column.[55] On his arrival, he learned that his partner in the operation, Siskovics, had reached Altstadt. Loudon informed the other commander that if he, Siskovics, still planned to attack the column, then Loudon would do all in his power to assist in the enterprise. Still, after his repulse that day, Loudon sounded a note of dejection, telling Siskovics 'I believed it was already too late, since the enemy general Zieten was already on the way with a considerable force, and was supposed to be already at Altliebe.'[56]

In explaining Siskovics's absence from the engagement on the 28th, Christopher Duffy initially observes that his delay was due to the commander's lack of experience in partisan tactics, though he was of Hungarian descent – as previously noted, Hungarians were, at this time, known for their facility in the employment of Small War tactics.[57] He had actually earned his reputation as a drillmaster in the line infantry. Siskovics's abilities as a trainer contributed to his rapid ascent through the ranks of the officer corps moving from *kapitän* to *major*, and only a few days later to *inhaber* of the regiment von Haller.[58] This blinding series of promotions came at a time when officers could spend literally decades in grade. Siskovics's rapid promotions so unnerved contemporaries that one, *Oberstleutnant* Robentisch, left the Austrian service for that of the Prussians. Siskovics's most recent promotion brought him the rank of *Generalfeldwachtmeister*.

Siskovics's skills as a trainer of men aside, he had been posted in Moravia, therefore, he actually had the longer distance to march to rendezvous with Loudon and attack the Prussian column. However, in order to preserve the secrecy of his intentions, Siskovics had been forced to delay his march until the same day that Loudon embarked. Further complicating matters, the *Generalfeldwachtmeister* spent the first day of his march being misled by his guides.[59]

Siskovics managed to regain the time lost on the following day, the 28th, through the execution of a forced march which brought his force to the hills just short of the rising ground from whence Loudon had launched his attack.[60] The colonel received further aid, unconsciously, from the Prussians.

Following the clash with Loudon on the 28th, Zieten arrived on the battlefield at about 4:00 p.m., and assumed overall command of the column. By that time, only a few stragglers from Loudon's force remained visible. Zieten spent the following day attempting to restore some sense of order.[61]

---

53   Loudon, quoted in Duffy, *By Force of Arms*, p.109.
54   Duffy, *By Force of Arms*, p.109.
55   Großen Generalstabe, *Krieges Friedrichs*, p.97.
56   Loudon quoted in Duffy, *By Force of Arms*, p.109.
57   Duffy, *By Force of Arms*, p.109.
58   Duffy, *By Force of Arms*, p.109. See also James R. McIntyre, 'Joseph Count Siskovics', in *Journal of the Seven Years War Association*, 23:2 (Winter 2019/2020), pp.54–66.
59   Duffy, *By Force of Arms*, p.109.
60   Duffy, *By Force of Arms*, p.109.
61   Großen Generalstabe, *Krieges Friedrichs*, pp.97–98.

A traffic jam occurred at the front of the column where, as previously noted, many of the drivers had cut their traces and fled for their lives. Zieten sent some of his patrols back to Troppau to bring up additional wagons which had been left there in reserve.[62] The press of abandoned vehicles was untangled, and the carts restored to some semblance of order. The delays this effort entailed allowed Siskovics to recover more time lost during his first days' meandering.

Once he reorganized the supply train, Zieten set it in motion out of the Gundersdorf valley and to the open country beyond. The topography in this area conspired against surprise, as it presented open views as far as the Carpathian Mountains.[63] Still, the General Staff History notes that Zieten's delay while making his arrangements only contributed to the ensuing disaster that befell the column.[64] The convoy made its way out of the plain, down to the hollow that contained the village of Altliebe. Zieten sent out strong patrols in the direction of the village.[65] Here Mosel set up a defensive position with a reformed Wagenberg as a precaution. Due to the reorganization necessary to change the wagons from the defensive burg to a column, they did not begin moving until 8:00 a.m.[66] Leaving Altliebe, the head of the column was once again on a forward slope where it prepared for the final stage of the march through Domstadtl.[67]

Through these manoeuvres, Zieten remained undisturbed as he continued his march. The lack of any sighting of the enemy caused him to relax his vigilance somewhat, a fatal error in this circumstance. The same lack of understanding concerning the overall situation dominated the Prussian headquarters, where confidence reigned following Loudon's repulse on the 28th. Many in the Prussian leadership seemed to perceive the event as a victory as opposed to a narrow escape. Even so, Frederick ordered two additional grenadier battalions as reinforcements to the column.[68]

Though Loudon's men were nearing exhaustion, the commander was willing to launch another attempt on the Prussian convoy. As noted above, Loudon was in contact with Siskovics by the end of the day of his repulse at Gundersdorf. While Loudon remained pessimistic of their chances for success, he was willing to give Siskovics his full support in launching another attack on the column. For his part, Siskovics determined to at least attempt to hold up its progress.[69] Doing so would further strain the Prussian siege operations at Olmütz. The two commanders began to develop a plan for a renewed attack on the Prussian supply train for the following day.[70]

Siskovics would take the lead with his troops since they were the less fatigued of the two Austrian forces. He deployed his troops to the east of

---

62 Großen Generalstabe, *Krieges Friedrichs*, p.98.
63 Duffy, *By Force of Arms*, p.109.
64 Großen Generalstabe, *Krieges Friedrichs*, p.98.
65 Großen Generalstabe, *Krieges Friedrichs*, p.98.
66 Wilson, 'Ambush', p.17.
67 Wilson, 'Ambush', p.17.
68 Großen Generalstabe, *Krieges Friedrichs*, p.98.
69 Großen Generalstabe, *Krieges Friedrichs*, p.99.
70 Wilson, 'Ambush', p.17.

the Prussian line of march. As one noted historian of the conflict explains, 'In detail, Siskovics planned to arrange his forces along the summit of a continuous ridge which ran parallel the Prussian route as it made the gradual descent a couple of miles from Neudörfel to Domstadtl.'[71]

Siskovics planned to use the terrain to his advantage. There were two tracts of woodland which extended along the rest of some high ground about 1,000 yards from the road. The left side, or southern wood would be occupied by the Warasdiner Croats, the Hungarian infantry Regiment Haller, and the Saxon Prince Karl Chevaulegers. They were supplemented by a force of Austrian grenadiers in their rear as a reserve, along with a battery of two light pieces and two 6-pounders on their right and the regimental 3-pounders of the Regiment Haller on the left. He intended to allow the convoy to begin moving and then attack its left flank. The far right-flank would be secured by mounted troops. These consisted of some dragoons, hussars and Polish-Saxon Uhlans. The left-hand wood was, in turn held by small bodies of infantry. All of these forces remained carefully concealed in the woods on either side of the road.[72] Siskovics's goal was to bring the Prussians to a complete halt and create a jam at the head of the column. Once the convoy halted Loudon would attack from the west with his troops. Their assault would complete the destruction of the Prussian convoy. Weather played his role in the clash as well, as a summer rain fell on the morning of 30 June.

At 9:00 a.m., an *Oberst* Nauendorf sent word that the head of the Prussian column had initiated their march. The first wagons actually left Altliebe an hour previously.[73] For their part, the Prussians were moving in a somewhat leisurely formation. The cavalry marched to the right of the road, where the road was fairly level. There were wide intervals between the squadrons. Likewise, the infantry were stationed on the right.[74] Interestingly, the German General Staff History places Prussian troops on both sides of the road.[75] Siskovics moved his troops forward into their ambush positions. For a time, the Hungarian commander allowed his unsuspecting quarry to pass by unmolested.[76]

With impeccable timing, Siskovics sprang the trap at 10:30 a.m. By then, the head of the convoy had reached Domstadtl.[77] No sooner had about 120 carts entered the town than the enemy sprang from hiding on the heights to the left of the road and at once opened a heavy fire of artillery on the village entrance. This cannonade had the desired effect of killing a number of horses, which in turn created an obstacle, bringing the column to a dead halt.[78]

Zieten reacted by sending every available man into a counter-attack against his Austrian assailants. As a result, 200 Puttkamer Hussars and three and a half battalions of infantry advanced up the slope. Since the rain

71   Duffy, *By Force of Arms*, pp.109–110.
72   Duffy, *By Force of Arms*, p.110.
73   Großen Generalstabe, *Krieges Friedrichs*, p.99.
74   Duffy, *By Force of Arms*, p.110.
75   Großen Generalstabe, *Krieges Friedrichs*, p.99.
76   Duffy, *By Force of Arms*, p.110.
77   Wilson, 'Ambush', p.17
78   Duffy, *By Force of Arms*, p.110.

made their muskets and carbines useless, the men pressed the attack with the cold steel. The Prussians thus chased their Croat assailants through the woods.[79] In spite of the rain, the Prussians enjoyed some success in ejecting the Warasdiner Croats from the wooded area on the left after a brief melee.[80] Consequently, they did prevent the attack from hitting that section of the column, at least for a time. Still, the fighting in the woods left the Prussian formations disorganized.[81] When it appeared that the counter-attack was succeeding, Zieten turned command over to *Major* von Rath and headed to the left flank of the column to shore up the defences there.[82]

Though the Austrian forces listed above seemed significant, they were in fact spread thinly on the ground, and the sudden Prussian assault threatened to overwhelm them. Seeing the danger, Nauendorf ordered *Oberstleutnant* Voit with 100 Löwenstein Chevaulegers to join in the attack. The added pressure of this new attack on their flank, while the troops remained disorganized, broke the sustaining motivation of the Prussians to the extent that they fell into a general rout. The Prussians abandoned all their colours, as well as five cannon. Six officers and 300 men fell into the hands of the Austrian as well.[83]

Zieten turned back down the road to Neudörfel and ordered an additional battalion and a half into an attack on the woods. This latest and last effort was short-lived however, as the Austrian horse threatened the Prussian right flank. By noon, all Zieten's attempts to organize a counterattack on the Austrians had come to naught.[84] As the General Staff History observes, 'Zieten had not yet deployed his cavalry, and six fresh battalions were still at his disposal at Altliebe, but the spearheads of Loudon's corps were already approaching the battlefield. This made Zieten's situation hopeless.'[85]

By this time, Loudon had finally organized his own forces in front of Bärn and was ready to attack the Prussians from the west. The surviving details of Loudon's attack are incomplete. What is known is that he formed his infantry into two groups on his left flank and threw them against Altliebe and Neudörfel. As the attack opened, a gap developed in the first line between the troops of the Alt-Wolfenbüttel and Kollowrat infantry. This was quickly filled by the perceptive work of *Major* Tom Caldwell who led the grenadiers of *Oberst* Lanjus' detachment. Caldwell led his men against some Prussian artillery posted on the high ground. At 80 yards, his men loosed two volleys and proceeded to overrun the Prussian guns, capturing the two pieces in the process.

Meanwhile the Nadasdy Hussars and the Zweibrucken Dragoons maintained their assault on Loudon's right. Together, they managed to drive back repeated attacks on the part of the Prussian cavalry, which was numerically superior.[86]

---

79   Duffy, *By Force of Arms*, p.110.
80   Wilson, 'Ambush', p.17
81   Großen Generalstabe, *Krieges Friedrichs*, p.100.
82   Großen Generalstabe, *Krieges Friedrichs*, p.100.
83   Duffy, *By Force of Arms*, p.110.
84   Großen Generalstabe, *Krieges Friedrichs*, p.101.
85   Großen Generalstabe, *Krieges Friedrichs*, p.101.
86   These were the Schmettau and Kyan Cuirassiers, and the Werner and Zieten Hussars. See Duffy, *By Force of Arms*, pp.110–111.

By the afternoon, Loudon's right wing soon swung to the north-east and joined with Siskovics's left wing, which was advancing on the Altliebe-Domstadtl road. As a result, Zieten was cut off from the rest of the army.[87] By this point, roughly 1,000 Prussian carts sat motionless, jammed up on the road that fed past Neudörfel to Domstadtl. Part of the reason for the pile-up lay in the fact that many of the drivers, who were civilians, had again cut their traces and rode off in the direction of Troppau in search of safety.[88] Two thousand additional carts had not even left Altliebe. Acting on his own initiative, and a fair amount of common sense, *General-Major* Puttkamer leaguered these vehicles up into a Wagenberg in a depression in some high ground southwest of Altliebe.[89] To hold this temporary defensive fortification Puttkamer mustered some eight and a half battalions from the escort. These now clustered in a semi-circle defending the remaining wagons.

While this formation offered an excellent defence against an infantry attack, the men being so closely formed presented the Austrian artillery with a tantalizing target, one they were not going to pass up. As one contemporary observed, 'through the skill of the artillery Captain Rouvroy the pieces were served so well that every shot scored a hit.'[90] Horses were killed, and ammunition wagons blown up. All the work of destruction sowed chaos among the already frazzled Prussian troops. An additional fault in the Prussian dispositions derived from the fact that they were forced to fight where they were, while the Austrians could redirect the focus of their attacks on certain sections of the Wagenberg. Eventually, the Austrians managed to break through the Prussian defences on the flank and in the rear.[91] Interestingly, the last Prussian unit to break and run were the battalion of Prinz Ferdinand. This unit was made up of new recruits who in the words of Christopher Duffy 'as was the way with the new soldiers, did not know when it was sensible to run away.'[92] Perhaps, but as one contemporary noted, 'Never did Spartans or Romans fight for their fatherland with more composure than these blooming youths of seventeen or twenty years.'[93] Likewise, their defence led Peter Wilson, another historian to study the raids in some detail, to observe 'Throughout the struggle, the Prussian infantry had shown considerable determination despite being composed entirely of new recruits and second line units.'[94] Wilson further singled out the Prinz Ferdinand battalion, the Tresckow infantry and the reconstituted grenadier battalions for particular praise for the stolid defence.[95] The men of the Tresckow infantry earned their laurels when the Croats penetrated the town of Altliebe and began to loot both the wagons that remained there and the town itself. The men of the Tresckow infantry succeeded in driving them out

---

87 Großen Generalstabe, *Krieges Friedrichs*, pp.101–102.
88 Großen Generalstabe, *Krieges Friedrichs*, p.102.
89 Duffy, *By Force of Arms*, p.111.
90 Duffy, *By Force of Arms*, p.111.
91 Großen Generalstabe, *Krieges Friedrichs*, p.102.
92 Duffy, *By Force of Arms*, p.112.
93 Quoted in Duffy, *By Force of Arms*, p.112.
94 Wilson, 'Ambush,' p.19.
95 Wilson, 'Ambush,' p.19.

of the town.[96] Most of the men defending the Wagenberg fell victim to the Austrian artillery, along with their leader, a *Kapitän* Pirch. Following a two-hour fight at the Wagenberg, out of 900, only 65 were taken prisoner, though a few wounded managed to make their way back to Troppau. Among the prisoners was *General-Major* von Puttkamer.[97]

Summing up the outcome of the engagement, Franz Szabo observes, 'Though the Austrians had only a slight superiority in numbers the ambush succeeded in part due to the concealment tactics of "little war," and in part because Loudon's two cavalry regiments were able to rout their larger Prussian counterparts.'[98]

The Prussian mounted troops, on this occasion, did little to enhance their reputation. Peter Wilson provides a more balanced assessment of their performance, observing,

> Apart from the hussars, the cavalry had proved unreliable and ineffective, though to be fair, the terrain was hardly suited for the optimal use of the two cuirassier regiments while the rest of the mounted escort comprised detachments drawn from 17 different units, rather than whole squadrons trained and used to operating together.[99]

He further adds that the Prussian artillery did not seem to engage on the 30th to the extent it had on the 28th. It is, therefore, impossible to determine if the artillery were deployed in support of Zieten's attack on the woods.

While there existed clear deficiencies on the force charged with defending the column, the Austrian attacks prevented any effective junction on the part of the Prussian defenders. Now, the remnants of the two forces retreated as best they could towards opposite ends of the plateau. Those who managed to escape the disaster were in full retreat toward Troppau. The Prussian Regiment Blankensee, which was sent out to restore some discipline to the refugees could not stem the flow.[100]

Initially, Siskovics pursued the surviving defenders of the Wagenberg. However, Zieten managed to break contact with the pursuit. He rallied at Troppau, where by 2 July he assembled a group of some 3,000 infantry and 1,200 cavalry. On the southern end of the plateau, *Feldzeugmeister* Krockow saw the smoke and felt the explosions of the assault on the Wagenberg. When these ceased, he assumed, correctly, that there was no purpose in marching towards that end of the column. He therefore moved on to Olmütz with the remnants of his forces. These included some eight battalions of infantry and six squadrons of cuirassiers along with about 500 hussars.[101]

On the Austrian side, while sustaining casualties of roughly 600, they had killed, wounded or captured 58 Prussian officers and 2,328 men. The

96   Großen Generalstabe, *Krieges Friedrichs*, p.102.
97   Großen Generalstabe, *Krieges Friedrichs*, p.104.
98   Szabo, *Seven Years War*, p.150.
99   Wilson, 'Ambush,' p.19
100 Großen Generalstabe, *Krieges Friedrichs*, p.104.
101 Duffy, *By Force of Arms*, p.112.

truly spectacular testament to their success encompassed the nearly 3,000 abandoned wagons stretched out from the Wagenberg at Altliebe along the road to the south. The convoy included far too much material to carry away, especially after many horses were killed in the fighting. Likewise, the Austrian troops were nearly exhausted from their exertions in driving off the Prussians escort.[102] The flour, necessary for the staple of the soldiers' diet, bread, was thrown to the wind or burned in its barrels.[103] In all, two months' supply of flour was destroyed for lack of transportation to bring it off from the battle site.[104] The only material carried off was the money captured during the fighting on the first day of the attacks. The proceeds, however, were too much for the Croats to carry with them. Instead, they exchanged it or used the money to purchase alcohol at incredibly inflated prices. Exchange rates soared as high as 30, 40 and even 50 silver crowns for a ducat. As Christopher Duffy reports, 'Our colonel [Otto Heinrich Rath], who had with him four horses and more than three hundred golden ducats, made a fortune and bought an estate in his own country with the profits.'[105]

Then there was the crucial strategic effect. The successful Austrian raids against the Prussian supply column broke the siege of Olmütz. On learning of the fate of the supply column, Frederick ordered the lifting of the siege. He determined against a retreat in the direction of Troppau as this risked a 'Domstadtl writ large.'[106] Instead, he resolved to march in a wide arc through northeast Bohemia into Lower Silesia. Before breaking up their positions around Olmütz, the Prussian gunners pummelled the city with an exceptionally heavy bombardment on 1 July. The Prussians then abandoned their positions by dawn the following morning.[107] The retreating Prussians were encumbered with 1,500 sick and wounded. Still, they reached Könnigrätz on the 13th and Frederick retired on Glatz by early August.[108] Even Prince Henry of Prussia, not one to heap praise freely on his royal brother called this Frederick's best managed manoeuvre of the entire conflict.[109] Considering the sometime fraught relationship between the royal siblings, this comment should perhaps be viewed as less than complimentary.

As seems the case with many great military successes, controversy erupted among the leaders over who deserved the majority of the credit for the Austrian success. In his report on the engagement, Loudon downplayed the efforts of Siskovics. Buccow probably deserves a significant share of the acclaim, as it was his idea to begin with. By the same token, Daun supported the scheme from the outset and made it part of his overall plan of campaign.[110] From the preceding, it should be clear that a significant portion of the laurels belong to Josef, Count Siskovics. Though Loudon grasped at

---

102 Duffy, *By Force of Arms*, p.112.
103 Duffy, *By Force of Arms*, p.112.
104 Wilson, 'Ambush,' p.20
105 Duffy, *By Force of Arms*, p.112.
106 Wilson, 'Ambush,' p.20.
107 Wilson, 'Ambush,' p.20.
108 Wilson, 'Ambush,' p.20.
109 Wilson, 'Ambush,' p.20.
110 Duffy, *By Force of Arms*, p.113.

the laurels for the operation by denigrating the efforts of Siskovics, he does deserve some credit, especially for not giving up after his initial attempt on the Prussian column was repulsed. Such determination stood out as a quality that separated many a successful leader of light troops, in both theatres, from their less successful contemporaries. Even with the best of leadership, it is the men in the ranks who contribute the lion's share to the fighting. In that vein, the Austrian artillery and cavalry deserve recognition as both acquitted themselves well in making the second attack especially a success.

Finally, the attacks on Domstadtl and Altliebe offer an excellent example of the potential operational effects that could on occasion be achieved by a raid. The Austrians conducted themselves with daring and flexibility. Likewise, on both days, they prevented the Prussians from utilizing their local numerical superiority due to uncertainty concerning the Austrians' strength and whereabouts.[111] They embodied the ancient Chinese military thinker Sun Tzu's observation that 'All warfare is based on deception.'[112] The inability of the Prussian commanders speaks to the notion that the Austrians read and utilized the terrain more adeptly and possessed greater local support from the civilian population. All of the preceding encompassed qualities of successful light troops.

At the same time, it underscores a dearth in Prussian scouting and intelligence gathering. Concerning the implications of the raid, the same informant cited at the outset noted, 'This was a fatal stroke; for had it arrived safe, the place would not have held out above a fortnight longer.'[113] Franz Szabo observes only that the attack forced Frederick to break off the siege of Olmütz and withdrawal.[114] Conversely, Christopher Duffy observes more accurately that, 'the great ambush made Frederick's position in Moravia untenable, and continued throwing him on the defensive for the rest of the war.'[115] Duffy goes on to liken the attack to those carried out by the Viet Minh on French convoys in Indo-China for its sheer scale.[116] For its operational effect, a more compelling comparison might be Washington's attack on the German garrison at Trenton in late December 1776.[117]

---

111 Wilson, 'Ambush', p.19.
112 Sun Tzu, Samuel B. Griffith (trans.), *The Art of War* (Oxford: Oxford University Press, 1966), p.66.
113 Anonymous, *A Complete History of the Present War*, p.264.
114 Szabo, *Seven Years War*, p.150.
115 Duffy, *By Force of Arms*, p.113.
116 Duffy, *By Force of Arms*, p.113.
117 Currently, the standard account of Trenton is David Hackett Fischer, *Washington's Crossing* (New York: Oxford University Press, 2004). Not to be discounted, however is William S. Stryker, *The Battles of Trenton and Princeton* (Trenton, NJ: The Old Barracks Association, 2001, reprint of 1898 orig.)

6

Warfare in North America in the Eighteenth Century

From the moment the first Europeans set foot in the Americas, they were confronted with a new set of military challenges. The indigenous peoples they came into contact with practiced a different approach to warfare, and one deeply rooted not just in the technological level of their society, but their culture as well. A complete examination of the various practices of warfare as they existed in the indigenous inhabitants of the Americas in the sixteenth to eighteenth centuries lies far beyond the scope of the present work. The focus for the present will be on the military practices of the various groups of the Great Lakes region of North America as they existed in the mid-eighteenth century as that encompasses the primary theatre under investigation.[1]

During the sixteenth and seventeenth centuries Europeans were moving in the direction of more organized, state-sponsored warfare involving standing armies that remained together to drill during times of peace. In many ways, this transformation, what some refer to as the Military Revolution, derived in large part from the use of gunpowder weapons on the battlefield. The debate among military historians concerning this topic was particularly intense in the last decade of the twentieth century.[2] One aspect is clear; the new gunpowder weapons required more training for their effective use than the edged and projectile weapons of previous period. At the same time, they

---

1   The standard works on Native American war in the region include: Daniel P. Barr, *Unconquered: The Iroquois League at War in Colonial America* (Wesptport, CT: Praeger, 2006); George Hunt, *The Wars of the Iroquois: A Study in Intertribal Trade Relations* (Madison: University of Wisconsin Press, 1978); David E. James, *Native North American Armor, Shields and Fortifications* (Austin: University of Texas Press, 2004); Wayne E. Lee, 'Peace Chiefs and Blood Revenge: Patterns of Restraint in Native American Warfare, 1500-1800', *Journal of Military History*, 71:3 (2007), pp.701–741; Arthur J. Ray, *Indians in the Fur Trade: Their Role as Trappers, Hunters and Middlemen in the Lands Southwest of Hudson Bay, 1660-1870* (Toronto: University of Toronto Press, 1998).

2   On the Military Revolution, see M. S. Anderson, *War and Society in Europe of the Old Regime 1618-1789* (Montreal: McGill-Queen's University Press, 1998); Jeremy Black, *Warfare in Europe, 1650-1792* (Aldershot: Ashgate, 2005); Howard, *War in European History*, pp.20–53, Geoffrey Parker, *The Military Revolution: Military Innovation and the Rise of the West,1500-1800* (Cambridge: Cambridge University Press, 1988); Frank Tallet, *War and Society in Early-Modern Europe, 1495-1715* (London: Routledge, 1992). This list is not exhaustive.

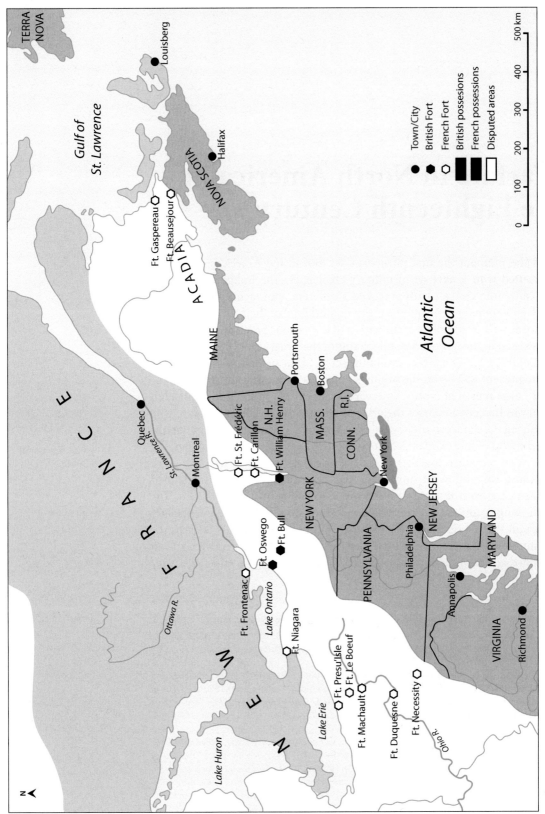

Eastern North America at the time of the Seven Years War.

were woefully inaccurate, and therefore the use of linear tactics became more prevalent. Consequently, battles were fought in the open with large blocks of troops manoeuvring around in an almost choreographed manner. The use of linear tactics and large blocks of infantry manoeuvring around a battlefield continued through much of the eighteenth century.[3]

The terrain of North America, at least that in the areas that will feature in the current examination, did not support linear warfare. Much of the area was heavily wooded, and especially along the east coast there were numerous hills that continued westward becoming mountain ranges. In addition, what roads existed there were often only narrow paths. These made deployment in the formations currently in vogue in Europe impossible. They did, however, support the tactical approaches favoured by the Native Americans.

The main form of warfare for the native groups that would participate in the Seven Years War was known as mourning war.[4] The underlying premise was that the death of a member of the tribe created a spiritual as well as the obvious physical gap in the tribe. 'Because an individual's death diminished the collective power of a lineage, clan, and village, Iroquois families conducted "Requickening" ceremonies in which the deceased's name, and with it the societal role and duties it represented, was transferred to a successor.'[5] Historian Daniel Richter continues, 'Such rites filled vacant positions in lineages and villages both literally and symbolically: they assured survivors that the social function and spiritual potency embodied in the departed's name had not disappeared and that the community would endure.'[6] This death could be from sickness as well as warfare. The only means to assuage the spirit of the departed, and formally conclude the grieving of their family lay in a war party bringing back a captive. Warfare therefore played an important role in the grieving process as prisoners taken while on a raid were often adopted into the family to help strengthen the group in the place of the deceased.[7]

'On a societal level, then, warfare (or, more specifically, the taking of war prisoners) helped the Iroquois to deal with deaths in their ranks.'[8] Likewise, the Iroquois tradition possessed an extended grieving process that for the loss of a family member could last upwards of a year. During this time, they would often show little concern for personal hygiene or social amenities. While those with close ties to the deceased manifested their grief, principles of reciprocity required members of a connected kin group to 'cover' the grief of the bereaved by conducting funeral rituals, providing funeral feasts and bestowing gifts.[9]

---

3   Steven T. Ross, *From Flintlock to Rifle: Infantry Tactics, 1740-1866* (London: Frank Cass, 1979), pp.17–50 provides a solid if dated overview of the warfare during this period.

4   The classic work on mourning war is Daniel K. Richter, *The Ordeal of the Longhouse: The Peoples of the Iroquois League in the Era of European Colonization* (Chapel Hill, NC: University of North Carolina Press, 1992)

5   Richter, *Ordeal of the Longhouse*, p.32.

6   Richter, *Ordeal of the Longhouse*, p.32.

7   Richter, *Ordeal of the Longhouse*, pp.32–33.

8   Richter, *Ordeal of the Longhouse*, p.33.

9   Richter, *Ordeal of the Longhouse*, p.33.

At times, however, all of the extended and in-depth rituals might not assuage the grief of the family. In such cases, the women would then call on the males of the community to go to war to seek prisoners to physically fill the gap created by the death of their loved one.[10] While the initial call for armed conflict might come from the women of the community, the actual organization and implementation of the raid was in the hands of the warriors.

The war party served as the basic tactical unit of conflict among the Native Americans of eastern North America. The size of the party varied contingent on several factors: the target in contemplation, the leader of the war party, and the likely chances of success. The measure of success lay not only in survival, but almost more importantly in the potential for taking enemy scalps, which will be discussed below, and prisoners.

To initiate the campaign, the prospective leader would approach a post in the centre of the village compound and strike their war club into it, thus 'burying the hatchet.' They would then sing their war song and perform their war dance. The song was individual to each warrior and the dance encompassed a performance of the actions that warrior intended to take on the group proposed as the target.

The other assembled warriors listened to the proposal, and one by one joined the initiator at the post, adding their war songs and dances to those of the initiator. Once the war party gathered, they would prepare and then leave on the raid.

Once on campaign, the warriors on travelled only at night, if at all possible. During the day, the majority would sleep while sentinels stood watch. They would go to elaborate lengths to conceal their numbers, walking single file (which came to be known among the colonists as 'Indian-file') often intentionally over rocky soil to leave fewer traces of their passing. The last warrior in the column would then use a branch to carefully efface the party's tracks.[11].

Often, if it was believed that the secrecy of the war party had been lost, the attackers would break off. The focus on concealment and secrecy were part of the larger goal of keeping their casualties down. At times, they might fight to the death in order to allow others, especially women and children to escape, to defend the reputation of their people as brave fighters, or in situations where they had no alternatives.[12] A major goal of their way of war, however, was to prevent any of the above possibilities from manifesting.

If they continued to successfully conceal their movements, the raiders often waited until just before dawn to launch their attack. They did this for several reasons. First, they gambled that the hour would have any sentinels around their target, be it a village or the hunting party of a rival group, dozing. Second, the predawn hours in the region were often characterised by heavy fog. This would further disguise the size and direction of their attack until the last possible moment.[13]

---

10   Richter, *Ordeal of the Longhouse*, p.33.
11   Richter, *Ordeal of the Longhouse*, p.37.
12   McLeod, *Canadian Iroquois in the Seven Years War*, p.35.
13   Richter, *Ordeal of the Longhouse*, p.38.

'Indians from the Six Nations at Newport, Rhode Island, 29 August–1 September 1780', by Jean Baptiste Antoine de Verger. (Anne S.K. Brown Military Collection)

Again, if all went well, the attackers would take their adversary's village by surprise and succeed in taking the scalps of several enemy warriors as well as some prisoners. The significance of scalping lay in the fact that it was believed that this was where the warrior's spirit resided. Thus, if an adversary was deemed worthy after being dispatched in battle, his opponent scalped him, and in the process added their martial prowess to his own. It is worth noting that over time, and due to European involvement in the form of scalp bounties, the taking of scalps denigrated to the point where any victim of an attack could be scalped. Initially, however, the scalps were dried and painted and used to decorate the warrior's lance. As such, they served as a visual record of that warrior's martial prowess.

One preferred tactic of the Native Americans was ambush. This could be prepared in several ways. One was simply to occupy a path that the members of raiding party knew enemies would travel along. More often, one picked warrior would go ahead and act as bait and lure opponents into the prepared attack.[14]

On the conclusion of fighting a sort of division occurred concerning the prisoners. Women and children, who were considered more malleable, possessed a greater likelihood of being adopted into a grieving family.[15] First, however, they had to survive the return journey to the attacker's village. On the way, the captives would have to maintain the pace set by their captors, regardless of age, injury, or physical conditions. Those who failed to keep up were often killed out of hand.

Males taken as prisoners were subjected to the same gruelling march back to the village. For the men, the journey might only be the beginning of their torments. On entering the village, they were often made to run the gauntlet. Running the gauntlet encompassed walking between two rows of villagers armed with sticks who subjected the male prisoners to heavy blows. If they should stumble and fall, they could count on being the recipient of a savage beating. Those who survived this ordeal were then tied to separate posts in the village. At that point, the women of the mourning families determined whether to accept them as members of their family or not.[16]

For women and children, again, the choice was often more forthcoming. They would be taken into the dwelling of their adoptive family where they would be introduced and given what was likely the first full meal they received since their capture. The same outcome befell men who were accepted into the tribe.

Men rejected as substitutes in the aggrieved families could expect to be slowly tortured to death at the stake. First, a fire would be kindled, and smouldering splinters driven under their fingernails. Then, the women would take turns cutting off strips of their flesh and scorching the wounds with hot embers. All these agonies the male was supposed to endure in stoic silence. Better yet, if the captured warrior taunted their captives as they inflicted the various torments on the doomed prisoner, he might be dispatched sooner for

---

14   Richter, *Ordeal of the Longhouse*, p.38.
15   Richter, *Ordeal of the Longhouse*, p.35.
16   Richter, *Ordeal of the Longhouse*, p.35.

displaying his bravado. In this way, the captive warrior could regain some of the honour they had lost in being taken alive rather than dying in combat.[17]

From their earliest contacts with Europeans, the above approach to war making on the part of the Native Americans began to change. The natives use of stealth and cover came to be referred to by the English as the 'skulking way of war.'[18] At the same time, Europeans quickly learned that they had to develop effective countermeasures to native practices or pay the price. The two main groups in the theatre under investigation, the English and French, developed different responses to the fighting practices of the Native Americans they encountered. For the settlers in England's North American colonies, countering native tactics meant two things: forts and rangers.

Forts developed as a means of creating local defensive centres. As Glenn F. Williams points out in his masterful study of Lord Dunmore's War, there were two types of forts. There were those which were designed as military outposts which often featured a garrison of some kind. Secondly, there were local homes which had been constructed with double-thick walls and were capable of providing some shelter to local inhabitants in a crisis. Names gave the hint to which type of fort was being utilized. For example, a military outpost might be named Fort Smith, whereas a reinforced home might be christened Smith's Fort.[19]

While the forts served as strong points, they could not effectively defend the frontier from native incursions. At best, they created a porous border. To try and plug some of the gaps, ranger units were developed. These were forces that attempted to copy indigenous tactical approaches and patrol or range between the forts. They were truly elite soldiers in the sense that they practiced a different mode of warfare from their brethren in the regular ranks. Like their native foes, they tended to travel at night and attack in the early morning in order to make the most use of deception and the element of surprise. They avoided contact with larger formations as well, tending to focus on hitting small detachments.

Unlike the regulars, the rangers continued to conduct active operations in winter, using skates on frozen waterways to travel quickly and conceal their movements.[20] The tracks left by skates on ice would be harder to detect than those left by men marching, even on snowshoes, overland. When they did travel on land in winter, the rangers again, copied the Native Americans and used snowshoes, and covered their tracks to efface any signs of their passage. On at least one occasion, they were known to dig pits in the snow three feet deep and set fires to dry their muskets. The pits were to ensure that any hostile scouts did not see the light of their fires.[21] Otherwise, they avoided lighting any fires at all either for cooking or heating.

17   Richter, *Ordeal of the Longhouse*, p.36.

18   Patrick Malone, *The Skulking Way of War Technology and Tactics among the New England Indians* (New York: Madison Books, 1991), pp.23–24.

19   Glenn F. Williams, *Dunmore's War: The Last Conflict of America's Colonial Era* (Yardley PA: Westholme Press, 2018), pp.48–50.

20   James H. Silcox, 'Rogers and Bouquet: The Origins of the American Light Infantry', *Military Review*, 65:12 (December 1985), p.70.

21   Bernd Horn, 'Hollow of Death: Rogers' Rangers Desperate Fight for Survival', *Canadian Military History*, 14:4 (2005), p.6

John Gorham is sometimes credited with raising the first true ranger unit in Massachusetts during King George's War (1744–1748). However, the ranger concept predated his activities for some time. As John Grenier has shown, the first ranger company was raised by Benjamin Church in 1676, during King Philip's War (1675).[22] The unit consisted of 60 English colonists and 140 friendly Native Americans.[23] The proportions within the unit are telling, as 'Americans in fact, never could have become rangers without the tutelage of Indian allies.'[24] The reason for the early reliance on native allies lay in the simple fact that from the first, Church's idea was to develop a force which could act offensively against the Native Americans by fighting them on their own terms and using their own tactics. Thus, Church 'endeavored to learn to fight like Indians from Indians.'[25] Church applied the same methods in King William's War (1688–1697), the North American name for the Nine Years' War.[26] Numerous colonists served under Church in this conflict. Consequently, Church's company and the other ranger companies raised in New England served as 'nurseries for successive generations of New England rangers.'[27]

The use of ranger companies in successive conflicts in colonial New England meant that certain families served in them repeatedly. To John Grenier this suggests that, 'ranging was a way of life for successive generations of New Englanders, among whom a "corporate knowledge" of ranger warfare was passed down from generation to generation.'[28] There thus grew up certain families who possessed a reputation for raising and leading ranger units successfully. Likewise, the knowledge and experience they accrued over time was passed on informally, without codification, becoming, in a sense, akin to the trade secrets guarded so zealously by the craft guilds in Europe. It resembled the informal practices of the Native Americans as well in that the decision to join a ranger company was often based on the success of the leader, much like the decision to join a war party. The employment of rangers, as well as the proclivity of certain families to serve in ranger units continued well into the eighteenth century. By the middle of the 1740s, therefore, most New Englanders who served in ranger companies were led by officers who could trace a lineage back to Benjamin Church.[29]

The rangers stood as something of a local solution to the defensive needs of the New England colonies, however, it would be in the French and Indian War, the North American portion of the Seven Years War, that British officers would gain significant exposure to the rangers' techniques. Probably the best-known ranger was Robert Rogers who served extensively during the French and Indian War and interacted with and inspired several British

---

22   Eric B. Schultz and Michael J. Tougias, *King Philip's War: The History and Legacy of America's Forgotten Conflict* (New York: W.W. Norton and Company, 1999) offers a solid history of this conflict.
23   Grenier, *First Way of War*, pp.32–33.
24   Grenier, *First Way of War*, p.33.
25   Grenier, *First Way of War*, p.37.
26   On this conflict, see Lynn, *Wars of Louis XIV*, pp.191–265.
27   Grenier, *First Way of War*, p.37.
28   Grenier, *First Way of War*, pp.37–38.
29   Grenier, *First Way of War*, p.37.

commanders. Born in Methuen, Massachusetts to Scots-Irish parents, at age eight, he and his family moved to the Great Meadow area of the New Hampshire frontier.[30] In 1746, during King George's War (War of the Austrian Succession), Rogers served as a private in Captain Daniel Ladd's Scouting Company of the New Hampshire militia. The following year Rogers served in one Ebeneezer Eastman's Scouting Company. Both of these tours were spent guarding the New Hampshire frontier. As noted above, service in a ranger company in one conflict often allowed young men to establish their credentials for leading such units in the next conflict. Rogers was no exception to this pattern. In 1756, he began to raise his own unit of rangers for the British crown. His company may have included several of Rogers' own brothers. Once completed, Rogers' Rangers served mainly in the Lake George and Lake Champlain area in New York. While many British regular officers took a condescending view of Rogers and his men, their record of success as compared with the failures of the regulars in the early years of the conflict spoke volumes all its own.

One of Rogers' major contributions came in the form of his 'Rules of Ranging'. Rogers' rulers were the first attempt to codify tactics which had been passed down informally to that point and will receive attention in the conclusion.

These factors combined to give the British colonists some capacity to respond to native threats, however, rangers never developed into forces as tactically proficient as their native foes, and so an additional factor was the use of native allies. While the rangers did provide the English colonists with some offensive capability, they never did wholly offset the tactical advantages displayed by their native foes. It was more the after effects of warfare, and especially of disease, which served to disperse their enemies.

The French, however, took a fairly different tack. New France never achieved anything remotely like the population levels of the British colonies. Likewise, the goal of their colonizing efforts was not so much about creating permanent settler colonies as trade, specifically in furs. The most efficient manner in which to conduct the fur trade was to work in cooperation with the Native Americans as much as possible. This cooperation included backing native allies against their foes. From early on, local colonists, the habitants, became fairly adept at copying native tactics and often fought alongside native allies.[31]

Consequently, a French expedition targeting a British outpost included local troops (known as Canadian militia), Troupes de la Marine and Native Americans. The Troupes de la Marine were regular soldiers who were assigned to garrison posts in New France. Their name derived from the fact that in France their administration fell under the auspices of the bureau de la Marine.[32] Both Troupes de la Marine and Canadian militia could be very effective fighting forces.

---

30   Unless otherwise noted, biographical information on Rogers is derived from John F. Ross, *War on the Run: The Epic Story of Robert Rogers and the Conquest of America's First Frontier* (New York: Random House, Inc., 2009).

31   Bernd Horn, 'La Petite Guerre: A Strategy of Survival', in Bernd Horn (ed.), *The Canadian Way of War* (Toronto, Ontario: Dundurn Press, 2006), pp.25–26.

32   Andrew Gallup, *La Marine: The French Colonial Soldier in Canada 1745-1761* (Bowie, MD: Heritage Books, 1992), pp.10–11.

Robert Rogers, 1775. (Anne S.K. Brown Military Collection)

'Canada: Bataille de Carillon 1758. Troupes de la Marine. Milices Canadiennes', by Henry Boisselier (1960). (Anne S.K. Brown Military Collection)

The French did construct forts at strategic locations across their colony, however, the purpose was different. In New France, forts served as concentration areas for expeditions to form up and draw supplies before moving off against their intended target. They were not meant as defensive points so much as offensive springboards.[33]

These were, in broad strokes, the two forms taken by the Europeans in responding to Native American fighting techniques. As can be seen, they developed as a result of the different forms of colonization being practiced by the two powers in North America.

---

33   Horn, 'La Petite Guerre', p.26.

From the Native American perspective, they practiced what one historian has dubbed parallel war, meaning that while Native Americans fought alongside their French allies, they did so for their own goals. Specifically, while the French fought to drive the British out of their territory, the Iroquois continued to fight to take scalps and prisoners which both added to their prestige as warriors and that they could possibly trade to the French allies for various commodities.[34]

The Native American method of warfare effected the tactics of the European colonists as well. It is likely that these exerted the most profound effect on the French settlements. Here, small populations and limited resources contributed to the development of a hybrid of military practices between European and Native American models. One author has called these practices petite guerre, which in the current context stands as something of a misnomer.[35] Consequently, the following pages will use the term North American Petite Guerre to differentiate these practices from those employed in Europe discussed above. As the term is sometimes defined,

> Petite Guerre is the designated term for the method of asymmetrical warfare inspired by the irregular warfare of North American Aboriginal peoples. The method has often been labeled as barbaric and as contrary to the ethics and morality of its time.[36]

Less confusing is the point that necessity drove the Canadians to conduct a distinct form of warfare. 'Their way of war also needed to be limited and cost-effective—both fiscally and in regards to resources and personnel— particularly in casualties.'[37] Horn further notes how the Canadians adopted 'a tactical outlook that was dependent on the clever use of ground and cover, the element of surprise, sudden ambushes, swift raids, and engagement in combat only when the likelihood of success was high and the possibility of casualties was low.'[38]

This approach to warfighting, which encompassed essentially a hybrid of Native American and European tactical approaches, was prevalent in Canada during the seventeenth and eighteenth centuries. These same historians note its marginalization during the Seven Years War.[39] While petite guerre existed in Europe at the same time, in New France it possessed a strategic dimension not often prevalent in Europe. North American Petite Guerre as used in New France constituted a means by which the underpopulated colony could survive.[40]

In practice, the North American Petite Guerre was a war of raids that went deep into the British colonies and left devastation in their wake. For

---

34   Peter D. McLeod, *The Canadian Iroquois and the Seven Years War* (Toronto: Dundurn, 2012), p.19.

35   Horn, 'Petite Guerre', pp.21–22.

36   Lacroix-Leclair and Ouellet, '*Petite Guerre*', p.49.

37   Horn, 'Petite Guerre', p.23.

38   Horn, 'Petite Guerre', p.25.

39   Lacroix-Leclair and Ouellet, '*Petite Guerre*', p.49.

40   Lacroix-Leclair and Ouellet, '*Petite Guerre*', p.50.

the French colonies, this was the point, to use terror to overawe the English colonies and thereby prevent them from moving north and westward, and thus threatening the existence of New France.[41]

Clearly, this bore a marked resemblance to the Native American tactics described above. By the same token, there existed some prominent differences. Prisoners were of less value as potential additions to the community. Further, scalps did not possess the same spiritual and cultural value they did for Natives. In addition as Horn notes, 'Petite guerre placed great reliance on cunning, furtiveness, the use of cover and especially marksmanship.'[42]

At the same time, North American Petite Guerre received something of an official sanction, as it was supported by the Royal Governors of the New France as well as both Louis XIII and Louis XIV. All seemed to realize that the method of warfare offered the best chance for the survival of the colony. It was incredibly effective, when it is considered, 'that asymmetrical method was effective against the enemy: it took almost 70 years for the British to triumph over their French-Canadian neighbors...'[43] The effectiveness of North American Petite Guerre is made all the more impressive when it is considered that it allowed French-Canadian colonists to hold out effectively against British encroachments although the latter outnumbered the former by a margin of 20 to 1 beginning in 1682.[44]

Finally, 'It was a strategy that was carried out year-round and it was cost effective and fruitful. It clearly represented an economy of effort. Small parties of Canadians and Indians, led by French—and in some cases Canadian—officers could in this manner make an effective contribution to the war effort.'[45]

Support for the method was easily obtained as New France constituted a military outpost of sorts whose main purpose was to facilitate the fur trade. Other factors, including the climate, effected the choice for North American Petite Guerre. Consider that the St Lawrence waterway, the chief artery of trade and communication into the interior of North America was closed due to ice for six months out of the year. This meant that no reinforcement, food or even communications could make their way to Quebec from France. Likewise, on the other side of the Atlantic, there existed a certain lack of interest among the French authorities. France was, after all, a continental power in Europe. Consequently, valuable and limited resources had to be focused there as opposed to the periphery. The beliefs of the French colonists supported the adoption and adaptation of various Native tactics to the defence of the colony for two reasons: First, it was the only method which offered a real chance of success. Second, and possibly more important than the first, North American Petite Guerre offered a means by which the colonists could conduct an offensive-defence. By using the forts they constructed as staging

---

41   Lacroix-Leclair and Ouellet, '*Petite Guerre*', p.50.
42   Horn, 'Petite Guerre', p.29.
43   Lacroix-Leclair and Ouellet, '*Petite Guerre*', p.50.
44   Lacroix-Leclair and Ouellet, '*Petite Guerre*', p.50.
45   Bernd Horn, 'Terror on the Frontier: The Role of the Indians in the Struggle for North America, 1754-1760', in Bernd Horn (ed.), *The Canadian Military Experience: Perspectives on the Canadian Military Experience* (St Catherines: Varnwell Publishing, 2002), p.59.

areas, they could launch raids deep into the British colonies, thereby keeping them off balance and preventing the superior numbers of colonists, backed by British regulars from marching northwards into their homeland. All of these factors contributed to make the North American Petite Guerre the most effective and the only real strategy with a chance of success for the French colonists in North America.[46]

Consequently, when what came to be referred to as the incident at Jumonville's Glen or the Jumonville Affair occurred on 28 May 1754, both sides employed irregular tactics to varying degrees. It was here that a unit of Virginia provincials under the command of Lieutenant Colonel George Washington surrounded and captured a French patrol commanded by *Enseigne en second* Jospeh Coulon de Jumonville after an initial skirmish. Washington then presented the Frenchman with a letter from the royal governor of Virginia, Robert Dinwiddie ordering the French out of the region. Passing the communique formed the crux of Washington's mission. His objective accomplished, Washington prepared to release the French and return to Virginia.

At this point, a native guide serving with the Virginians, the Seneca Half-King Tanaghrisson attacked and killed Jumonville who had already been wounded in the initial encounter.[47] Washington now hastily reformed the Virginia provincials and sought to exit the area as quickly as possible. While the Virginia governor might claim the lands he was marching through, Washington stood under no illusions to the fact that he was in fact operating deep in French-controlled territory.

Responding to the news of the incident, the French at Fort Duquesne (modern Pittsburgh, Pennsylvania) dispatched a force numbering some 600 and composed of French troops and Canadian militia on 28 June. The French were led by *Capitaine* Louis Coulon de Villiers, de Jumonville's brother. They were joined by a number of Native Americans who agreed to take part in the pursuit. The force caught up with Washington's retreating Virginians at a place known as the Great Meadows on 3 July 1754. The Virginians hurriedly erected a field fortification, really little more than a slit-trench, which they dubbed Fort Necessity. In doing so, they conceded the surrounding high ground to the French and their native allies. The latter poured fire into the works, inflicting heavy casualties on the defenders. In the evening, seeing little alternative, Washington asked for terms.[48]

The two incidents described above presented the leadership in London and Paris with a clear casus belli, should they decide to accept it. The diplomatic efforts aimed at avoiding the conflict on both sides, as well as the views of the ministers and their monarchs fall beyond the scope of the present work. Suffice it to say that while neither side perceived itself as prepared for a

---

46   Lacroix-Leclair and Ouellet, '*Petite Guerre*', p.50.
47   The preceding account of the actions at Jumonville's Glen is derived from Fred Anderson, *Crucible of War: The Seven Years War and the Fate of Empire in North America, 1754-1766* (New York: Alfred A. Knopf, 2000), pp.53–58. See also David L. Preston, *Braddock's Defeat: The Battle of the Monongahela and the Road to Revolution* (Oxford: Oxford University Press, 2015), pp.26–27.
48   Anderson, *Crucible of War*, pp.59–61. See also, Preston, *Braddock's Defeat*, pp.28–29.

return of hostilities, both viewed the provocations of the other as too serious to let pass. The House of Hanover and the House of Bourbon drifted towards war once again.

At the outset of the French and Indian War in 1754, the French perceived the Native Americans as a key factor in how they would prosecute the conflict. Native troops would help to level out the numerical disparity between the French and their British foes. Likewise, the governor of New France, Pierre de Rigaud, marquis de Vaudreuil, was a proponent of the Native American way of warfare. He grasped that in the Petite Guerre lay New France's best means of preservation. With a population that was too small to stand against the British in open battle, and an uncertainty of support from the home country, he would have to wage a protracted war of attrition. His approach would be one of active defence, wherein the forces of New France, while fighting a strategically defensive war, would launch various offensive raids in order to keep the British and their colonists off balance.

When the British ministry in London decided to support the Virginia colony in their war against the French, they dispatched two regiments from the Irish establishment, the 44th and 48th under the command of Major General Edward Braddock. Historians have often criticized Braddock's lack of combat command experience, and his unfamiliarity with the colonies. David Preston offers a much-needed corrective when he notes that 'Unlike modern conceptions that equate military effectiveness with combat experience, in the eighteenth century experience was demonstrated by competent and lengthy service.'[49] These qualities, long and competent service, stood as the metric by which Braddock was selected by George II for the American command. The patronage of the Duke of Cumberland certainly aided as well.[50] The problem, then, was not so much with the man as with the military institution which placed him in the wrong place in charge of the wrong expedition.

Much has been made of Braddock's seeming low opinion of the colonists by scholars over the centuries, as well as the general's perceived arrogance as well.[51] The most recent scholarship to examine the commander and his ill-fated campaign to the Monongahela presents a much more balanced portrait.[52] They argue that to some extent Braddock did attempt to work with colonial leaders, however, he never fully grasped the nuances of colonial politics.

Whatever historians have determined concerning the man, and his plan, which formed one prong of a four-pronged British offensive, was to march on Fort Duquesne. The problem was that there was no direct route from Fort Cumberland in Maryland to the French outpost. Braddock determined to build one, and his force, bulked up to some 2,200 through the recruiting of provincial forces, marched out on 29 May. As can be imagined, the movement of supplies, including heavy artillery, through the wilderness, which included

---

49 Preston, *Braddock's Defeat*, p.52.
50 Preston, *Braddock's Defeat*, pp.52–53.
51 This trend goes at least as far back as Francis Parkman, *Montcalm and Wolfe. France and England in North America* (Boston: Little Brown and Company, 1884).
52 Preston, *Braddock's Defeat*, pp.53–54.

a section of the Appalachian Mountains, while constructing a road, slowed the advance to a crawl.

Responding to the situation, Braddock created a 1,300-man flying camp to advance ahead of the main column and make its way forward. Lieutenant Colonel Thomas Gage commanded the advanced force. Just as the advanced force completed the crossing the Monongahela River within 10 miles (16 kilometres) of Fort Duquesne, on 9 July they came into contact with a composite force of some 800 French and their Native American allies under the command of *Capitaine* Daniel Liénard de Beaujeu.[53] The French and their native allies had arrayed themselves in a half-moon formation and unleashed the first volley. Ironically, de Beaujeu fell in that initial volley due to friendly fire. A *Capitaine* Dumas rallied the men and continued the attack. The initial onslaught was enough to bring confusion among the British advance, who began falling back on the flying column. Panic and confusion spread through the British and provincial forces as retreating advanced parties ran into men trying to form up and receive the attack. Soon all order collapsed. In the end, some 457 British and provincial troops, including Braddock, were killed, with another 450 or more wounded. On the French side, they lost on 39 killed and 57 wounded.[54] In many ways, the Battle of the Monongahela stands as an example of the Small War on the scale that sometimes occurred in the western European theatre of the conflict as well. It was a well-positioned and generally well conducted ambush of the advanced guard. Likewise, it fit very well within the predominating French-Canadian conceptions of North American Petite Guerre. They had taken the fight to the enemy rather than wait for the enemy to invade their territory. Likewise, the scale of the defeat sowed terror along the frontier of the British colonies, and drove down the reputation of the British regulars – all significant accomplishments for such a small outlay of men and materials.

The rout of the British and provincial troops at the Battle of the Monongahela is often and rightly pointed to as providing the impetus for the British Army to develop their own light infantry formations. This assessment is borne out by the fact that one of the first British officers to develop a light formation for the British army, Thomas Gage, commanded the advanced guard that marched into the ambush. Other factors were at work as well. These will be discussed below. First, however, another example of the Small War as well as the Petite Guerre as it was conducted in the French and Indian War will serve to underline the talents of the French and their native allies in this approach to war making.

---

53   Specifically, there were 108 Troupe de la Marine, 146 Canadian militia, and roughly 600 Native Americans

54   The preceding account of the battle of Monongahela or Braddock's defeat as it is sometimes termed is based on Preston, *Braddock's Defeat*, pp.217–225, and Anderson, *The Crucible of War*, pp.94–107.

7

The Fort Bull Raid

The men broke cover into a clearing along a snow-covered treeline. They were hungry, tired, and cold. Numb with the kind of exposure that penetrates muscles to the bone, making both ache with fatigue and exertion.

Still, they had reached their objective. Soon, the winter silence of the woods was broken by the sounds of sleds sliding across the snow. It was a train of supplies making its way from Fort Williams to Fort Bull.

Rapidly, shots erupted from the silence and drivers fell from their sleds, wounded or killed. One driver quickly reigned in his sled and turned, heading rapidly back the way he had come. This was a moment of decision. Cover had already been lost when the raiders attacked the sled train. Now Fort Williams would certainly be alerted to their presence by the escaped driver. Should the column, composed of a mixture of French Troupes de la Marine, Canadian militia and Native American allies push on and attack the fort? Or should they grab what supplies they could carry, scalp the dead and dying and make their back the way they had come?

After a brief consultation with the Natives, the French commander determined to push on to the post. A few of the native troops joined the detachment. The remainder waited in ambush should any reinforcements make their way down the path from Oswego to Fort Bull…

The above episode began the Fort Bull Raid of 1756. As with the Gundersdorf and Domstadtl attacks, the Fort Bull Raid constituted a prime example of a tactical action with strategic outcomes. As will be seen below, while the numbers engaged were fairly small even for North America, and infinitesimal in the context of European warfare, the results of the attack put a major roadblock in the British plan of campaign in North America for 1756.

To place the raid in strategic context, Fort Oswego was the centre of British power in the area, nonetheless, it sat at the end of a very long logistics line that stretched back to Albany. The chief means for the transport of supplies to the fort involved navigating the Mohawk River through Wood Creek and the various subsidiary waterways. These served to get supplies through from Schenectady. In all, the supply line was over 90 miles long and terminated near present-day Rome, New York. From there, supplies had to be carried overland via the portage known as the Great Carrying Place, or the Oneida Carry, to Wood Creek. For the final leg of the journey, supplies were then

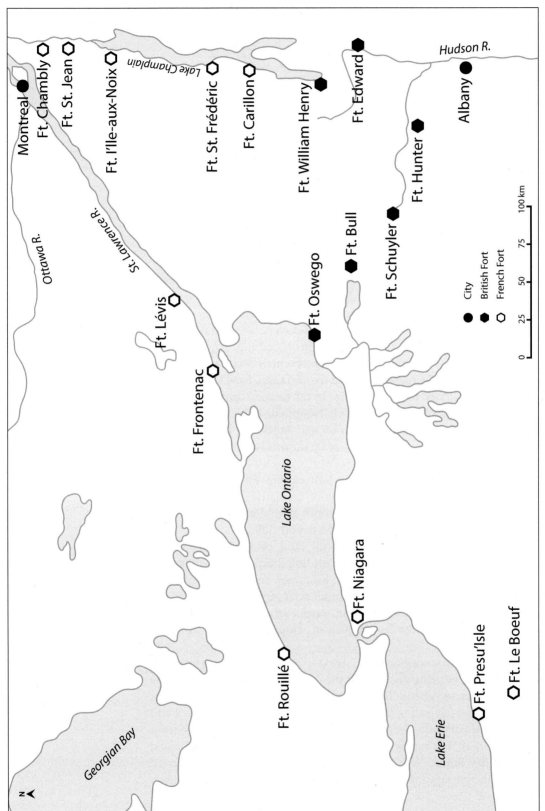

The region around Fort Bull.

moved again by water to the fort. Looking over the length of this logistics line, the weakest link was the Great Carrying Place. It served as the key to the line as well. To protect the portage, the British constructed two forts, Fort Williams on the eastern end and Fort Bull on the western end, nearest to Oswego. The two forts were sited at the halfway point on the route to Oswego. They served as warehouses for supplies, especially during the winter when weather conditions prevented them being sent forward to their final destination. Likewise, they guarded both ends of the Great Carrying Place. If either of the two were destroyed, Oswego would be cut off from resupply and reinforcements.

Native American scouts informed Pierre de Rigaud, marquis de Vaudreuil, the royal governor of New France, on the status of the forts and their garrisons. Significantly, they provided him with details of the condition of the garrison of Fort Bull. The post was held by the remnants of the 50th and 51st Regiments of Foot. The forts were rumoured to contain some cannon as well. Still, Vaudreuil saw the opportunity to launch a strike that would derail any British thrust into New France in the following campaign season. Likewise, it might make the post at Oswego untenable. Vaudreuil favoured a Petite Guerre approach to carrying out the strike as opposed to a formal military investment and siege for the simple fact that the former was more in keeping with the capacity of the local forces to make war. Destroying the post and the supplies stockpiled therein would actually stand as the more straightforward part of the operation as these were not heavily guarded. Vaudreuil dispatched two separate Native American scouting parties to determine the strength and status of the post.[1] One of these patrols included an Oswegatchie scout named Ou8atory who informed Vaudreuil that the eastern warehouse was guarded by a force of 100 men while the western one was protected by only 40. Lastly, according to Ou8atory's report, instead of living in the palisaded forts the men were camped in tents and bark huts outside the fort's stockaded walls.[2]

Other factors may have influenced Vaudreuil's decision to launch a winter expedition as well. First, due to the conditions prevalent at that season, the post would likely be low on supplies as it was at the end of the long logistics train stretching back to Albany. Second, and building on the first, the British defenders were unlikely to expect an attack during such an inclement time of the year. In this regard the French governor was correct, as one historian of the raid noted, 'The British continued to think that they were safe in the wintertime and continually failed to learn the lessons of raids during all seasons of the previous wars.'[3]

The more difficult aspect of the raid would be to get the men in position. Considering the distance the attackers would have to travel from the assembly

---

1   Ian K. Steele *Warpaths: Invasions of North America* (New York: Oxford University Press, 1995), p.199.

2   McLeod, *The Canadian Iroquois and the Seven Years War*, p.23. 8 is a ligature of the Greek letters o and υ.

3   Adam Bancroft, 'Savages in a Civilized War: The Native Americans as French Allies in the Seven Years War, 1754-1763', MA Thesis (U.S. Army Command and General Staff College, Fort Leavenworth, KS, 2013), p.87.

point at Montreal and the random thaws and freezes that characterised the month of March in the area through which they would march, this constituted no small effort. The weather would make river crossings even more hazardous than usual. Consequently, Native American assistance would be essential as the area through which the raiders passed served as a hunting ground and was therefore well known to them.[4] Add to these risks the fact that the expedition would be crossing into territory controlled by the Six Nations. If a skirmish should occur between the expedition and a group of Iroquois on the New York side, it could drive the latter firmly into the British camp and away from their declared neutrality. In Vaudreuil's estimation, however, the threat to New France posed by the British supply bases stood as so profound that he was willing to risk such a conflict in order to forestall British designs for the following campaign season. As he stated, 'the situation became urgent and I could not defer without the risk of being forestalled by the enemy at Niagara and at Frontenac.'[5]

To conduct the mission, Vaudreuil called on Gaspard Joseph Chaussegros de Léry. Léry was the son of an army engineer Joseph Gaspard Chaussegros de Léry. The younger Léry received an education in Quebec from the Jesuits prior to joining the Troupes de la Marine in 1739. He spent much of his career up to this time ranging between Montreal and Detroit. He had previously visited Oswego as well as serving in New England frontier raids during King George's War or the War of the Austrian Succession (1740–1748). He had constructed or modified a number of the French forts in the region as a part of his service. Finally, Léry also accompanied Pierre-Joseph de Céloron de Blainville on his famed expedition and as a result had become acquainted with a number of the Native American tribes in the area as well. The purpose of Céloron's expedition was to restore the Native Americans, in particular the Miami, in the Ohio country, to their trading partnership with the French, and to map out the extent of the French claims in the region.[6] The mission is sometimes referred to as the 'lead plate expedition' because as Céloron progressed through the Ohio country he placed lead plates in the ground to mark the boundaries of New France.

Léry commanded a raiding force composed of 360 men including some 90 Canadian Iroquois, 166 Canadian militia, 84 Troupes de la Marine and 20 Huron.[7] When Léry met with Vaudreuil to discuss the plan, the two Frenchmen included the Native Americans in their planning process through a number of conferences, demonstrating a grasp of the concept of parallel war. The participants in these meetings included delegations of Kahnawakes, Kanesetakes and Oswegatchies. While many of the native delegates remained dubious about undertaking the expedition in winter, they provided information that was vital in the planning phase. It is worth observing that

---

4   McLeod, *Canadian Iroquois in the Seven Years War*, p.24.
5   Vaudreuil quoted in McLeod, *Canadian Iroquois in the Seven Years War*, p.24.
6   Anderson, *Crucible of War*, pp.25–29.
7   Bancroft, 'Savages', p.87. Starkey gives the figure of 362, which seems more accurate. See Armstrong Starkey, *European and Native American Warfare 1675-1815* (Norman: University of Oklahoma Press, 1998), p.1.

the presence of the Canadian Iroquois was vital to the mission's success, so much so that Léry's orders contained a clause ordering him to return to New France if the Native contingent abandoned the enterprise.[8]

The planning and assembly of the force complete, the expedition left Montreal on 29 February and moved out westward along the St Lawrence. Their first stop was at Oswegatchie. Here, a pattern emerged that would be repeated at each successive native village the expedition arrived at. A council was held during which interested warriors were invited to join the expedition. During these conferences, it was essential to gain the support of one of the main war chiefs of the community so that other warriors would be swayed to join in the operation.[9] It was only following considerable persuasion that the various chiefs agreed to join the expedition. For instance, Missakin, an Ojibwa chief, met with Léry beginning on the evening of 23/24 February and when the plan was explained to him showed no enthusiasm for it. The two talked through the night and only on the following morning did he agree to join the enterprise with his band. In the end, Léry expected some 18 Kahnawakes, 33 Kanestakes, 67 Algonquins and 11 Nipissings to join his force of regulars and Canadian militia. An additional undetermined group of Akwesasnes, three Abenakis and 66 Oswegatchies later joined in the expedition as well.[10]

While the raiding party was taking shape, other native troops were raiding along the Anglo-American frontier. Their activities provided the natives with the opportunity to gain additional information concerning the condition and strength of the British forts as well as their garrisons, which they passed along to their French allies. For instance, on 9 March, just as Léry's force was preparing to depart on their trek, a raiding party of Akwesasne returned from the Oswego area with nine prisoners. These prisoners proved invaluable to the expedition for upon interrogation, they revealed to Léry's interpreter that instead of being stored in unfortified warehouses the munitions at the portage were in fact defended by the two forts.[11] Further, they explained that the garrison was not housed in tents but in barracks inside the forts. The information gleaned from the prisoners clearly complicated the situation for Léry.

The commander initially kept this information to himself out of fear that informing his native troops would cause them to back out of the expedition. In this regard, Léry acted in much the same fashion as Pandour Trenck in incident described above.[12] The force departed the French fort at La Presentation for the Great Carrying Place on 12 March.[13] Léry's deception did not last long. Two days into the march, an Oswegatchie traveller informed the Native Americans that the storehouses at the portage were now fortified, and that the British were on the alert.[14] On learning of the conditions at the Great Carrying Place, the chiefs called a halt to the march declaring that to

8   McLeod, *Canadian Iroquois*, p.25.
9   McLeod, *Canadian Iroquois*, p.25.
10   McLeod, *Canadian Iroquois*, p.25.
11   McLeod, *Canadian Iroquois*, pp.25–26.
12   See pages 20–21 of this work.
13   Bancroft, 'Savages', p.87.
14   MacLeod, *Canadian Iroquois in the Seven Years War*, p.26.

proceed further would be futile and dangerous. Their concern brought them into direct confrontation with their French allies.[15]

Here again, different perspectives on warfare emerged. For the French, if the target was destroyed, even should they sustain heavy casualties in the process, the mission still counted as a victory. This represented a fundamental difference in the approaches to war-making of the two groups. For the natives in his force, the prestige of a successful attack was not important when achieved with heavy casualties since for them the purpose of the raid was to take booty, prisoners, and scalps, and it would be successful only if these goals were accomplished with the least casualties. Consequently, the native warriors applied many of the skills they derived from the hunt to their warfighting techniques. These techniques included such attributes as stealth, cleverness, and deception. Likewise, in their culture, if an engagement appeared as if it were going against them or if they began to sustain heavy casualties, withdrawal was the permissible, even advisable, response. It was not considered cowardly, rather a practical solution to the situation.[16] At the same time, it should be kept in mind, that while officers such as Léry might be willing to sustain significant casualties in achieving their objective, the men under their command might hold different views on the matter. The revelations of the Akwesasne brought the differing perspectives of the two groups to loggerheads.

These contrasting approaches to warfare came to the fore once the native warriors learned of the fortifications at the Great Carrying Place. The two groups occupied the remainder of the day in discussions as to the appropriate course of action moving forward. In these discussions, Léry reminded his Troupes de la Marine and the Canadian militia under his command that he expected them to obey his orders. By way of contrast, the Canadian Iroquois leaders, Missakin and Collière, an Oswegatchie chief, first sought to gain the consensus of the warriors in their bands and then communicated that decision to the French. [17] As one historian of the raid noted, 'They spoke in council not as commanders, but as advocates, who could be relied upon to make sure that the views of their compatriots were heard, and their sensibilities respected.'[18]

As a result of these consultations, the Canadian Iroquois leaders reported to Léry that it was the consensus of their followers that the original plan was no longer viable. Instead, they presented an alternative more in keeping with their approach to combat. The chiefs proposed that the force should raid the settlements along the Mohawk Valley as opposed to attacking the British forts. As they noted, they had been invited to attack soldiers living in bark huts, not attack a fortification, an action that guaranteed heavy casualties.[19]

---

15   MacLeod, *Canadian Iroquois in the Seven Years War*, p.27.
16   MacLeod, *Canadian Iroquois in the Seven Years War*, p.27. See also Williams, *Dunmore's War*, pp.277–278.
17   MacLeod, *Canadian Iroquois in the Seven Years War*, p.27.
18   MacLeod, *Canadian Iroquois in the Seven Years War*, p.27.
19   MacLeod, *Canadian Iroquois in the Seven Years War*, p.27.

Their declaration likely came as no surprise to Léry as he possessed significant experience operating in tandem with native warriors. As a result, the Frenchman would have been well aware of their aversion to attacking fortified places. While such concerns received fair hearings from French officers in the past, on this occasion, Léry showed himself to be much less accommodating. There were reasons for his determination to attack the post.

On the commander's side, there was the awareness that if the British maintained their supply depots at the current location, they could serve as springboards for a major campaign into New France, one which the French colonists, numerically inferior to begin with, would have little chance of successfully repelling.[20]

In the short term, Léry chose to delay the decision by telling his native auxiliaries that they could determine whether there were fortifications for themselves on their arrival. His ploy worked, as the Native American contingent accepted this delay of the final decision. Still, they reserved the right to reopen the issue.[21]

Not only did the members of the expedition often disagree on whether the plan should be carried out and how. The expedition encountered all the vicissitudes of March weather on their trek as well. These ranged from snowstorms and freezing rains to sub-freezing temperatures.[22] Their exertions on the march were exacerbated by the fact that the men carried only enough supplies for a one-way journey, the expectation being that they could replenish their packs from the plunder taken in the raid. Consequently, if the raid failed, it amounted to a virtual death sentence for the men in Léry's command. One final factor increased the men's misery – no fires were allowed as these could give away the location of the raiders' camps to British spies.[23]

The conditions the men encountered on the march exacted their own toll. Seventeen Frenchmen were sent back to La Presentation due to exposure and frostbite while five additional soldiers were lost to food poisoning.[24]

As the expedition neared the portage on 20 March, the natives asked Léry again what his intentions were concerning the attack. He again avoided giving a firm answer. This time he stated that they would decide when they reached the portage. As he stated,

> I assured them that I would not attack the fort, that I had not come to give glory
> to the English and that, if I could not find an opportunity to fight them without
> suffering heavy losses, I would return without doing anything: but that it was
> necessary for me to see the situation there to report to their father [Vaudreuil].[25]

In all of the conferences with the Native Americans Léry never mentioned the true purpose of the attack for the French, to prevent the British from

---

20   MacLeod, *Canadian Iroquois in the Seven Years War*, p.27.
21   MacLeod, *Canadian Iroquois in the Seven Years War*, p.27.
22   Bancroft, 'Savages', p.87.
23   Bancroft, 'Savages', p.87.
24   Bancroft, 'Savages', pp.87–88.
25   Vaudreuil quoted in MacLeod, *Canadian Iroquois in the Seven Years War*, pp.28–29.

launching an invasion of New France by destroying the supplies they had gathered to support it. While Léry maintained this deception of his erstwhile allies, some chose to abandon the expedition of their own accord. In this way, the Native Americans demonstrated that they were in fact allies, and not under the jurisdiction of the French.[26]

At the same time, some left due to concerns about their community as opposed to demonstrating their status. On 15 March, word arrived with the expedition of a fire at Oswegatchie, and 30 of the warriors from that town returned home to inspect the damage.[27]

Others who left the expedition professed their continued willingness to engage against the British. They simply preferred to do so on their own terms. For instance, 19 Canadian Iroquois and four Algonquins left the main expedition and divided themselves into five war parties. They proceeded to make their way to Oswego and the Mohawk Valley settlements in search of prisoners. These parties were successful in taking a total of 10 prisoners.[28] At the same time, it could be argued that their assertion of their independence actually supported the main expedition, as it served to distract the attention of the British authorities away from the forts and the portage. In this case, the impromptu dispersal of some elements of the raiding force served it well as it confused the enemy as to the actual intent of the main party. In this, the Native warriors contributed an act of impromptu deception.

Still, the remainder of the Native allies remained with the French expeditionary force and continued on southward to the target. By 26 March, the expedition was close to the forts. At the same time, they were in a poor position to fight as they had been without food for two days. Furthermore, they had made an arduous march through heavy snow and torrential rains.[29]

On the morning of 27 March, the fatigued party emerged from the woods in range of their target. At this point, scouts who formed something of an advanced guard for the expedition spotted convoys of sleighs carrying provisions from Fort Williams at the eastern end of the portage to Fort Bull on the western flank. The leading warriors held a brief council with Léry in which they decided to attack the supply convoy in order to gain provisions for their men.

The Amerindians launched the attack and demonstrated a high level of discipline in carrying it out. They set up an ambush and waited in silence for the convoy to make its way into position. Meanwhile the French officers had to forcibly restrain their men from joining the attack too soon and thus giving away the entire enterprise.[30]

When the convoy was in range, the Native Americans sprang the trap, once again moving in silence and without firing a shot. As a result, they were able to capture nine of the sleighs and 10 men. One of the drivers, in some accounts an African American servant, managed to escape the ambush and

26   MacLeod, *Canadian Iroquois in the Seven Years War*, p.29.
27   MacLeod, *Canadian Iroquois in the Seven Years War*, p.30.
28   MacLeod, *Canadian Iroquois in the Seven Years War*, p.30.
29   Starkey, *European and Native American Warfare*, p.1.
30   MacLeod, *Canadian Iroquois in the Seven Years War*, p.30.

fled in the direction of Fort Williams.[31] Some assert that discipline broke down as the starving men of the expedition broke the cover of the woods and sought to plunder the supplies on the captured wagons.[32]

The escape of the lone driver meant the British would soon have warning as to the presence of the raiding force. Once again, there emerged a difference of opinion between the natives and the French and Canadian contingents as to what course of action to follow. For Léry, their discovery meant that it was time for the French to press their attack without delay, before their British adversaries could mount any kind of organized resistance. In advocating for this course of action, wittingly or not, Léry was applying the same sort of irregular tactics used in Europe. He thus ordered an immediate attack on Fort Bull. For the Native Americans, on the other hand, their success in capturing the convoy without sustaining any losses stood as a victory in its own right and it was time to retire instead. They had captured enough food for the return journey and taken some scalps as well as prisoners. Again, they had no desire to make an attack on a fortified post, especially one now alerted to their presence. The native leaders supported their position with references to the 1755 battle of Lake George in which the French commander baron Jean Armand de Dieskau launched a failed assault on the British in entrenched positions.[33]

Still, aware that the French were their allies, the Native American contingent agreed to provide two guides to Léry to lead the French party to the target. The Native Americans further agreed to guard the prisoners already taken and to remain on the portage road and watch for any activity from the direction of Fort Williams. The force that remained on the portage road comprised 56 Canadian Iroquois, 11 Nipissings and three Abenakis.[34] Thirty other Canadian Iroquois then went off with the 259 French troops towards Fort Bull, which was occupied by a garrison of 25 soldiers of the 50th (Shirley's) Regiment and an additional 34 carpenters, boatmen, carters and at least three women.[35] According to some sources, the 30 warriors who joined the attack on Fort Bull were fired by brandy taken from the sleighs.[36] If true, the effects would have been exacerbated by the lack of food over the preceding days. By the same token, it would help to explain some of the erratic behaviour that followed.

As the mixed column of French and Amerindians made their way through the woods towards Fort Bull, they came upon a group of six British, likely cutting wood for heating in Fort Bull. Whether they were soldiers or colonists remains unclear to this day. Twenty-four of the Native Americans took off in pursuit of the British as they fled. They may have seen in this unfortunate group an easy means to absent themselves from what they

---

31 MacLeod, *Canadian Iroquois in the Seven Years War*, p.30; Starkey, *European and Native American Warfare*, p.1.

32 Bancroft, 'Savages', p.88.

33 MacLeod, *Canadian Iroquois in the Seven Years War*, p.31. On the battle of Lake George, see Anderson, *Crucible of War*, pp.119–121.

34 MacLeod, *Canadian Iroquois in the Seven Years War*, p.31.

35 MacLeod, *Canadian Iroquois in the Seven Years War*, p.31.

36 Starkey, *European and Native American Warfare*, p.2.

perceived to be a suicidal attack. The loss of these warriors meant that only Collière, a war chief, and five other Canadian Iroquois actually played any part in the attack on the fort.[37]

At roughly 11:00 a.m., the attackers were about 900 metres from the fort. Léry had hoped to utilize surprise as an advantage and storm through the gate before the garrison realized they were under attack. However, he failed to communicate this ambition to his native allies, and they gave their war whoops and proceeded to storm out of the woods. The British working party was the reason for their exclamation.[38] The garrison, duly alerted, quickly slammed the gate shut as the attackers approached.[39]

Some note that Fort Bull was not a fort in the European sense, as in a trace Italienne structure with stone bastions. Instead, it was of the type more common on the frontiers of the British colonies in North America, a wooden stockade with firing loops cut into the walls.[40] Léry's determination to attack the post was favoured by the fact that some of the intelligence the expedition received on their march proved incorrect. The post did not mount any cannon, nor was it designed to.[41]

Some of the French regulars began to try and chop away at the gate with axes, however, this proved ineffectual. Likewise, some of the Canadian militia attempted to open a breach in the northern palisade. The remainder of the attacking force, noticing that the defenders, while closing the gate, had not deployed to the walls, began to fire into the fort through the loopholes as well as through gaps in the south wall.[42] They targeted anyone brazen enough to break cover within the fort. Their fire effectively reversed the purpose of the firing loops. In doing so, the attackers turned the open areas on the inside of the fort into a killing ground.[43]

Many of the garrison sought refuge in the buildings within the fort's walls and became trapped by the hostile fire. Through an interpreter, Léry called on the defenders to surrender, and they replied by increasing their rate of fire. Among those killed by the defenders' fire was Collière who was shot by the commandant of the fort.[44] The refusal of the garrison to surrender, now that all reasonable hope of defending the post had passed might have justified what transpired next.

The fighting at Fort Bull continued for about an hour during which Léry called upon the garrison to surrender a total of three times. During the fight, the attackers contrived a makeshift ram, which they used to break through the gate. Historian Armstrong Starkey asserts that the defenders were distracted by the fire coming into the fort, which allowed Léry's regulars to complete

---

37 MacLeod, *Canadian Iroquois in the Seven Years War*, p.31.
38 Starkey, *Native American and European Warfare*, p.2.
39 McLeod, *Canadian Iroquois in the Seven Years War*, p.31.
40 On frontier fortifications, see Horn, 'La Petite Guerre', pp.25–26 and Williams, *Dunmore's War*, pp.48–50.
41 Starkey, *Native American and European Warfare*, p.2. Bancroft, 'Savages', p.88.
42 Bancroft, 'Savages', p.88.
43 McLeod, *Canadian Iroquois in the Seven Years War*, p.31.
44 McLeod, *Canadian Iroquois in the Seven Years War*, p.31.

chopping a hole through which they could enter the fort.[45] However, they gained entry, and once inside the fort, the attackers fell upon soldiers and civilians alike. Among the first four through the broken gate was a Canadian Iroquois who struck down Collière's killer, the commandant.[46]

Given the type of fight that had occurred thus far outside the fort, the breaching of the walls set the stage for a massacre. The men were at the end of their logistical rope, and there were supplies within the fort vital to their survival. The fort was out matched, it had been called upon to surrender, and the garrison refused. Under the rules of war as they existed at the time, the garrison and the civilians inside were under no guarantee of receiving mercy.

Léry later testified that he had trouble restraining his troops, both the regulars and the Canadians. Some of the soldiers barricaded themselves in the barracks in the fort, which were broken open. Once the attackers breached the stockade, it transformed into a death-trap. The defenders had nowhere to escape to. Only a few soldiers and one woman, named Ann Bowman, were lucky enough to hide themselves from the initial onslaught of the soldiers and their native allies.[47] The remainder of the post, some 59 people composed almost equally of soldiers and civilians, were killed. In the end, only three soldiers, one carpenter and Ann Bowman survived, making for a total death toll of some 58, soldiers and civilians combined.[48]

The garrison now disposed of; the French turned their attention on what they perceived as the main target of the expedition, the contents of the fort's magazines and warehouses.[49] This encompassed a truly massive haul of booty. There were 2,200 kilograms of gunpowder contained in 260 kegs. In addition to the gunpowder, there were large quantities of shells, grenades and cannon balls, as well as clothing for 600 men. Likewise, the warehouses contained 1,000 blankets, as well as barrels of salt pork, biscuit, butter, chocolate and spirits. There were about a hundred horses, whom the raiders killed or took. Likewise, they were roughly 16 bateaux and a number of wagons that the men destroyed.[50] Some of the provisions were taken off to supply the raiders on their long return journey. The remainder of the supplies stored in Fort Bull were destroyed. In destroying the loot they could not transport, Léry's men resembled their European counterparts.[51]

Léry ordered the powder, musket and cannon balls dumped into the river and the fort fired as well. Unfortunately, his orders were carried out simultaneously. Before all the powder could be dumped in the river, the attackers began setting the fort's buildings aflame. Léry noticed the fires and apprehended the danger, ordering his men to abandon the post immediately.

45   McLeod, *Canadian Iroquois in the Seven Years War*, p.31; Starkey, *Native American and European*, p.2.
46   McLeod, *Canadian Iroquois in the Seven Years War*, p.32.
47   McLeod, *Canadian Iroquois in the Seven Years War*, p.32.
48   McLeod, *Canadian Iroquois in the Seven Years War*, p.32.
49   McLeod, *Canadian Iroquois in the Seven Years War*, p.32.
50   McLeod, *Canadian Iroquois in the Seven Years War*, p.32.
51   Duffy, *Military Experience*, p.277.

Fire spread to the main magazine which disintegrated in a massive explosion. Fort Bull was now little more than a pile of smoking debris.[52]

Just as Léry and his men were brushing themselves down from the explosion, a messenger arrived informing the French commander that a contingent from Fort Williams was making a sortie towards their location.[53] It seems that just after the initial encounter, at about 10:00 a.m., the driver who escaped the initial ambush made his way into Fort Williams and raised the alarm. The commander of the garrison responded by dispatching a patrol composed of a sergeant, 15 men and one colonial volunteer, a man named Robert Eastburn, to go and investigate the situation. The bulk of the Native Americans who had previously refused to take part in the attack on Fort Bull stationed themselves about 500 metres from Fort Williams. When they caught sight of the patrol, they opened fire. The men in the patrol responded with a single volley and then tried to fall back on Fort Williams. In attempting to break off, the British contingent fell back into a bog. Adding to their woes, a recent snowfall made it so that their tracks were clearly visible in the snow, allowing their assailants to follow them and round them up with relative ease.[54]

There exists some debate as to whether Léry considered turning his force on Fort Williams once he had learned of the fate of the relief force. While Armstrong Starkey asserts he might have considered doing so, most of the other sources consulted refute this idea.[55] The latter proposition seems more realistic. As someone experienced with Native Americans and their approach to warfare, Léry would no doubt understand that his allies were satisfied with the loot and prisoners they had so far taken, and the low number of casualties. Even from the Frenchman's perspective, he had succeeded in his mission of destroying the supplies stockpiled at the fort. Oswego would be weakened, and thus less capable of withstanding Montcalm's assault in the coming spring. Furthermore, without the supplies he and his men had managed to incinerate, any thrust northward would be significantly delayed if not cancelled altogether for the coming campaign season.[56] Attacking an alerted garrison in a prepared position with the benefit of artillery on their side could easily turn the victory thus far achieved into a crippling defeat. Whatever the decision-making process, Léry opted to break off the attack and retreat. He and his men made their way back to Sackets Harbor, New York and there awaited their relief force, a detachment from the Bearn Regiment of the Troupes de Terre.[57]

The prisoners were bound and stripped of their coats in order to make it difficult for them to attempt to escape. As one historian of the attack notes, 'Thus, at one end of the portage, the occupants of Fort Bull, soldiers and civilians alike, were being massacred almost to the last man and woman by

52   Bancroft, 'Savages', p.89.
53   McLeod, *Canadian Iroquois in the Seven Years War*, p.32.
54   McLeod, *Canadian Iroquois in the Seven Years War*, pp.32–33.
55   Starkey, *Native American and European Warfare*, p.2. McLeod, *Canadian Iroquois in the Seven Years War*, p.33. Bancroft, 'Savages', pp.86–87.
56   Bancroft, 'Savages', p.87.
57   Bancroft, 'Savages', p.89.

the French soldiers and militiamen. At the other, British soldiers who ceased to resist were taken prisoner by Amerindian warriors.'[58]

Following the two clashes, the disparate components of the raiding force reunited. At the direction of their chaplain, the French briefly gave prayers of thanksgiving for their success. Prior to departing, they destroyed 15 bateaux as well.[59] The destruction of these craft would effectively prevent any pursuit of the departing force. Likewise, it would further hinder efforts to bring supplies up to succour the post at Oswego.

The attack on Fort Bull had indeed been very successful for the French considering the context. They had lost only one regular killed and two wounded. Their native allies were not as fortunate. As noted above, Collière fell in the fighting that preceded the storming of the post. In addition, two Kanestakes and one Kahawake were wounded by flying debris when the magazine of the fort exploded. The latter succumbed to his wounds. These losses confirmed for many of the warriors the foolishness of assaulting a fortified post in the open.[60] In his journal, Léry undercounted the losses to his native contingent. Whether this was accidental or by design is unclear.[61]

Soon, the raiders began the long return journey to Canada, where the two groups separated, each to celebrate their victory in accordance with their own customs. Each side accomplished the goals they set out to. The Native Americans had taken scalps and prisoners, as well as booty, the latter two would be very useful to their people. They demonstrated their prowess as warriors as well. Concerning the prisoners, approximately 14 were taken in the fighting at the Great Carrying Place. The prisoners were taken on a tour of sorts of the various native villages. One of the prisoners taken at Fort Bull, Robert Eastburn, left an account of his time among the natives.[62]

The French, on the other hand, succeeded in the destruction of an important enemy staging area, which prevented a British thrust into Canada in the coming campaign season. They returned from the raid on Fort Bull believing that the destruction of the post had achieved safety for New France by destroying the post and the stores it contained. Doing so disrupted the British plans for a spring campaign on Lake Ontario. Further, the destruction of the post provided time for Vaudreuil to plan for a major move against Oswego.[63] Interestingly, François, chevalier de Lévis, who served as the second in command to the marquis de Montcalm, commented that 'Few provisions were found in the fort, which was only a warehouse.'[64] This may be due to several factors. First,

---

58   McLeod, *Canadian Iroquois in the Seven Years War*, p.33.

59   Douglas Leach, *Arms for Empire: A Military History of the British Colonies in North America 1607-1763* (New York: The Macmillan Company, 1973), p.382.

60   McLeod, *Canadian Iroquois in the Seven Years War*, p.33.

61   Bancroft, 'Savages', pp.89–90.

62   Robert Eastburn, *A Faithful Narrative, of the many Dangers and Sufferings, as well as Wonderful and Surprizing Deliverances of Robert Eastburn, during his late Captivity among the Indians: together with some remarks upon the country of Canada, and the Religion and Policy of its Inhabitants; the whole Intermixed with Devout Reflections* (Philadelphia: Green and Russell, 1758).

63   McLeod, *Canadian Iroquois in the Seven Years War*, p.34.

64   François-Gaston du Chevalier de Lévis, *Journal des Campagne du Chevalier de Lévis de 1756 à 1760* (Montreal: C.O. Beauchemin and Fils, 1889), p.44.

Lévis did not take part in the expedition, and consequently, his account gets a number of details incorrect. Second, he was an officer sent from metropolitan France, and may therefore reflect the condescension many regular officers felt towards their French-Canadian contemporaries.

The broader effects of the Fort Bull raid were profound as well. It left Oswego in a dangerous position through the rest of the spring. War parties moved through the region with impunity, attacking supply convoys headed for the outpost and taking prisoners with ease. It took until May to get the first supply convoy from Albany through to the beleaguered post, and until June before the garrison, much reduced by disease, was able to begin work on repairing the defences of the post.[65] These delays cut deeply into the campaign season and effected British plans for what they could possibly hope to achieve in 1756.

Finally, the raid against Fort Bull demonstrates the varied approaches to warfare of the French and their native allies working in tandem. The French launched an attack in the open against a fortified post, rushing over open terrain and engaging in an hour-long fire fight with the defenders. In order to achieve his strategic and tactical goals, Léry willingly risked sustaining significant casualties. Once his men managed to enter the post, he accepted the slaughter of the bulk of the garrison as well. The French perception was that the risk of major losses was worth attaining the objective.[66] Likewise, the failure of the defenders to surrender, even when they no longer possessed a realistic chance off driving of the attack deprived them of Léry's protection.

On the Native American side, the French willingness to accept the possibility of high casualties seemed absurd. While they were willing to risk their lives in battle, they would not do so without some overarching reason. As the Kahnawake war chief Tecaughretango aptly summarized the perspective of his people on warfare, which was to them 'the art of war ambushing and surprising our enemies, and in preventing them from ambushing and surprising us.'[67] For the Native Americans who took part in the raid, their interests were not at stake, beyond honouring their alliance with the French. Thus, once they had secured supplies and prisoners, they accomplished their mission and for them, the goal was achieved, and it was time to return home rather than risk sustaining heavy casualties. This view would be borne out by the losses sustained by those who followed the French force on to Fort Bull.

In the end, as one historian of the raid observed, 'The actions and decisions of the French and Iroquois in the expedition to Fort Bull mirrored their respective role in the Seven Years War.'[68]

The destruction of Fort Bull meant that there was now no safety for bateaux men and British supply convoys moving to the Oswego forts. Subsequent raids combined with poor weather to cut the flow of supplies to a mere trickle. As a result, the situation of the garrison at Oswego deteriorated significantly.[69]

---

65 Anderson, *War that Made America*, p.93.
66 McLeod, *Canadian Iroquois in the Seven Years War*, p.34.
67 Tecaughretango quoted in McLeod, *Canadian Iroquois in the Seven Years War*, pp.34–35.
68 McLeod, *Canadian Iroquois in the Seven Years War*, p.36.
69 Bancroft, 'Savages', p.90.

The fort, under the command Lieutenant Colonel James Mercer, lacked sufficient supply. Over time, this contributed to rising losses from disease, the combination generated low morale as well.[70] Consequently, by the time Louis-Joseph, marquis de Montcalm-Gozon de Saint Véran, arrived before the fort on 10 August 1756 with a force of 3,000 troops, the garrison was reduced to 1,135, many of these being in poor condition.

Montcalm's arrival surprised the garrison, and there followed only a short siege, during which the besiegers employed a very effective combination of regular and irregular warfare.[71] During the French cannonade of the post, Lieutenant Colonel Mercer was decapitated by a cannonball on 13 August, causing his subordinate to surrender the post on the following day.[72] The irregulars in Montcalm's force, especially the Native Americans helped to shorten the siege by driving back all attempts to sally from the post and at the same time intercepting any messengers attempting to get out calls for reinforcements. At the same time, the Native Americans shocked the French regular officers by killing at least 30 wounded prisoners after the surrender of the fort.[73] Historian Ian K. Steele noted, 'In the conduct of the Oswego campaign, there had been some tensions between Canadians and regulars, but few serious problems. However, Montcalm was becoming increasingly uncomfortable'.[74] While there did not as yet exist any formal, universally accepted, rules of war in Europe, prisoners were considered as being under the protection of the victorious army commander. Thus, any injury sustained by the prisoners reflected dishonour on the commander, a theme that will receive further examination below.

Still, the capture of Oswego, in turn, provided the French with secure control of waterborne communications between Quebec and the *pays d'en haut*, an asset they would maintain until 1758.[75] The raid therefore allowed New France to hold out longer than would have been possible had the connection be severed.

Thus, the raid on Fort Bull exerted the effect of softening up the garrison at Oswego. Lack of supply and its subsequent effects on the garrison of the post certainly made it more susceptible to a siege. The fact that the commander of the British garrison was killed shortly into the French investment, and the manner in which he was killed likely deflated already flagging morale on the part of the defenders. In essence, the Fort Bull raid not only had a short-term consequence of disrupting the supply lines from Albany, vital to the maintenance of Oswego, but it exerted an interim operational effect as well. All of this in return for the risk of some 350 troops and the actual loss of only one dead and two wounded. Clearly, this was a small action with very large ramifications.

---

70   Bancroft, 'Savages', p.90.
71   Steele, *Warpaths*, p.199.
72   Bancroft, 'Savages', p.90.
73   Steele, *Warpaths*, p.200.
74   Steele, *Warpaths*, p.200.
75   Bancroft, 'Savages', p.90.

8

The Continuing Small War in North America and the Emergence of British Light Infantry in the 'American Army'

If, as it is usually presented, the battle of the Monongahela made the British army aware of the need for light troops in the North American theatre, the Fort Bull Raid and incidents like it drove home that awareness. A standard account of the British experience of the conflict in North America reads as follows: 'the harrowing experiences of 1755 had illustrated to the British that numbers alone could not win this war.'[1] It continues, 'In 1757, British commanders formed an experimental temporary corps that stemmed from the nature of the terrain as well as the tactics of the enemy. Those troops were called "light troops," or "light infantry," and sometimes "light bobs," to distinguish them from the heavy infantry in the marching regiments.'[2] The preceding pages amply demonstrate that the reality was somewhat different. The Fort Bull Raid, especially, illustrates in stark relief the problem that British regular forces were confronted with on entering the North American theatre. Put succinctly, their opponents possessed a tactical system which was much more effective than theirs.

J.A. Houlding sums up the British predicament aptly,

Whereas in Germany the burden of the light service could be borne by the assorted *Freikorps*, *jägers*, hussars and legions of the Hanoverians and Hessians, in America the British had themselves to make a major effort, and to rely on their own resources. The Canadians and their Indian allies were past-masters at the *petite guerre*, while the nature of the country made them formidable; and

---

1   Ruth Sheppard, *Empires Collide: The French and Indian War 1754-63* (Oxford: Osprey, 2006), p.149.
2   Sheppard, *Empires Collide*, p.151.

the forces from metropolitan France—the *Troupes de la Marine* in particular—showed themselves adept at many aspects of the light service.[3]

Rory Cory aptly supplements Houlding's analysis: 'The British Army did not exist in a vacuum.'[4] Not only did the officers who aided in the development of the British light infantry observe the tactical doctrines of their French and native foes. They combined these with the concepts they had seen or heard of concerning the light troops in Europe as well. 'Although European light troops may have provided some of the inspiration for British light infantry, they did not provide a direct example for them to copy.'[5]

Developing a solution had to be done quickly and at the lowest cost in blood and treasure possible. Initially, British leaders placed greater confidence in the colonial rangers following Braddock's defeat.[6]

John Campbell, 4th Earl of Loudoun writing to the Duke of Cumberland from Albany on 22 November 1756, offers some insights into the initial British response to the Native American depredations:

> I am afraid, I shall be blamed for the *Ranging* Companies; but as realy [*sic*] in Effect we have no *Indians,* it is impossible for an Army to Act in this Country, without *Rangers*; and there ought to be a considerable body of them, and the breeding them up to that, will be a great advantage to this Country, for they will be able to deal with Indians in their own way; and from all I see, are much stronger and hardier fellows than the Indians who are many of them *tall,* as most of the People here are, but have a *small feeble* Arm, and are a *loose-made indolent* sett of People and hardly any of them, have the least degree of *Faith* or *honesty,* and I doubt a good deal of their *Courage*: better times, may shew them in a different light.[7]

Among the most successful ranger units in the British service was that of Major Robert Rogers. Roger's background is addressed above. As a young man, he tried a number of different occupations before finally achieving some local prominence as a guide and frontier fighter. During the early stages of the French and Indian War, Rogers emerged as one of the few men on the side of the British and their colonial allies who enjoyed some success against the Native Americans.[8] Rogers thus offered an example that British officers had to take seriously, though many looked down upon the colonists, seeing them as amateurish.

While they were effective as a counter to the French and their native allies, several factors served to mitigate against the reliance on rangers as scouts and advanced guards for the British forces deployed to North America. Among

---

3   J.A. Houlding, *Fit for Service: The Training of the British Army, 1715–1795* (Oxford: Clarendon Press, 1981), p.374.

4   Cory, 'British Light Infantry', p.5.

5   Cory, 'British Light Infantry', p.6.

6   Cory, 'British Light Infantry', p.41.

7   Loudoun to Cumberland, Albany, 22 November 1756, concluded 26 December 1756, quoted in Stanley Pargellis, *Military Affairs in North America, 1755-1763: Selected Documents from the Cumberland Papers in Windsor Castle.* (New York: D. Appleton Century Company, 1936), p.317.

8   See Ross, *War on the Run*, pp.71–134.

these factors stood the sense of corporate identity among the British officer corps. This was exacerbated by the conduct of the rangers themselves who demonstrated a proclivity for indiscipline. Consequently, the British sought a solution to their tactical conundrum which fit more seamlessly with their military institution.

Faced with the tactical problem posed by the French and their native allies, the British leadership drew on their experience dating back to the War of the Austrian Succession. After all, many of the tactics utilized by their foes resembled those used by the Pandours and Croats very closely. Likewise, many of the officers who played prominent roles in the creation of the light bobs, such as Thomas Gage and George Augustus Howe, gained their initial military experience fighting in Europe during the War of the Austrian Succession. The argument proposed herein is that the British Army, when confronted by the challenges posed their Native American and French allies, did not, as is usually presented, adapt ideas solely from colonial rangers. It seems more accurate that they took the experiences they had already encountered in Europe and combined them with the practices current among the colonists.

Still, the successes of Rogers and his men, contrasted with the humiliating failure of the British regulars, could not be ignored. Based on the New Englander's successes, the British commander in North America at the time, Lord Loudoun, sent Rogers a list of some 50 men he drew from the regular battalions, whom he wanted to be trained in Ranger methods.[9] In selecting men for ranger training, officers sought out men who were in good physical condition and skilled marksmen.[10] In the end, 55 'gentlemen voluteers' were selected to undergo seven weeks of training with Rogers.[11] Gentleman volunteers accompanied units into the field in the hopes of gaining experience and potentially filling an officer vacancy that opened up due to attrition. Consequently, they were often out to display their willingness to serve to their superiors. Rogers opened the first of these 'ranging schools' on 5 September 1757. The school was run specifically for volunteer officers who sought to mimic Rogers' methods. Colonel George Augustus Howe of the 55th Foot participated as one of the students in the first class.[12] Lord Loudoun had hoped that the men so trained would bring back the knowledge they had acquired and that it would disseminate through their regiments via that route.[13] While Rogers' school no doubt exerted a major impact on the British officers who formed light companies in North America, they did not completely abandon the knowledge base they previously acquired in Europe. Peter Russell notes that both John Forbes and Henry Bouquet studied the work of Turpin de Crissé prior to launching their attack on Fort Duquesne in

---

9   King Lawrence Parker, *Anglo-American Wilderness Campaigning 1754-1764: Logistics and Tactical Developments*, PhD dissertation, (Columbia University, 1970), p.238.
10   Sheppard, *Empires Collide*, p.152.
11   Ian M. McPherson and Tim J. Todish, *British Light Infantryman of the Seven Years War North America 1757-1763* (Oxford: Osprey, 2004), p.20.
12   McCulloch and Todish, *British Light Infantryman*, p.20.
13   Brumwell, *Redcoats*, p.228.

1758. Likewise, James Wolfe supposedly recommended both Turpin's and La Croix's works as 'must reads' for aspiring young officers.[14]

The preceding plan gave way when Lieutenant Colonel Thomas Gage of the 44th Foot, who had commanded Braddock's advanced guard at the battle of the Monongahela, offered to raise a unit of 'good, active, healthy, young men,'[15] at his own expense.[16] The regiment was to number 500.[17] As Stephen Brumwell notes, Gage's proposal had two winning attributes: first, it provided a unit of men trained as rangers, but paid at the same rate as British regulars. Second, it provided a force of rangers led by regular army officers and held to the same code of discipline as the regulars.[18] In essence, Gage's idea gave Loudoun a hybrid: rangers under stricter discipline and greater control of the British leadership. Pay did prove something of an issue, as some of the men enlisted in the belief that they would be given the higher pay of the rangers.[19]

These men were drafted from other regiments to form an elite unit. To initiate the program, Lord Loudoun sent an initial detachment of 96 men from the regular battalions under his command.[20] All were to be 'alert, Spirited soldiers, able to endure fatigue.'[21] Other attributes the officers sought were men who could climb trees, and who were deemed as capable of detached service, essentially, that they would not take such service as an opportunity to desert of go marauding. Again, the pattern of selection, the criteria and the training given those selected were all at the discretion of the commanding officer. As a result, no standards were established.[22] Interestingly, the men who were selected resembled the rangers in that many chafed at the strict discipline of the regulars.[23] The rejection of discipline by the light troops is exemplified by the following entry from Josiah Goodrich's Orderly Book, dated 9 July 1759, 'A soldier of [the] brigade of Light Infantry Accused of Desartion Is found guilty of ye crime Laid to his charge And Is to Reicev 1000 Lashes with a Cat of nine tails.'[24]

The light infantry were to be armed with muskets that were cut down to approximately the length of carbines.[25] These weapons were less cumbersome than the musket. Those who distinguished themselves as the most capable marksmen were issued rifles. Likewise, they were issued with cartridge boxes of a lighter manufacture and capable of holding more rounds than those of

---

14   Peter E. Russell, 'Redcoats in the Wilderness: British Officers and Irregular Warfare in Europe and America, 1740-1760', *William and Mary Quarterly*, Series 3, 35:4 (October 1978), p.641.

15   Sheppard, *Empires Collide*, p.152.

16   Brumwell, *Redcoats*, p.228.

17   Brumwell, *Redcoats*, p.228.

18   Brumwell, *Redcoats*, pp.228–229.

19   Brumwell, *Redcoats*, p.229.

20   Brumwell, *Redcoats*, p.229.

21   John Knox, *Journal*, quoted in Brumwell, *Redcoats*, pp.229–230.

22   Sheppard, *Empires Collide*, p.152.

23   Brumwell, *Redcoats*, p.229.

24   Josiah Goodrich, 'The Josiah Goodrich Orderbook', *The Bulleting of the Fort Ticonderoga Museum*, 14:1 (Summer 1981), pp.44–45.

25   Eric Robson, 'British Light Infantry in the Mid-Eighteenth Century: The Effect of American Conditions', *Army Quarterly*, (1952), p.210.

the regular units. The cartridge boxes were covered in tin as well to guard against moisture.

Many were equipped with powder horns as well, filled with pistol powder, which was of a finer grain, to use in priming their weapons. Again, mimicking their native opponents, the men were issued with tomahawks and knives as well for close quarter combat.[26] The men of Gage's unit, officially designated the 80th Foot, wore brown, skirtless coats without any lace. The officers were expected to set the example for their men by doing their own washing.[27] This, in turn, removed the need to bring along any women for the unit.

The following presents one of the most complete descriptions of the ideal type of uniform for the light infantry on campaign in North America:

> The following order for the dress of the Light Infantry, as approved of by his excellency General Amherst: Major-General Wolfe desires the same may be exactly conformed to by the light troops under his command: the sleeves of the [red] coat are put on the waistcoat and, instead of coat-sleeves, he has two wings like the grenadiers, but fuller; and a round slope reaching about halfway down his arm; which makes his coat no encumbrance to him, but can be slipt off with pleasure; he has no lace, but the lapels remain; besides the usual pockets, he has two, not quite so high as his breast, made of leather, for balls and flints; and a flap of red cloth on the inside, which secures the ball from rolling out, if he should fall. His knapsack is carried very high between his shoulders, and is fastened with a strap of web over his shoulder, as the Indians carry their pack. His cartouch-box hangs under his arm on the left side, slung with a leathern strap; and his horn under the other arm on the right; canteen down his back, under his knapsack and covered with cloth; he has a rough case for his tomahock, with a button; and it hangs in a leathern sling down his side like a hanger, between his coat and waist-coat. No bayonet; his leggings have leathern straps under his shoes like spatterdashes, his hat is made into a cap, with a flap and a button, and with as much blackcloth added as will come under his chin and keep him warm when he lies down; it hooks in the front, and is made like the old velvet caps in England.[28]

Note the amalgamation of European and Native American accoutrements. On campaign the light infantryman was expected to carry his own provisions as there was no supply train. The lack of a lumbering supply train stood as one factor that increased the speed and mobility of light troops in the North American wilderness. The provisions carried by the light infantry included salted meat, parched Indian corn, peas, rice, biscuits and possibly chocolate or sugar. These could, at times, be supplemented while on campaign through hunting and fishing. By the same token, such activities were often forbidden, especially when the force was close to its

---

26 Sheppard, *Empires Collide*, p.153.
27 H.C.B. Rogers, *The British Army of the Eighteenth Century* (New York: Hippocrene Books, 1977), p.72.
28 Anonymous, quoted in McCulloch and Todish, *British Light Infantryman*, pp.16–17.

target to prevent them giving away their location. Campaigning in winter was something to be avoided as well due to the hardships it bought on the men.[29] Gage's unit coalesced in early 1758 and participated in each of the campaigns of the next six years, seeing a great deal of service.[30]

Essentially, Gage stripped down his force to make it more mobile and effective in the terrain of North America. At the same time, it conformed to the ideals then prevalent among Europeans concerning Native American ways of war.[31] Thomas Gage 'pioneered the first true light infantry in the British army, though his 80th Regiment of Foot ultimately reflected the inherent conservatism of senior British commanders who were unwilling to permit their light infantrymen to become true irregulars.'[32] While Gage's regiment was innovative in establishing the British light infantry, in many ways it remained a fairly conservative approach.

'The officer who brought Gage's conservatism into sharp relief was George Augustus, Lord Howe, the commanding officer of the 55th Regiment in 1757 and 1758. Lord Howe fully embraced techniques practiced by Rogers and was especially beloved by the American provincials who knew that he respected their martial abilities.'[33] Howe had gained his first military experience in the War of the Austrian Succession, fighting in the Low Countries, where he came into contact with the light forces then developing in large numbers.[34]

Howe took his reforms much further than Gage, and set the example himself, to the extent that one student of his efforts asserted 'Howe's progressivism might have revolutionized the British infantry training had he not died at Ticonderoga.'[35] The alteration he made in the uniforms and tactics of his men aided them in adapting to the realities of campaigning in North America. He cut down his own uniform coat. He ordered the barrels of the muskets carried by his men blued or browned to reduce the glare caused by sunlight. This would help keep them concealed both on the march and when setting an ambush as well. Further, he ordered that the coats worn by his men were to be quite plain. The general consensus, as put forth by one officer, seemed to be 'the less they are seen in the Woods the better.'[36] Officers gave up their gorgets, and many began to dress in more drab uniforms to match those of their men as well. In adopting these modifications to their dress, the officers made themselves less visible targets to the aimed fire of their foes. Likewise, the men were encouraged to 'break up the whiteness of their face before going on operations by growing a beard or "smutting" it with

---

29   Sheppard, *Empires Collide*, p.155.
30   Brumwell, *Redcoats*, p.229.
31   On this point, a useful discussion of culture conceptions influencing tactical developments may be found in John A. Lynn, 'The Battle Culture of Forbearance,' in Wayne E. Lee (ed.), *Warfare and Culture in World History*. (New York: New York University Press, 2011), pp.89–114.
32   Preston, *Braddock's Defeat*, p.303.
33   Preston, *Braddock's Defeat*, p.309.
34   See, James R. McIntyre, 'George Augustus Howe: Father of the British Light Infantry?', *Journal of the Seven Years War Association*, 19:3 (Summer 2014), pp.12–14.
35   Silcox, 'Rogers and Bouquet', p.70.
36   Moneypenny Orderly Book, quoted in Horn, 'Terror', p.60.

charcoal.'[37] Many of George Augustus Howe's reforms were implemented in James Abercromby's army in the 1758 campaign.[38]

At the same time, George Washington, never known to be a great military innovator, was experimenting with some reforms to make his Virginia troops more mobile and thus more of a challenge to their native foes. Writing to Henry Bouquet on 3 July 1758, Washington expressed his plans for modifications in the uniforms of his men:

> My men are very bare of Cloaths/Regimentals I mean and I have no prospect of a Supply—this want, so far from regretting during this Campaigne, that were I left to pursue my own Inclinations, I would not only cause the Men to Adopt the Indian Dress but Officers also, and set example myself: nothing but the uncertainty of its taking with the General causes me to hesitate a moment at leaving Regiments at this place, and proceeding as light as any Indian in the Woods—tis an unbecoming dress I confess for an Officer, but convenience rather than shew I think should be consulted—the Reduction of Bat-Horses alone is sufficient to recommend it, for nothing is more certain than that less Baggage will be required, and that the Publick will be benefitted in Proportion.
>
> I was desirous of being this full in my letter to you, how far it may be consistent with good Policy, as there is at least a possibility of its falling into the Enemy's hands I know not, but I shall be directed in these Affairs by you.[39]

By 1758, men were being trained and selected for new battalions based on their marksmanship as well as their physical condition. As mentioned above, the better marksmen among the light infantry in the period prior to 1758 were issued with a new weapon before embarking on that years' campaign. Eighty 'riffled barrel pieces' were issued to the 10 best shots in each regiment of Major General James Abercromby's army.[40]

Initially, their missions were simply scouting activities, however, as the lights grew in proficiency, the missions developed to where the detachments could engage the enemy independently of the main force. These newly developed light companies were deployed on the left of the parent regiment when drawn up in line of battle.[41] At least this was their stipulated place according to regulations. In actual practice, more often than not, the light companies of several units were brigaded together in special light battalions. In whatever manner the units were deployed, they were, as of 1758 designated light companies in order differentiate them from the bulk of the regiment on the one hand, and colonial rangers on the other.[42] By the same token, they continued to operate with the rangers.[43] The duties of the light infantry mirrored those of the rangers in

---

37   McCulloch and Todish, *British Light Infantryman*, p.15.
38   McCulloch and Todish, *British Light Infantryman*, pp.15–16.
39   George Washington to Henry Bouquet 3 July 1758, in Sylvester K. Stevens and Donald H. Kent (eds.), *The Papers of Colonel Henry Bouquet* (Harrisburg: Pennsylvania Historical Commission, 1940), vol.2, p.159.
40   McCulloch and Todish, *British Light Infantryman*, p.19.
41   Parker, *Anglo-American Wilderness*, p.239.
42   Parker, *Anglo-American Wilderness*, p.239.
43   Cory, 'British Light Infantry', p.47.

many ways. An example of the combined service comes from the Moneypenny Orderly Book, and is dated 1 September 1758:

> A detachment of 4 Subs., & 100 Volunteers from the Regulars, the three Companys of Light Infantry, 110, of M. Roger's Rangers, 100, of Colonel Partridge's Rangers, & 110 of the Connecticut Rangers to march tomorrow morning at seven o'clock with seven Days Provisions, under the command of Capt Dalzell of the Light Infantry. They are to take a convoy under their Escort to Halfway Brook.[44]

It could be observed that the light infantry developed by the British army in North America seemed to mirror in ways the process occurring in Europe in which irregular troops were brought more and more under regular discipline. Even with the development of light troops, the Native Americans especially continued to raid British columns. These raids could be quite damaging. Take as an example the following incident recorded by captain Samuel Cobb of Colonel Jedidiah Prebble's Massachusetts Regiment on Thursday, 27 July 1758, 'Indians Waylaid the road between fort Edward and halfway Brook and they killed and took about 80 of our Men and women and Destroyed about 80 Teams Oxen and Loading.'[45] Here, again, is a similarity with the activities of light troops in the European Small War. Aside from the prisoners, supplies that could not be carried off were destroyed on the spot and valuable draft animals were killed.

Among the more prominent figures in inculcating light infantry tactics and ideas into the British Army in North America was Henri Bouquet, a Swiss born soldier of fortune who served as second in command of the 1758 campaign to take Fort Duquesne.[46] Probably Bouquet's most significant innovation was that he adopted some of the Native Americans' own tactics and trained his men in them, thus turning their practices against them.[47] One of Bouquet's numerous innovations lay in his practice of arming and equipping his men much like the Native Americans.[48] Likewise, he trained them in rapid changes in formation as well as silent movements through forested areas. In Bouquet's organization, the company served as the primary manoeuvre unit as opposed to the battalion. Other innovations Bouquet introduced included such practices as teaching the men to wheel on the run in broken terrain, swim, and walk on snowshoes.[49] Thus, he introduced a number of practices which had the effect to acclimating the tactics of the British troops to the conditions they would operate in in the North American Theatre. Still, as one author observed, 'Only time in the wilderness could build up the expertise that a light infantryman needed to be able to confidently take on his adversaries.'[50]

---

44 Anonymous, 'Monepenny Orderly Book', *The Bulletin of the Fort Ticonderoga Museum*, 13:1 (1970), pp.97–98.

45 Samuel Cobb, 'Journal of Captain Samuel Cobb', *The Bulletin of the Fort Ticonderoga Museum*, 14:1 (Summer 1981), p.21.

46 Douglas E. Branch, 'Henry Bouquet: Professional Soldier', *The Pennsylvania Magazine of History and Biography*, 62:1 (January 1938), pp.41–51.

47 Sheppard, *Empires Collide*, p.152.

48 Branch, 'Bouquet', p.45.

49 Sheppard, *Empires Collide*, p.152.

50 Sheppard, *Empires Collide*, p.153.

The light troops took a very active role in the campaign of 1759. As noted in … 'on July 7th 'Brigadfier Townsend with Regimts. 4 Compys of Grenadiers & the light Infantry under Colo. How, cross'd the North Channel about 12 oClock this Night & Encamp'd close to the Falls of the Montmorency, that small River separating our army from the French'.[51] The account continued the following day: ·

> Early this Morning Capt Dante's Compy of Rangers were Attack'd in the Woods by a large body of Canadians and Indians, they were soon drove by our Troops who lay nearest, but the Rangers suffer'd so much that they did not act afterwards during the Campaign, having above 30 Men Kill'd & Wounded; some Indians were found kill'd after the skirmish.[52]

Another skirmish ensued on 11 August. On this occasion, 'A large body of Canadians & Savages fell upon a Party of our soldiers, making Fascines on the Montmorency side, the light Infantry push'd them, & put them to flight, however, they kill'd & wounded us a good many men & our loss Exceeded theirs greatly…'[53]

Similarly, in late July 1759, as Wolfe engaged in the campaign that would eventually bring him to the Plains of Abraham, his forces encountered increasing resistance from Native Americans and Canadian militia.[54] Their Small War tactics proved a constant drain on men and morale. By this point in time, however, the British light infantry were becoming more capable, as witnessed by the following where Wolfe ordered his light troops to move against the camp of some Native Americans and Canadian militia:

> Anstruther's regiment, the light infantry, and rangers, are to march at nine, under colonel Howe's command, about a mile into the woods, towards the ford where the Canadians and Indians are encamped; this body must skirt about within the wood from the camp of the light infantry to the road, but so as just to be seen from the opposite side of the river by the enemy … colonel Howe will lengthen his line of march, so as to appear numerous …[55]

Over time, the grinding nature of the campaign began to wear on the discipline of the troops under Wolfe's command. Such is evidence by the entry made on 10 August 1759:

> The general was extremely surprised to see the disorders that seemed to run through the working parties this morning, and foresees, that if a stop is not immediately put to such unsoldier-like proceedings, the consequences must be

---

51   William Bamford, John B. Hattendorf (ed.), *A Redcoat in America: The Diaries of Lieutenant William Bamford, 1757-1765 and 1776* (Warwick: Helion, 2019), pp.74–75.
52   Bamford, *Recoat in America*, p.75.
53   Bamford, *Recoat in America*, p.79.
54   This campaign is covered very thoroughly in Matthew C. Ward, *The Battle for Quebec 1759* (Stroud: The History Press, 2005).
55   James Wolfe, *General Wolfe's Instructions to Young Officers: Also Orders for a Battalion and an Army* (London: J. Millan, 1780), pp.90–91.

very dangerous. The men fired this day upon one another, fired upon the light infantry, and were scattered in such a manner, that a few resolute people would have easily defeated them; it is therefore ordered and commanded that when there is an alarm of this kind, every soldier remains at his post till ordered to march by his proper officer.[56]

Later in the same entry, Wolfe noted:

As the enemy's light troops are continually hovering about the camp, in hopes of surprising some small guard, so some of the centinels [sic], it is necessary to be very vigilant on duty; the out-posts and guards in the redoubts are not to have less than a third of their men under arms; and for an hour before and for at least half an hour after broad day-light, the whole are to be under arms.[57]

Over time, the men selected to undergo training as light troops helped to forge a type of soldier – the British light infantryman. Since their training set them apart from their brethren in the regular and grenadier companies, those men who were selected to become part of the light units considered themselves to be 'chosen'.[58] As Ian M. McCulloch and Earl Chapman observe, 'By the end of the Seven Years War in North America, these "chosen men" had become the most seasoned and useful veterans of Britain's "American Army."'[59] They reached the point where they formed the vanguard of the assault on Quebec in September of 1759, scaling the cliffs before the city and silently dispensing with the French sentinels. On this occasion, they were led by Lieutenant Colonel William Howe, younger brother of George Augustus, and viewed as one of the more capable leaders of light troops in North America. By then Wolfe deemed Howe to be his best battalion commander. Likewise, his light infantry had already proven extremely useful in driving off the French and Indian irregulars who were constantly nipping at the periphery of the besieger's camp.[60] Following the Peace of Paris in 1763, William Howe would go on to conduct a series of exercises in Britain demonstrating the utility of the light companies.

Interestingly, the light infantry experiments embarked upon in North America began to flow back to the Home Islands. They manifested in 1759 with the raising of the 90th regiment of light infantry in Ireland. The 90th stood out as the first unit raised by the British Army outside of North America designed to act specifically as light infantry.[61]

1759 also witnessed Rogers' most famous, and in some circles infamous, exploit during the war in his raid on the Abenaki settlement of St Francis. This attack is worth examining in some detail as it provides an excellent

---

56   Wolfe, *Instructions to Young Officers*, p.95.
57   Wolfe, *Instructions to Young Officers*, p.96.
58   Sheppard, *Empires Collide*, p.152.
59   John Grant, Ian McPherson McCulloch and Earl John Chapman (eds.), *A Dangerous Service: A Soldier's View of the Seven Years War in the Caribbean and North America* (Montreal: Robin Brass Studio, 2017), p.34.
60   McCulloch and Todish, *British Light Infantryman*, p.58.
61   McCulloch and Todish, *British Light Infantryman*, p.18.

'A view of the landing place above the town of Quebec, describing the assault of the enemys post, on the banks of the River St. Lawrence, with a distant view of the action between the British & French armys, on the Hauteurs d'Abraham, Septr. 13th 1759', by Hervey Smyth, and Francis Swain. (Anne S.K. Brown Military Collection)

example of the sort of the tactics employed by ranger forces. At the same time, it highlights the brutality of the conflict as it transpired in the North American wilderness. Robert Kirk(wood), a member of the 77th Foot's Light Company who served with Rogers on the expedition, left an extremely rare first-hand account of action from the soldiers' perspective. After traveling to their target, Rogers' men prepared for the assault:

> It was determined, that we should march to the town that night, and lie until the morning at dawn, and then our orders were to proceed by two and two, and place ourselves severally at each house, and on firing of a shot by way of signal from Major Rogers, we were to fire the town at once and kill every one without mercy.[62]

Attacking the village at dawn mimicked the tactics of the Native Americans. The difference here was the decision to kill all the inhabitants. The following morning, 'The alarms however took place, and in less than a quarter of an hour the whole town was in a blaze, and carnage terrible, hardly any of the enemy escaping; those who the flames did not devour, were either shot or tomohawk'd.'[63] Kirkwood's descriptions as well as his opinions hold particular

---

62   Robert Kirk(wood), Ian M McCullough and Timothy J. Todish (eds.), *Through so Many Dangers: the Memoirs and Adventures of the Robert Kirk, Late of the Royal Highland Regiment* (Fleischmanns, NY: Purple Mountain Press, 2004), p.66.

63   Kirk(wood), *Through so Many Dangers*, p.66.

merit as he was one of the few soldiers who could claim to have experienced the war from both sides.

He had come to America as part of the British forces sent by the Crown but had also spent several years as a captive of the Shawnee. It is clear that his experience with the Native Americans did not completely efface his identity as he stated, 'The whole was reduced to ashes in about an hour; thus the inhumanity of these savages was rewarded with a calamity dreadful indeed, but justly deserved.'[64] Kirkwood concluded by asserting 'This was I believe the bloodiest scene in all America, our revenge being completed.'[65]

Finally, it is worth noting that war, to paraphrase the great Prussian military theorist Carl von Clausewitz, consists in interaction. The enemy gets a vote, or sometimes abstains. As the British solution to the challenges of campaign in North American and against their Native American and French foes coalesced, their opponents' approach fell apart. Parallel war generated its own tensions between the allies as since they fought for their own agendas, these did not always merge well. A case in point from the French and Indian War was the famed Fort William Henry Massacre. On this occasion, the French commander, the marquis de Montcalm, had provided the garrison and its civilians with a safe passage, giving his word of honour for their protection, and allowed them to leave the surrendered fort unmolested. For his native auxiliaries, this proved a great affront as they were being deprived, what was form their perspective their just rewards for participating in the campaign.

The result constituted a turning moment in the conflict, as the natives attacked the retreating column and captured or killed many of the members. In the process, they broke Montcalm's promise of safe conduct, besmirching his honour. As a result, the French commander avoided using native auxiliaries for the remainder of the conflict. Montcalm's actions also served to widen the dispute between him and the governor of New France, Pierre de Rigaud de Vaudreuil de Cavagnal, marquis de Vaudreuil.[66]

---

64 Kirk(wood), *Through so Many Dangers*, p.66.
65 Kirk(wood), *Through so Many Dangers*, p.66.
66 On the Fort William Henry Massacre, see Ian K. Steele, *Betrayals: Fort William Henry and the Massacre*. (New York: Oxford University Press, 1993). A more recent account can be found in David Starbuck, *Massacre at Fort William Henry* (Hanover, NH: University Press of New England, 2002).

9

Conclusion

As the guns ceased firing and the smoke gradually began to clear from battlefields across the globe, the various belligerents surveyed the results of the conflict. One colonial empire was essentially gone, and another vastly increased, at least for the moment, with numerous new colonies. In Europe itself, Prussia had survived, against seemingly impossible odds. Several themes emerge from the examination of the role played by light troops in both Europe and North America.

One factor which emerges from the preceding study of light troops in both theatres is the importance of leadership. When commanded by men who understood the strengths and liabilities of the formations they led, the light troops could render exemplary service. When they were treated the same as other infantry or mounted troops, their performance declined accordingly. Christopher Duffy presents a list of skilled Austrian leaders of light troops which includes Beck, Brentano, Draskovich, Hadik, Jahnus, Kleefeld, Loudon, Luzinsky, Siskovics, Ried and Wied.[1] To these could be added Fischer for the French, Freytag and Luckner for the Hanoverians, as could von Wunsch from the Prussian army. Certainly, Monkewitz from Schaumburg-Lippe earned a place in the pantheon of skilled leaders of light troops for his exploits.

In the North American theatre, Léry's conduct of the Fort Bull raid set him apart as a skilled leader of irregulars. While Robert Rogers would, of course, earn a place for his ranging techniques, one should be set aside as well for George Augustus Howe who successfully transmitted Rogers' lessons to the British regulars, and added innovations of his own. As noted above, the Austrian irregulars seemed to lose their combat edge over the course of the conflict. One of the reasons for their decline, at least according to Christopher Duffy, was the fact that they 'were exposed to repeated maulings by superior enemy forces, and became less and less inclined to show their faces.'[2] Over the course of the conflict, the Prussians grew more adept at using their conventional tactics as countermeasures against the Austrian irregulars, to the degree that they became willing to venture into wooded areas in pursuit of their foes.[3]

---

1   Duffy, *Instrument of War*, p.397.
2   Duffy, *Instrument of War*, p.396.
3   Duffy, *Instrument of War*, p.396.

Another theme that emerges implicitly in the preceding deserves explicit discussion at this juncture, this was the disposition of the civilian population in the area in which the light troops were operating. If they were well disposed to the forces, such as the Moravian civilians were to the austrians in the case of the raids on Domstadtl and Gundersdorf, then they could provide valuable operational intelligence.

Military professionals surveyed the results of the conflict as well. For many, the Seven Years War seemed to prove the utility of light formations. Following this conflict, while many of these units were reduced in keeping with peacetime economizing, they were not struck off the military establishments completely. For many, light troops had become a standard formation in their respective military establishments. Consequently, there appeared fresh works from various commentators who sought to inform readers of which troops made the best irregular fighters and why, the qualities necessary for successful leaders of light troops and so forth.

As occurred following the War of the Austrian Succession, there were attempts to codify the experiences of light forces in the war and preserve them for future reference. The Frenchman, De la Roche observed in his *Essai sur La Petite Guerre*, 'Hungarians seem to be naturally destined to the little war; the men are number, sober, dexterous and vigorous.'[4] He went on, noting, 'From the earliest childhood, they exercised the handling horses and knives, and their horses seemed to be prepared by nature for this trade.'[5] De la Roche listed other groups as well, including Croats, the Talpaches, the Moldavians, and the Licanians, who we commonly designate under the name of pandours...'[6] He observed of these groups, that they 'are all people peculiarly suited to the little war.'[7]

Johann Ewald, who would go on to win great renown as a leader of light troops in the War for American Independence, produced his first treatise, *Thoughts of a solider on What to Do when leading troops on Detachment*. In the work, Ewald demonstrated a great deal of concern with the leadership of these formations. He first observed, 'the majority of writers believe those who lead light troops do so unwillingly.'[8] He went on to reject this proposition vehemently. This developed into a theme he would return to in later works as well.[9]

Still, there were voices in opposition. One of the most influential of these belonged to the comte de Guibert. As his most recent biographer noted, Guibert observed that light formations drew off as much as 20 percent of the strength from the line regiments and disapproved of this practice, 'noting that skirmishers serve their specialized role but could not fight in any other

---

4   Comte de la Roche, *Essai sur La Petite Guerre, Ou Méthode de diriger les différentes operations d'un Corps de deux mille cinq cens Hommes de Troupes légères, don't seize cens d'Infanterie & neuf cens de Cavalerie* (Paris: Saillant & Nyon, 1770), p.14.

5   Roche, *Essai sur La Petite Guerre*, p.14.

6   Roche, *Essai sur La Petite Guerre*, p.14.

7   Roche, *Essai sur La Petite Guerre*, p.14.

8   Ewald, *Gedanken*, p.19.

9   See specifically, Johann Ewald, Robert A. Selig and David Curtiss Skaggs (trans.), *Treatise on Partisan Warfare* (New York: Greenwood Press, 1991).

manner.'[10] In his *Essai general de tactique*, he focused on the line infantry as the core of his vision of a reformed French army, and thus rejected the use of these troops for the most part. For instance, he titled the eleventh chapter of his work, 'It is Possible to Create a System that Renders Light Troops Little Necessary', which should provide a clear indication of the direction in which he was taking his reforms.[11] From there, he observed that if the regular line infantry were better trained, there would be less need for light troops altogether.[12] He lays out his argument a few pages later:

> Finally not only can line troops accomplish a part of the functions assigned to light troops, but it will be advantageous that they be accomplished, not by pickets, [or] by detachments, as was done in the past in France [and] as we practiced in the first campaigns of the last war, which was the source of our daily checks and of the ascendancy that the enemy took over us [and] which caused all our expeditions to fail, but as Marshal Broglie did in 1760.[13]

He observed that Broglie conditioned the grenadiers and dragoons of his army to act as a truly elite force and then 'employed them at every turn, whether in the war of detail of the war of mass'.[14] This goes to the core of some of Guibert's prevailing concerns in the *Essay*. He believed that through better training of the line infantry, they could become more flexible and thus obviate the need for specialized troops dedicated to the Small War. As he noted, concerning Broglie, 'he accustomed them [his reformed infantry and cavalry] to departing from the line for daily service and returning to it for the day of combat.'[15]

Even Guibert, however, did retain a very limited number of light infantry who were to act as scouts, screen the army and harass enemy formations both on and off the battlefield.[16] The light formations Guibert would have the army retain were not composed along the same lines as some of the larger formations he had seen, which equalled 2,000 to 3,000 men. He noted that one problem with such large formations of light troops was finding commanders capable of handling them. Guibert further indicated that these troops acting in detachment often times focused solely on their own missions and neglected that of the army overall.[17]

Guibert devised some very logical criticisms of the light forces he witnessed in action during the Seven Years War. These would certainly serve as grist for the mill of the mind of a young Corsican who would later

10   Jonathan Abel, *Guibert: Father of Napoleon's Grande Armée* (Norman: University of Oklahoma Press, 2016), p.65.
11   Jacques-Antoine-Hippolyte, Comte de Guibert Guibert, Jonathan Abel (trans.), *Guibert's General Essay on Tactics* (Leiden: Brill, 2022), p.144.
12   Guibert, *General Essay*, p.144.
13   Guibert, *General Essay*, p.146.
14   Guibert, *General Essay*, p.146.
15   Guibert, *General Essay*, p.146.
16   Abel, *Guibert*, p.65.
17   Guibert, *General Essay*, p.146.

implement these reforms. For the moment, however, the use of specialized light troops continued, though not without some debate as to their efficacy.

Numerous authors point out that the use of light troops waned in Europe following the end of the Seven Years War. There were several reasons for this change. First, the activities of the light troops often bordered on brigandage. The destruction they wrought went against the grain of Enlightenment thought which sought to impost reasonable limits on the use of force.[18] George Satterfield postulates that among the more affluent and influential in European society, 'we can speculate that there existed scarcely a difference between brigands and partisans or bands of highwaymen and companies of dragoons.'[19] At the same time, authors continued to write on the subject of light troops. Many now sought to place their experiences in an ethically acceptable context. For instance, Georg von Wissel, author of *Der jäger im Felde* noted in his introduction that he had served in the corps of Freytag and Stockhausen, two recognized and respectable leaders of light troops.[20]

An additional reason for the suppression of light troops in the continent of Europe emerged from the research. For several of the leaders described, specifically Luckner and to a lesser extent, Fischer, their service with the irregulars proved to be something of a path to social advancement. The same was true for Johann Ewald as well, whose his rise from common origins into the Hessian officer corps began during the Seven Years War. With the reassertion of noble privilege which came about in the years just prior to the French Revolution as evidenced in such reforms of the de Segur law, it seems possible that suppressing the light troops may have been another way for entrenched privilege to block the social mobility such service offered. It should be emphasized that this is only conjecture at present and additional research is necessary prior to drawing any firm conclusions.

One aspect that stuck out was the attempt, in both theatres, to force the irregulars to operate under greater military discipline. In both the result was the same, they became less effective as a result. This was certainly more the case in Europe than in North America.[21] The shift in perception as well as disciplining the light troops was more profound in Europe than in North America. Still, there were some efforts aimed at codifying the experiences of the last war. In 1765, Robert Rogers' journals were published in London. The journals included numerous general accounts of Rogers exploits such as the following:

January 26, 1756. I marched from Lake George with a part of fifty men, with a design to discover the strength and works of the enemy at Crown Point.

On the 2d of February, we arrived within a mile of that fortress, where we climbed a very steep mountain, from which we had a very clear and full prospect

---

18 Bruce Buchan, 'Pandours, Partisans and *Petite Guerre*: Two Dimensions of Enlightenment Discourse on War', *Intellectual History Review*, 23:3 (2013), pp.329–347.

19 Satterfield, 'Petite Guerre', pp.55–56.

20 Georg von Wissel, *Der jäger im Felde oder kurze Abhandlung wie der Dienst bei leichten Truppen im Felde* (Göttingen: Johann Christian Dietrich, 1778), p.8.

21 Rink, 'Partisan's Metamorphosis', pp.34–36.

of the fort, and an opportunity of taking a plan of the works there. In the evening we retired to a small village, half a mile from the fort, and formed an ambuscade on each side of the road leading from the fort to the village.

Next morning a Frenchman fell into our hands; soon after we discovered two more, but they unluckily got sight of us before they were in our power, and hastily retired to the fort. Finding ourselves discovered by the enemy by this accident, we employed ourselves while we dared to stay in setting fire to the houses and barns of the village, with which were consumed large quantities of wheat, and other grains; we also killed about fifty cattle, and then retired, leaving the whole village in flames, and arrived safe at our fort, with out prisoner, the 6th of February.[22]

Many aspects of the operations described in the preceding account accord with both the exploits of Baron Trenck discussed in the first chapter, and the general exploits of European irregulars. Rogers' account glosses over any difficulties he and his men encountered while on their reconnaissance and paints a generally rosy picture of their exploits. At the same time, it does provide some insight on how his unit operated; setting up ambushes and taking prisoners in order to augment the intelligence gained from their own observations.

Of much greater utility was the fact that Rogers included in his journal what came to be known as his Rules of Ranging. These were developed out of his experiences, and supposedly written down when he raised his own volunteer company.[23] They included such practical insights on irregular warfare as the following, Rule Two:

> When you are ordered out to the enemies forts or frontiers for discoveries, if your number be small, march in single file, keeping at such a distance from each other as to prevent one shot from killing two men, sending one man, or more, forward, and the like on each side, at the distance of twenty yards from the main body, if the ground you march over will admit of it, to give the signal to the officer of the approach of an enemy, and their number...[24]

The spacing of men in his reconnaissance or scouting party was important in order to reduce casualties should they be caught in an ambush. Likewise, moving single-file served to prevent disclosing their numbers to anyone following the party.

Rule Seven enjoined 'If you are obliged to receive the enemies [sic] fire, fall, or squat down, till it is over, then rise and discharge at them.'[25] Falling down or squatting would allow for the enemy's fire to pass over head of the party.

While there were efforts, such as the publication of Rogers' journals, to bring some order to the colonial irregulars, they remained an important force for local defence. Consider, at the outset of the war of American

---

22   Robert Rogers, *Journals of Major Robert Rogers* (London: J. Millan, 1765), pp.11–12.
23   Rogers, *Journals of Major Robert Rogers*, p.59.
24   Rogers, *Journals of Major Robert Rogers*, p.60.
25   Rogers, *Journals of Major Robert Rogers*, p.62.

Independence, one of the first actions taken by the Continental Congress after adopting the New England Army of Observation besieging Boston called on middle colonies to raise units of riflemen, six from Pennsylvania, and two each from Maryland and Virginia. These troops were armed with a distinctive hybrid firearm, the Pennsylvania longrifle. The riflemen were to serve as light infantry.

Consequently, the Americans early on utilized riflemen to serve as light infantry, however, they quickly learned that these troops had some critical vulnerabilities. These included the slow reloading time of the rifle (up to a minute), and the fact that it could not mount a bayonet.[26] As a result, commanders, such a Brigadier General Anthony Wayne of Pennsylvania, determined that the riflemen were ineffective and rearmed these troops with muskets. Another response by the Americans was to develop their own light infantry formations. These men, armed with muskets and bayonets could provide fire support for the riflemen while they reloaded. The American commander who most effectively practiced this approach was Brigadier General Daniel Morgan, and it was best exemplified in his conduct of the Battle of Cowpens, 17 January 1781.[27]

The British brought light troops to the war in North America as well. By this time, each regiment in the British army had its company of light infantry. There were often grouped together to form light infantry battalions which were used to scout ahead of the regulars, skirmish with enemy light units and defend against possible ambushes. The light battalions often served as rear guards as well. The British continued to experiment with light troops as well as rifles during the War for America as well. Major Patrick Ferguson stands as a prime example of this innovative streak. Ferguson served briefly in the Seven Years War in the European theatre and went on to take part in the light infantry training supervised by William Howe.[28] In 1777 he received permission to form an experimental company equipped with a breech-loading rifle of his own design.[29] Unfortunately, Ferguson was wounded at the Battle of Brandywine, 11 September 1777, and his corps was dissolved.

The British contracted with six of the German states to provide subsidy troops to serve in North America. The contingents from Hessen Kassel and Anspach Bayreuth in particular contained *jäger*. The *jäger* were specifically sought by the British Crown to serve as light infantry in North America based on the previous experience fighting there in the Seven Years War. As the most recent scholar of these German auxiliaries notes, 'Jager participated

---

26   Neil L. York, 'Pennsylvania Rifle: Revolutionary Weapon in a Conventional War', *Pennsylvania Magazine of History and Biography*, 103 (July 1979), pp.302–324. See also John W. Wright, 'The Corps of Light Infantry in the Continental Army', *American Historical Review*, 31:3 (April 1964), pp.454–461.

27   The most complete tactical analysis of Cowpens remains, Lawrence E. Babits, *A Devil of a Whipping the Battle of Cowpens* (Chapel Hill: University of North Carolina Press, 1998).

28   M.M. Gilchrist, *Patrick Fergusson A Man of Some Genius* (Edinburgh: NMS Publishing, 2003).

29   De Witt Bailey, *British Military Flintlock Rifles 1740-1840* (Lincoln, RI: Andrew Mowbray Publishers, 2002), pp.35–54.

in every significant engagement between Britain and its enemies.'[30] Several of those who served in the *jäger* in North America went on to write about their experiences and use them as examples in the conduct of Small War. These included Andreas Emmerich whose work, *The Partisan in War* was published in an English edition in 1789.[31] More prolific, and more relevant for the long-term development of light troops was Johann Ewald, who served with the 2nd company Hessen Kassel Jäger Corps. In the years following his return to Europe in 1784, Ewald produced a number of works on Small War which drew on his experiences in the American War, as well as the Seven Years War for examples. Among his works was *Abhandlung von dem Deinst der Leichten Truppen*, or *Treatise on the Duties of Light Troops*.[32] This work, in an early English language translation by a Lieutenant A. Maimburg served as a guide for Sir John Moore's troops in the Peninsular War.[33]

It should be evident at this juncture that the experience of light troops in one conflict, especially those who rose to become officers, often led to them distilling their experiences in writing. These writings, in turn, provided intellectual fodder for the next generation of partisan leaders. It should also be clear that the Seven Years War produced a host of practitioners of, and later authors on, Small War.

---

30 Frederike Baer, *Hessians: German Soldiers in the American Revolutionary War* (Oxford: Oxford University Press, 2022), p.92.
31 Andreas Emmerich, *The Partisan in War or the Use of a Corps of Light Troops to an Army* (London: H. Reynell, 1789).
32 Johann Ewald, *Abhandlung von dem Deinst der Leichten Truppen* (Schleswig: J.G. Schloss, 1790 and 1796).
33 Mc Intrye, *Johann Ewald*, p.293. See also Robert A. Selig and David Curtiss Skaggs (trans.), *Treatise on Partisan Warfare* (New York: Greenwood Press, 1991), p.3.

Bibliography

Primary Sources

Anon., 'Memoir on the Defense of the Fort of Carillon', *The Bulletin of the Fort Ticonderoga Museum*, 13:2 (June 1972), pp.197–226

Anon., 'Moneypenny Orderly Book', *The Bulletin of the Fort Ticonderoga Museum*, 12:5 (December 1969), pp. 328-357; 12:6 (October 1970), pp.434-461; 13:1 (December 1970), pp. 89-116; 13:2 (June 1971), pp.151–184

Anon., *A Complete History of the Present War, from its Commencement in 1756, to the End of the Campaign, 1760* (London: Owen, Davis & Reymers, 1761)

Anon., *The Operations of the Allied Amy under the command of his Serene Highness Prince Ferdinand Duke of Brunswick and Luneberg beginning in the year 1757 and ending in the year 1762* (London: T. Jefferys, 1764)

Bamford, William, John B. Hattendorf, (ed.), *A Redcoat in America: The Diaries of Lieutenant William Bamford, 1757-1765 and 1776* (Warwick: Helion, 2019)

Bell, Thomas A., *A Short Essay on Military First Principles* (London: Becket and De Hondt, 1770)

Bland, Humphrey, *A Treatise of Military Discipline; In Which is Lain Down and Explained the Duty of the Officer and Soldier thro' the Several Branches of the Service* (London: D. Midwinter, J. and P. Knapton, 1743)

Bouquet, Henry, *An Historical Account of the expedition against the Ohio Indians in the Year 1764* (Philadelphia: William Bradford, 1765)

Broglie, Victor-François de, *Correspondance inédite de Victor-François Duc de Broglie Maréchal de France avec le Prince Xavier de Saxe, Comte de Lusace* (Paris: Albin Michel, 1903)

Broglie, Victor-François de, *L'Instruction pour l'Armee du Roi, Commandée par Mr. le Maréchal Duc de Broglie* (Frankfurt: Freres van Duren, 1760)

Chapman, Earl John, 'A New Account of the Battle of the Plains of Abraham', *Journal of the Society for Army Historical Research*, 94:379 (Autumn 2016), pp.193–197

Clausewitz, Carl von, Michael Howard and Peter Paret (trans.), *On War* (Princeton: Princeton University Press, 1976)

Cobb, Samuel, 'The Journal of Captain Samuel Cobb', *Bulletin of the Fort Ticonderoga Museum*, 14:1 (Summer 1981), pp.12–31.

Cointe, M. la, *The Science of Military Posts, for the use of Regimental Officers, who Frequently Command Detached Parties, in which is shewn the manner of Attacking and Defending Posts.* (Nismes: Royal Academy, 1761)

Crissé, Lancelot Turpin de, *Essai sur l'art de la Guerre* (Paris: Prault, 1754)

Crissé, Lancelot Turpin de, Joseph Otway (trans.), *Essay on the Art of War* (London: A. Hamilton, 1761)

Croix, M. de la, *Traité de la Petite Guerre pour les Compagnies Franches, Dans lequel on voit utilité, la différence de leur Service d'avec celui des autres Corps, la manière la plus avantageuse de les condiuré, de les équiper, de les commandeur & les discipliner; & les ruses de Guerre qui leur sont propres* (Paris: Antoine Boudet, 1759)

Eastburn, Robert, *A Faithful Narrative, of the many Dangers and Sufferings, as well as Wonderful and Surprizing Deliverances of Robert Eastburn, during his late Captivity among the Indians: together with some remarks upon the country of Canada, and the Religion and Policy of its Inhabitants; the whole Intermixed with Devout Reflections.* (Philadelphia: Green and Russell, 1758)

Emmerich, Andreas *The Partisan in War or the Use of a Corps of Light Troops to an Army* (London: H. Reynell, 1789)

Ewald, Johann, *Gedanken eines hessischen Offiziers uber sa, was man bei Fuhrung eines Detachments im Felde zu thun hat* (Cassel: Johann Jacob Cramer, 1774)

Ewald, Johann, *Abhandlung von dem Deinst der Leichten Truppen* (Schleswig: J.G. Schloss, 1790 and 1796)

Ewald, Johann, Robert A. Selig and David Curtiss Skaggs (trans.), *Treatise on Partisan Warfare* (New York: Greenwood Press, 1991)

Ford, Worthington C. (ed.), *Journals of the Continental Congress, 1774-1789* (Washington, D.C.: U.S. Government Printing Office, 1904–1937)

Fraser, Malcolm, R.O. Alexander (ed.), 'The Capture of Quebec: A Manuscript Journal Relating to Operations before Quebec from 8th May, 1759 to 17th May, 1760. Kept by Col. Malcom Fraser', *Journal of the Society for Army Historical Research*, 18:71 (Autumn, 1939), pp.135–168.

Goodrich, Josiah, 'The Josiah Goodrich Orderbook', *The Bulletin of the Fort Ticonderoga Museum*, 14:1 (Summer 1981), pp.39–61

Grandmaison, Thomas Le Roy de, *La Petit Guerre ou Traité de Service les Toupes Legeres en Campagne* (Paris, n.p., 1756)

Grandmaison, Thomas Le Roy de, Lewis Nicola (trans.), *A Treatise on the Military Service, of Light Horse, and Light Infantry, and in the Fortified Places. By Major General de Grandmaison, Formerly a Captain, With the Rank of Lieutenant Colonel of Cavalry.* (Philadelphia: Robert Bell, 1777)

Grant, John, Ian McPherson McCulloch and Earl John Chapman (eds.), *A Dangerous Service: A Soldier's View of the Seven Years War in the Caribbean and North America.* (Montreal: Robin Brass Studio, 2017)

Guibert, Jacques-Antoine-Hippolyte, Comte de, Jonathan Abel (trans.), *Guibert's General Essay on Tactics* (Leiden: Brill, 2022)

Hohenzollern, Frederick II, Anon. (trans.), *Military Instructions, written by the King of Prussia, for the Generals of his Army* (London: Becket & de Hondt, 1762)

Hohenzollern, Frederick II, Jay Luvaas (ed. and trans.), *Frederick the Great on the Art of War* (New York: De Capo Press, 1999)

Hordt, Ludwig Count von, Stephen Summerfield (ed.), *The Adventures of a Freikorps Commander: Memoirs of Frederick the Great's Swedish Adventurer* (Huntingdon: Ken Trotman Publishing, 2022)

Jeney, Louis Michel de, *The Partisan: Or the Art of Making War in Detachments* (London: n.p., 1760)

Lévis, François-Gaston du Chevalier de, *Journal des Campagne du Chevalier de Lévis de 1756 à 1760* (Montreal: C.O. Beauchemin and Fils, 1889)

Mante Thomas, *The History of the Late War in North American and the Islands of the West Indies* (London: W. Strahan and T. Caldwell, 1772)

Roche, Comte de la, *Essai sue La Petite Guerre, Ou Méthode de diriger les différentes operations d'un Corps de deux mille zxinq cens Hommes de Troupes légères, don't seize cens d'Infanterie & neuf cens de Cavalerie* (Paris: Saillant & Nyon, 1770)

Rogers, Robert, *Journals of Major Robert Rogers* (London: J. Millan, 1765)

Rousseau, Abbé, G.T. Nafziger (ed.), *The King of France's 1744-1745 Campaign* (Westchester, OH: The Nafziger Collection, 2012)

Simcoe, John Graves, *Simcoe's Military Journal* (New York: Bartlett and Welford, 1844)

Simes, Thomas, *The military guide for young officers, containing a system of the art of war; parade, camp, field duty; manoeuvers, standing and general orders; warrants, regulations, returns; tables, forms, extracts from military acts; battles, sieges, forts, ports, military dictionary, &c., with twenty-five maps and copper plates* (London: J. Millan, 1776)

Stevens, Sylvester K. and Donald H. Kent (eds.), *The Papers of Colonel Henry Bouquet* (Harrisburg: Pennsylvania Historical Commission, 1940)

Tarleton, Banastre, *A History of the Campaigns of 1780 and 1781 in the Southern Provinces of North America.* (Dublin: Colles, Exshaw, et al, 1787)

Tielke, Johann Gottlieb, *The Field Engineer Or, Instruction upon every Branch of Field Fortification: Demonstrated by Examples which occurred in the Seven Years War between the Prussians, Austrians and the Russians* (London: J. Walter, 1789)

Todd, William, Andrew Cormack and Alan Jones (eds), *The Journal of Corporal Todd, 1745–62* (Thrupp: Sutton Publishing for the Army Records Society, 2001)

Tory, John, *Journal of the Allied Army's Marches from the First Arrival of the British Troops, in Germany to the Present Time; with An Accurate Account of all the particular Battles and Skirmishes they have had with the French Army* (Osnabruck: J.W. Kisling, 1762)

Trenck, Franciscus von der, *Memoirs of the Life of the Illustrious Francis Baron Trenck* (London: W. Owen, 1748)

Wissel, Georg von, *Der jäger im Felde oder keine Abhandlung wie der Dienst der leichten Truppe im Feld* (Göttigen: Johann Christian Dietrich, 1778)

Wolfe, James, *General Wolfes Instructions to Young Officers: Also Orders for a Battalion and an Army* (London: J. Millan, 1780)

Secondary Sources

Unpublished Secondary Sources

Bancroft, Maj. Adam, *Savages in a Civilized War: The Native Americans as French Allies in the Seven Years War, 1754-1763*, MA Thesis, (U.S. Army Command and General Staff College, 2013)

Cory, Rory M., *British Light Infantry in North America in the Seven Years War*, MA Thesis, (Simon Fraser University, 1993)

Danley, Mark H., *Combat Motivation in the Eighteenth-Century British Army*, MA Thesis (Viginia Polytechnic Institute, 1991)

Dodson, Samuel James, *Battle of Vellinghausen: Lessons Learnt? A study of the British army in the closing Stages of the Seven Years War in Western Europe as studies through the Battle of Vellinghausen*, MA Thesis (University of Leeds, 2019)

Hannum, Patrick H., *Henry Bouquet: A Study of Three Campaigns in North America, 1758- 1764*, MA Thesis (Youngstown State University, 1976)

Kiefer, Anna Elizabeth, *'Through an Almost Impenetrable Wood': Logistics and the British Army in North America, 1755-1758*, MA Thesis (University of New Hampshire, 2006)

Parker, King Lawrence, *Anglo-American Wilderness Campaigning 1754-1764: Logistics and Tactical Developments*, PhD Dissertation (Columbia University, 1970)

Wernitz, Franz, *Britische leichte Truppen in der Armee Herzog Ferdinand von Braunschweig*, PhD Dissertation (Ludwig Maximillians Universtät Munich, 1993)

Books

Abel, Jonathan, *Guibert: Father of Napoleon's Grande Armée* (Norman: University of Oklahoma Press, 2016)

Anderson, Fred, *The War that Made America: A Short History of the French and Indian War* (New York: Penguin Books, 2006)

Anderson, Fred, *Crucible of War: The Seven Years War and the Fate of Empire in North America, 1754-1766* (New York: Alfred A. Knopf, 2000)

Anderson, M.S., *War and Society in Europe of the Old Regime 1618-1789* (Montreal: McGill- Queen's University Press, 1998)

Anderson, M.S., *The War of the Austrian Succession 1740-1748* (London: Longman, 1995)

Archenholz, Johann von, F.A. Catz (trans.), *The History of the Seven Years War in Germany* (Frankfurt am Main: C. Jugel, 1843)

Askan, Virginia H., *Ottoman Wars 1700-1870: An Empire Besieged* (London: Longman, 2007)

Aspery, Robert, *War in the Shadows the Guerrilla in History: Two Thousand Years of the Guerrilla at War from Ancient Persia to the Present* (New York: William Morrow and Company, 1994)

Babits, Lawrence E., *A Devil of a Whipping the Battle of Cowpens* (Chapel Hill: University of North Carolina Press, 1998)

Baer, Frederike *Hessians: German Soldiers in the American Revolutionary War* (Oxford: Oxford University Press, 2022)

Bailey, De Witt, *British Military Flintlock Rifles 1740-1840* (Lincoln, RI: Andrew Mowbray Publishers, 2002)

Bamford, Andrew, *The Lillies and the Thistle French Troops in the Jacobite '45* (Warwick: Helion, 2018)

Barr, Daniel P., *Unconquered: The Iroquois League at War in Colonial America* (Westport, CT: Praeger, 2006)

Berkovich, Ilya, *Motivation in War: The Experience of Common Soldiers in Old Regime Europe* (Cambridge: Cambridge University Press, 2017)

Black, Jeremy, *Warfare in the Eighteenth Century* (London: Cassell, 1999)

Black, Jeremy (ed.), *Warfare in Europe, 1650-1792* (Aldershot: Ashgate, 2005)

Bois, Jean-Pierre, *Maurice de Saxe* (Lille: Fayard, 1992)

Brown, Peter, *The Army of George II 1727-1760: The Soldiers who Forged an Empire* (Warwick: Helion, 2020)

Browning, Reed, *The War of the Austrian Succession* (New York: St. Martin's Griffin, 1995)

Brumwell, Steven, *Redcoats: The British Soldier and War in the Americas, 1755-1763* (New York: Cambridge University Press, 2002)

Carmichael, Ewan, *Like a Brazen Wall: The Battle of Minden, 1759, and its Place in the Seven Years War* (Warwick: Helion, 2021)

Childs, John, *Armies and Warfare in Europe, 1648-1789* (Manchester: Manchester University Press, 1982)

Cogswell, Neil (trans. and ed.), *Zweybruecken in Command: The Reichsarmee in the Campaign of 1758* (Warwick: Helion, 2019)

Colin, Jean, *L'Infanterie au XVIIIe Siècle: La Tactique* (Paris: Bergerevrault, 1907)

Colin, Jean, L.H.R. Pope-Hennessy (trans.), *The Transformations of War* (Westport, CT: Greenwood Press, 1977 reprint of 1912 original)

Corvisier, André, Abigail T. Siddal (trans.), *Armies and Societies in Europe, 1494-1789* (Bloomington: Indiana University Press, 1979)

Crowdy, Terry, *French Light Infantry 1784-1815, from the Chasseurs of Louis XVI to Napoleon's Grande Armée.* (Warwick: Helion, 2021)

Darling, Anthony D., *Red Coat and Brown Bess* (Alexandria Bay, NY: Museum Restoration Service, 1971)

Duffy, Christopher, *Russia's Military Way to the West: Origins and Nature of Russian Military Power 1700-1800* (London: Routledge, 1981)

Duffy, Christopher, *The Military Experience in the Age of Reason 1715-1789* (New York: Hippocrene Books, 1987)

Duffy, Christopher, *The Army of Frederick the Great* (Chicago: The Emperor's Press, 1996)

Duffy, Christopher, *Instrument of War: The Austrian Army in the Seven Years War.* (Chicago: The Emperor's Press, 2000)

Duffy, Christopher, *By Force of Arms: The Austrian Army in the Seven Years War* (Chicago: The Emperor's Press, 2008)

Duffy, Christopher, *Fight for a Throne: The Jacobite '45 Reconsidered* (Solihull: Helion, 2015)

Düring, G. W. von, *Geschichte des Schaumburg-Lippe-Bückeburgeschen Karabinier- und jäger– Korps im Siebenjährigen Kriegs* (Berlin: Graf Sigfried Mittler, 1828)

Fischer, David Hackett, *Washington's Crossing* (New York: Oxford University Press, 2004)

Falkner, James, *The Battle of Fontenoy 1745: Saxe Against Cumberland in the War of the Austrian Succession* (Philadelphia: Pen and Sword, 2019)

Fuller, J.F.C., *British Light Infantry in the Eighteenth Century* (London: Hutchinson & Co., 1925)

Gallup, Andrew and Donald F. Schaffer, *La Marine: The French Colonial Soldier in Canada 1745-1761* (Bowie, MD: Heritage Books, 1992)

Gat, Azar, *The Origins of Military Thought: From the Enlightenment to Clausewitz* (Oxford: Clarendon Press, 1989)

Gates, David, *The British Light Infantry Arm c. 1790-1815* (London: B.T. Batsford Ltd., 1987)

Gilchrist, M.M., *Patrick Fergusson A Man of Some Genius* (Edinburgh: NMS Publishing, 2003)

Grenier, John, *The First Way of War: American War Making on the Frontier* (Cambridge: Cambridge University Press, 2005)

Großen Generalstabe, *Die Kriege Friedrichs des Großen, Dritter Theil: der Siebenjährige Krieg 1756-1763* (Berlin: Ernst Siegfried Mittler und Sohn, 1902)

Großen Generalstabe, *Die Kriege Friedrichs des Großen, der Siebenjährige Krieg 1756-1763* Siebenter Bande: Olmütz und Crefeld (Berlin: Ernst Siegfried Mittler und Sohn, 1909)

Hagerty, Gilbert, *Massacre at Fort Bull the De Lery Expedition against Oneida Carry, 1756* (Providence, RI: Mowbray Publishers, 1971)

Houlding, J.A., *Fit for Service: The Training of the British Army, 1715–1795* (Oxford: Clarendon Press, 1981)

Howard, Michael, *War in European History* (Oxford: Oxford University Press, 1976)

Hotham-Thompson, Sir Charles, *Operations of the Allied Army under the Command of His Serene Highness Prince Ferdinand, Duke of Brunswick and Lüneburg, 1757-1762* (Point Pleasant, NJ: Winged Hussar Publishing, 2016)

Hunt, George T., *The Wars of the Iroquois: A Study in Intertribal Trade Relations* (Madison: University of Wisconsin Press, 1978)

James. David E., *Native North American Armor, Shields and Fortifications* (Austin: University of Texas Press, 2004)

Kennett, Lee, *The French Armies in the Seven Years War A Study in Military Organization and Administration* (Durham, NC: Duke University Press, 1967)

Kolbe, Wilhelm, *Marburg und der Siebenjährige Krieg: Ein Vortrag gehalten in der Versammlung des Hessischen Geschichtsvereins zu Marburg am 28 Januar 1880* (Marburg: R.G. Elwert Verlagsbuchhandlung, 1880)

Kunnisch, Johannes, *Der Kleinen Krieg: Studien zum Heerwesen des Absolutismus* (Weisbaden: Steiner, 1973)

Lapray, Olivier, *Hastenbeck 1757: The French Army and the Opening Campaign of the Seven Years War* (Warwick: Helion, 2021)

Leach, Douglas Edward, *Arms for Empire: A Military History of the British Colonies in North America, 1607-1763* (New York: The Macmillan Company, 1973)

Lenk, Torsten, J.F. Hayward (ed.), G.A. Urquhart (trans.), *The Flintlock: Its Origin and Development* (New York: J.F. Bramwell House, 1965)

Lynn, John A., *The Wars of Louis XIV 1667-1714* (London: Longman, 1999)

MacLeod, D. Peter, *The Canadian Iroquois and the Seven Years War* (Toronto: Dundurn, 2012)

Malone, Patrick, *The Skulking Way of War Technology and Tactics among the New England Indians* (New York: Madison Books, 1991)

Marston, Daniel *The Seven Years War* (Oxford: Osprey Publishing, 2001)

Martiny, Richard J., *Military Beginnings: Early Development of American and Maryland Forces* (North Charleston, SC: CreateSpace Independence Publishing, 2013)

McCulloch, Ian M. and Tim J. Todish, *British Light Infantryman of the Seven Years War North America 1757-1763* (Oxford: Osprey, 2004)

McIntyre, James R., *The Development of the British Light Infantry, Continental and North American Influences, 1740-1765* (Point Pleasant, NJ: Winged Hussar Publishing, 2015)

McIntyre, James R., *Johann Ewald: Jäger Commander* (New York: Knox Press, 2020)

McGuire, Thomas, *The Battle of Paoli* (Mechanicsburg, PA: Stackpole Books, 2000)

Mediger, Walther, *Herzog Ferdinand von Braunschweig-Lüneberg und die alliierte Armmee im Siebenjährigen Krieg (1757-1762)* (Hannover: Hahnsche Buchhandlung, 2011)

Miakinkov, Eugene, *War and Enlightenment in Russia: Military Culture in the Age of Catherine II* (Toronto: University of Toronto Press, 2020)

Möbius, Katrin and Sascha, *Prussian Army Soldiers and the Seven Years War: The Psychology of Honour* (New York: Bloomsbury Academic, 2020)

Neimeyer, Joachim, *The Hanoverian Army during the Seven Years War 'Gmundener Prachtwerk'* (Copenhagen: Bent Carlsens Forlag, 1977)

Nester, William R., *The First Global War: Britain, France, and the Fate of North America, 1756-1775* (Westport, CT: Praeger, 2000)

Nosworthy, Brent, *The Anatomy of Victory: Battle Tactics 1689-1763* (New York: Hippocrene Books, 1990)

Pajol, Comte Charles Paul Victor, *Les Guerres sous Louis XV* (Paris: Librarie de Fernin-Dioderot et Cie, Imprimeurs de l'Institut, 1891)

Pargellis, Stanley M. (ed.) *Military Affairs in North America, 1755-1763: Selected Documents from the Cumberland Papers in Windsor Castle* (New York: D. Appleton Century Company, 1936)

Parker, Geoffrey, *The Military Revolution: Military Innovation and the Rise of the West, 1500-1800* (Cambridge: Cambridge University Press, 1988)

Parkman, Francis, *Montcalm and Wolfe. France and England in North America* (Boston: LittleBrown and Company, 1884)

Phillips, Thomas R. (ed.), *The Roots of Strategy: A Collection of Military Classics* (London: John Lane, 1943)

Pichat, Henry, George Nafziger (trans.), *Maurice de Saxe's 1745 Campaign in Belgium* (Westchester, OH: The Nafziger Collection, 2011)

Picaud-Monnerat, Sandrine, *La Petite Guerre au XVIIIe Siecle* (Paris: Economica, 2010)

Preston, David L., *Braddock's Defeat: The Battle of the Monongahela and the Road to Revolution* (Oxford: Oxford University Press, 2015)

Quimby, Robert S., *The Background of Napoleonic Warfare: The Theory of Military Tactics in Eighteenth-Century France* (New York: Columbia University Press, 1957)

Ray, Arthur J., *Indians in the Fur Trade: Their Role as Trappers, Hunters, and Middlemen in the Lands Southwest of Hudson Bay, 1660-1870* (Toronto: University of Toronto Press, 1998)

Ribaucourt, E. de, George Nafziger (trans.), *The Military Life and Exploits of J.-C. Fischer Brigadier of the Armies of King Louis XV Founder and Commander of the Corps of Chasseurs (1743-1761)* (West Chester, OH: The Nafziger Collection, 2022)

Richter, Daniel K., *The Ordeal of the Longhouse: The Peoples of the Iroquois League in the Era of European Colonization* (Chapel Hill, NC: University of North Carolina Press, 1992)

Riding, Jacqueline, *Jacobites: A New History of the '45 Rebellion* (London: Bloomsbury, 2016)

Rogers, H.C.B., *The British Army of the Eighteenth Century* (London: Allen and Unwin, 1977)

Ross, John F., *War on the Run: The Epic Story of Robert Rogers and the Conquest of America's First Frontier* (New York: Random House, 2009)

Ross, Stephen T., *From Flintlock to Rifle, 1740-1866* (London: Portland, 1996)

Rothenberg, Gunther E., *The Military Border in Croatia, 1740-1881: A Study of an Imperial Institution* (Chicago: University of Chicago Press, 1966)

Rothenberg, Gunther E., *The Art of Warfare in the Age of Napoleon* (London: B.T. Batsford, 1977)

Satterfield, George, *Princes, Posts, and Partisans the Army of Louis XIV and Partisan Warfare in the Netherlands (1673-1678)* (Leiden: Brill, 2003)

Savory, Sir Reginald, *His Britannic Majesty's Army in Germany during the Seven Years War* (Oxford: Clarendon Press, 1966)

Schultz, Eric B. and Michael J. Tougias, *King Philip's War: The History and Legacy of America's Forgotten Conflict* (New York: W.W. Norton and Company, 1999)

Sheppard, Ruth, *Empires Collide: The French and Indian War 1754-63* (Oxford: Osprey, 2006)

Showalter, Dennis, *The Wars of Frederick the Great* (London: Longman, 1996)

Shumway, George, *Jaeger Rifles* (York, PA: George Shumway Publisher, 2003)

Smith, Digby, *A New History of the Seven Years War* (Huntingdon: Ken Trotman Publishers, 2016)

Sonntag, Kurt, *Trenck, der Pandur und die Brandschatzung Bayerns* (Munchen: Nusser, 1976)

Starbuck, David, *Massacre at Fort William Henry* (Hanover, NH: University Press of New England, 2002)

Starkey, Armstrong, *European and Native American Warfare 1675-1815* (Norman: University of Oklahoma Press, 1998)

Starkey, Armstrong, *War in the Age of Enlightenment, 1700-1789* (Westport, CT: Praeger, 2003)

Steele, Ian K., *Guerillas and Grenadiers* (Toronto: Ryerson Press, 1969)

Steele, Ian K., *Betrayals: Fort William Henry and the Massacre* (New York: Oxford University Press, 1993)

Stryker, William S., *The Battles of Trenton and Princeton* (Trenton, NJ: The Old Barracks Association, 2001)

Sulicki, Karl von, *Der Siebenjährige Krieg in Pommern und in den benachbarten Marken, Studie des Detachments-und des kleinen Krieges* (Berlin: Mittler, 1867)

Summerfield, Stephen, *Prussian Freikorps and Jager of the Seven Years War* (Huntingdon: Ken Trotman, 2018)

Summerfield, Stephen, *Prussian Frei-Infantrie, Militia and Navy of the Seven Years War.* (Huntingdon: Ken Trotman, 2018)

Summerfield, Stephen, *Hanoverian Army of the Seven Years War: Uniforms, Organization and Equipment* (Huntingdon: Ken Trotman, 2018)

Summerfield, Stephen, *Saxon Army of the War of the Austrian Succession and the Seven Years War: Uniforms, Organization and Equipment* (Huntingdon: Ken Trotman, 2018)

Summerfield, Stephen, *Austrian Light Cavalry and Staff, 1740-1765* (Huntingdon: Ken Trotman Publishing, 2021)

Sutton, John L., *The King's Honor and the King's Cardinal: The Wear of the Polish Succession* (Lexington: University Press of Kentucky, 1980)

Szabo, Franz J., *The Seven Years War in Europe 1756-1763* (New York: Longman, 2008)

Tallet, Frank, *War and Society in Early-Modern Europe, 1495-1715* (London: Routledge, 1992)

Teichman, Oscar, *Pandour Trenck: An Account of the Life of Franciscus von der Trenck, 1710-1749* (London: John Murray, 1927)

Tuck, Christopher, *Understanding Land Warfare* (London: Routledge, 2014)

Vajiravudh, Maha, *The War of the Polish Succession* (Oxford: Blackwell, 1901)

Ward, Matthew C., *Breaking the Backcountry: The Seven Years War in Virginia and Pennsylvania, 1754-1765* (Pittsburgh, PA: University of Pittsburgh Press, 2003)

Ward, Matthew C., *The Battle for Quebec 1759* (Stroud: The History Press, 2005)

Weigley Russell F., *The Age of Battles: The Quest for Decisive Warfare from Breitenfeld to Waterloo* (Bloomington: Indiana University Press, 1991)

Wernitz, Frank, *Die Preussisichen Freitruppen im Siebenjährigen Krieg 1756-1763* (n.p.: Podzun-Pallas, 1994)

Wetzel, Georg Heinz, *Die Hessischen Jager: einer deutche Truppenhistorie in politischen Wandlungsprozess von vier Jahrhunderten (1631-1987)* (Kassel: Verlag George, 1987)

White, Jon Manchip, *Marshal of France: The Life and Times of Maurice, Comte de Saxe, 1696- 1750* (Chicago: Rand McNally, 1962)

Williams, Glenn F., *Dunmore's War: The Last Conflict of America's Colonial Era* (Yardley, PA: Westholme Press, 2018)

Witzel, Rudolf, *Hessen-Kassels Regimenter in der Alliierten Armee 1762* (Norderstedt: Books on Demand GmbH, 2008)

Whitworth, Rex, *Field Marshal Lord Ligonier, The British Army 1702–1770* (Oxford: Clarendon Press, 1958)

Chapters in Edited Books

Horn, Bernd, 'La Petite Guerre: A Strategy of Survival', in Horn, Bernd (ed.), *The Canadian Way of War* (Toronto, Ontario: Dundurn Press, 2006), pp.21–56

Horn, Bernd, 'Terror on the Frontier: The Role of the Indians in the Struggle for North America, 1754-1760', in Berndt Horn (ed.), *The Canadian Military Experience* (Ontario: Varnwell Publishing), pp.39–63

Lynn, John A., 'The Battle Culture of Forbearance', in Wayne E. Lee (ed.), *Warfare and Culture in World History* (New York: New York University Press, 2011), pp.89–114

McIntyre, James R., 'Pandours, Partisans and Freikorps: The Development of Irregular Warfare and Light Troops across the Eighteenth Century', in Alexander S., Burns (ed.), *The Changing Face of Old Regime Warfare Essays in Honour of Christopher Duffy* (Warwick: Helion, 2022), pp.161–180

Picaud-Monnerat, Sandrine, 'La guerre de partis au XVIIe siècle en Europe', Coutau-Bégarie (dir), *Stratégies irrégulières* (Paris: Economica, 2010), pp.202–234

Querengässer, Alexander, 'Prussia's Army on the Eve of the Battle of Rossbach', in Alexander Querengässer (ed.), Rick Sanders (trans.), *The Battle of Rossbach*

1757: New Perspectives on the Battle and Campaign (Warwick: Helion, 2022), pp.15–47

Articles

Atkinson, C.T., 'Highlanders in Westphalia, 1760–62: and the Development of Light Infantry', *Journal of the Society for Army Historical Research*, 20:40 (1941), pp.208–223

Atkinson, C.T., 'British Strategy and Battles in the Westphalian Campaigns of 1758-1762', *Journal of the Royal United Service Institution*, 79:516 (1934), pp.733–740

Barker, Thomas M. and Paul R. Huey, 'Military jägers: Their Civilian Background and Weaponry', in *The Hessians: The Journal of the Johannes Schwalm Historical Association*, 15 (2012), pp.1–15

Branch, E. Douglas, 'Henry Bouquet: Professional Soldier', *The Pennsylvania Magazine of History and Biography*, 62:1 (January 1938), pp.41–51

Buchan, Bruce, 'Pandours, Partisans and *Petite Guerre*: Two Dimensions of Enlightenment Discourse on War', *Intellectual History Review*, 23:3 (2013), pp.329–347

Fuller, J.F.C., 'The Revival and Training of Light Infantry in the British Army', *Journal of the Royal United Services Institution*, 57 (1913), pp.1187–1214

Gadue, Col. Michael R., 'Lieutenant Colonel Friedrich S. Baum, Officer Commanding, the Bennington Expedition A Figure Little Known to History', *The Hessians: Journal of the Johannes Schwalm Historical Association*, 11 (2008), pp.37–54

Heuser, Beatrice, 'Small Wars in the Age of Clausewitz: The Watershed between Partisan War and People's War', *Journal of Strategic Studies*, 33:1 (February 19, 2010), pp.139–162

Horn, Bernd, 'Hollow of Death: Rogers' Rangers Desperate Fight for Survival, 21 January 1757', *Canadian Military History*, 14:4 (2005), pp.5–14.

Jankó, Annamária 'An Outstanding Person of the First Military Survey: Mihály Lajos Jeney', *Cartographic Studies*, 13. Studies in honor of Professor István Klinghammer's 65th birthday. ELTE Department of Cartography and Geoinformatics (2006), pp.201–207

Lacroix-Leclair, Jérôme and Eric Ouellet, 'The *Petite Guerre* in New France, 1660-1759: An Institutional Analysis', *Canadian Military History*, 11:4 (Autumn 2011), pp.48–54

Lasconjarais, Guillaume, 'Guerre limitée ou guerre à moyens limités? Le rôle de la petite guerre sur un espace frontalier au temps de Guerre de Succession d'Autriche', *Revue Historique des Armées*, 286:1 (2017), pp.60–68

Leach, Jeff, 'Swedish Jäger Units of the Seven Years War', *Seven Years War Association Journal*, 10:1 (Winter 1997), pp.33–42

Lee, Wayne E., 'Peace Chiefs and Blood Revenge: Patterns of Restraint in Native American Warfare, 1500-1800', *Journal of Military History*, 71:3 (2007), pp.701–741

Lynn, John A., 'The Treatment of Military Subjects in Diderot's Encyclopédie', *The Journal of Military History*, 65:1 (January 2001), pp.131–165

Lynn, John A., 'The Evolution of Army Style in the Modern West, 800-2000', *The International History Review*, 18:3 (August 1996), pp.505–545

McCulloch, Ian, '"Within Ourselves…", The Development of British Light Infantry in North America during the Seven Years War', *Canadian Military History*, 7:2 (Spring 1998), pp.41–55

McIntyre, James R., 'Eighteenth Century Heavy Metal: The Amusette and the Musketoon', *Eighteenth Century Warfare*, < https://18thcenturywarfare. wordpress.com/articles-2/>, (August 2022) accessed 4 July 2023

McIntyre, James R., 'Joseph Count Siskovics', *Journal of the Seven Years War Association*, 23:2 (Winter 2019/2020), pp.54–66

McIntyre, James R., 'The Ambushes at Gundersdorf and Domstadtl: Tactical Engagements with Strategic Results', *Journal of the Seven Years War Association*, 23:2 (Winter 2019/2020), pp.45–64

McIntyre, James R., 'The Freytag jäger Corps in the Seven Years War: Their Organization and Employment', *Journal of the Seven Years War Association*, 22:4 (Summer 2019), pp.13–21

McIntyre, James R., 'Field Marshal Freytag's Records', *Journal of the Seven Years War Association*, 22:4 (Summer 2019), pp.30–66

McIntyre, James R., 'Heavyweight of the Lights: Andreas Count Hadik von Futak', *Journal of the Seven Years War Association*, 22:3 (Spring 2019), pp.5–19

McIntyre, James R., 'The Raid on Berlin, 1757', *Journal of the Seven Years War Association*, 22:3 (Spring 2019), pp.20–42

McIntyre, James R., 'Frederick's Mentor: Santa Cruz de Marcenado', *Journal of the Seven Years War Association*, 22:2 (Winter 2018/2019), pp.18–25

McIntyre, James R., 'The Popularizer Friedrich Wilhelm von Zanthier and the Works of Santa Cruz de Marcenado', *Journal of the Seven Years War Association*, 22:2 (Winter 2018/2019), pp.26–31

McIntyre, James R., 'On the Origins and Development of the Pennsylvania-American Longrifle, 1500-1700', *Seven Years War Association Journal*, 14:1 (Fall, 2005), pp.40–55

McIntyre, James R., 'Vanished into Obscurity: Humphrey Bland', *Seven Years War Association Journal*, 14:3 (Fall 2005), pp.80–82

McIntyre, James R., 'Enlightened Rogues: Light Infantry and Partisan Theorists of the Eighteenth Century, 1740-1800', *Journal of the Seven Years War Association*, 18:2 (Fall 2013), pp.4–28

McIntyre, James R., 'A Scoundrel's Scoundrel: The Life and Exploits of Baron Franciscus von der Trenck, Pandour Leader', *Journal of the Seven Years War Association*, 19:1 (Winter 2014), pp.27–42

McIntyre, James R., 'George Augustus Howe: Father of the British Light Infantry?', *Journal of the Seven Years War Association*, 19:3 (Summer 2014), pp.12–14

Nicolai, Martin L., 'Military and the Canadian Irregular Soldiers during the Seven Years War', *Canadian Historical Review*, 70:1 (1989), pp.53–75

Nosworthy, Brent, 'Arquebussier de Grassin', *Seven Years War Association Journal*, 13:3 (Winter 2003), pp. 22–23

Paret, Peter, 'Colonial Experience and European Military Reform at the End of the Eighteenth Century', *Bulletin of the Institute of Historical Research*, 37:1 (January 1964), pp.47–59

Preston, David L., '"Make Indians of Our White Men": British Soldiers and Indian Warriors from Braddock's to Forbes's Campaigns, 1755-1758', *Pennsylvania History*, 74:3 (Summer 2007), pp.280–306

Picaud-Monnerat, Sandrine, 'Thomas -Auguste Le Roy de Grandmaison (1715-1801) un officier au service de la petite guerre', *Revue Internationale de Histoire Militaire*, 81 (2001), pp.101–114

Purky, Jim, 'Light Infantry Forces in the Austrian-Prussian Theaters of the SYW', *Seven Years War Association* Journal, 8:4 (Winter 1996), pp.38–45

Rink, Martin, 'The Partisan's Metamorphosis: From Freelance Military Entrepreneur to German Freedom Fighter, 1740-1815', *War in History*, 17:1 (January 2010), pp.6–36

Rink, Martin, 'Der kleine Krieg: Entwicklung und Teens asymmetrischer Gewalt bis 1740 bis 1815', *Militärgeschichte Zeitschrift*, 65:2 (2006), pp.355–388

Robson, Eric, 'British Light Infantry in the Mid-Eighteenth Century: The Effect of American Conditions', *Army Quarterly* (1952), pp.109–122

Russell, P.E., 'Redcoats in the Wilderness: British Officers and Irregular Warfare in Europe and America, 1740-1760', *William and Mary Quarterly*, Series 3, 35:4 (October 1978), pp.629–652

Satterfield, George, 'The Fate of Petite Guerre in Early Modern Europe', *Revue Historique des Armées*, 286:1 (2017), pp.48–59

Savory, Sir Reginald, 'John Tory's Journal, 1758-1762', *Journal of the Society for Army Historical Research*, 54:218 (1976), pp.70–95

Silcox, James H., 'Rogers and Bouquet: The Origins of the American Light Infantry', *Military Review*, 65:12 (December 1985), pp.62–74

Storkel, Arno, 'The Anspach Jägers', *The Hessians: Journal of the Johannes Schwalm Historical Association*, 14 (2011), pp.1–31

Szabo, Franz A.J., 'Prince Kaunitz and the Balance of Power', *International Historical Review* (1979), pp.399–408

White, Charles E., 'Scharnhorst's Mentor: Count Wilhelm zu Schaumburg-Lippe and the Origins of the Modern National Army', *War in History*, 24:3 (March 2017), pp.258–285

Wilson, Peter, 'Glasenapp's Freikorps', *Seven Years War Association Journal*, 10:4 (Summer 1999), pp.10–19

Wilson, Peter, 'The Ambush of the Olmütz Convoy at Domstadtl, June 28-30, 1758', *Seven Years War Association Journal*, 8:4 (Winter, 1996), pp.10–25

Wright, John W., 'Military Contributions during the Eighteenth Century', *The Journal of the American Military Institute*, 3:1 (Spring 1939), pp.3–13

Wright, John W., 'The Corps of Light Infantry in the Continental Army', *American Historical Review*, 31:3 (April 1964), pp.454–461

York, Neil L., 'Pennsylvania Rifle: Revolutionary Weapon in a Conventional War', *Pennsylvania Magazine of History and Biography*, 103 (July 1979), pp.302–324

Unpublished Papers

McIntyre, James R., 'With Sword in Hand: Johann Ewald in the Seven Years War', Sir William Johnson and the Wars for Empire Conference, Johnstown, NY, 23 October, 2022

McIntyre, James R., 'Crucible of the Partisan: Johann Ewald in the Seven Years War', Twenty-Sixth Annual College of the Seven Years War, Fort Ticonderoga, NY, 21 May, 2022

McIntyre, James R., 'The Elusive Partisan: Thomas Le Roy de Grandmaison', Seven Years War Convention, South Bend, IN, 2 April, 2022

McIntyre, James R., 'Atrocity in the Seven Years War in Europe: A Critical Reevaluation', 10 May, 2019, 86th Annual Meeting of the Society for Military History, Columbus, Ohio

McIntyre, James R., 'Freemen of a Freikorps? Light Horse Harry Lee and His Legion, American Partisans', 27 April, 2013, Wedded to My Sword: 'Light Horse Harry' Lee Symposium, Greensboro, N.C.

From Reason to Revolution – Warfare 1721-1815

http://www.helion.co.uk/series/from-reason-to-revolution-1721-1815.php

The 'From Reason to Revolution' series covers the period of military history 1721–1815, an era in which fortress-based strategy and linear battles gave way to the nation-in-arms and the beginnings of total war.

This era saw the evolution and growth of light troops of all arms, and of increasingly flexible command systems to cope with the growing armies fielded by nations able to mobilise far greater proportions of their manpower than ever before. Many of these developments were fired by the great political upheavals of the era, with revolutions in America and France bringing about social change which in turn fed back into the military sphere as whole nations readied themselves for war. Only in the closing years of the period, as the reactionary powers began to regain the upper hand, did a military synthesis of the best of the old and the new become possible.

The series will examine the military and naval history of the period in a greater degree of detail than has hitherto been attempted, and has a very wide brief, with the intention of covering all aspects from the battles, campaigns, logistics, and tactics, to the personalities, armies, uniforms, and equipment.

Submissions

The publishers would be pleased to receive submissions for this series. Please contact series editor Andrew Bamford via email (andrewbamford@helion.co.uk), or in writing to Helion & Company Limited, Unit 8 Amherst Business Centre, Budbrooke Road, Warwick, CV34 5WE

Titles